VISIT US AT

www.syngress.co

Syngress is committed to publishing high-quality books for IT Professionals and delivering those books in media and formats that fit the demands of our customers. We are also committed to extending the utility of the book you purchase via additional materials available from our Web site.

SOLUTIONS WEB SITE

To register your book, visit www.syngress.com/solutions. Once registered, you can access our solutions@syngress.com Web pages. There you may find an assortment of value-added features such as free e-books related to the topic of this book, URLs of related Web site, FAQs from the book, corrections, and any updates from the author(s).

ULTIMATE CDs

Our Ultimate CD product line offers our readers budget-conscious compilations of some of our best-selling backlist titles in Adobe PDF form. These CDs are the perfect way to extend your reference library on key topics pertaining to your area of expertise, including Cisco Engineering, Microsoft Windows System Administration, CyberCrime Investigation, Open Source Security, and Firewall Configuration, to name a few.

DOWNLOADABLE E-BOOKS

For readers who can't wait for hard copy, we offer most of our titles in downloadable Adobe PDF form. These e-books are often available weeks before hard copies, and are priced affordably.

SYNGRESS OUTLET

Our outlet store at syngress.com features overstocked, out-of-print, or slightly hurt books at significant savings.

SITE LICENSING

Syngress has a well-established program for site licensing our ebbooks onto servers in corporations, educational institutions, and large organizations. Contact us at sales@syngress.com for more information.

CUSTOM PUBLISHING

Many organizations welcome the ability to combine parts of multiple Syngress books, as well as their own content, into a single volume for their own internal use. Contact us at sales@syngress.com for more information.

SYNGRESS®

SYNGRESS®

Network
Security
Assessment

FROM VULNERABILITY TO PATCH

Steve Manzuik

André Gold

Chris Gatford

KEY	SERIAL NUMBER
001	HJIRTCV764
002	PO9873D5FG
003	829KM8NJH2
004	62234BPPLQ
005	CVPLQ6WQ23
006	VBP965T5T5
007	HJJJ863WD3E
008	2987GVTWMK
009	629MP5SDJT
010	IMWQ295T6T

PUBLISHED BY
Syngress Publishing, Inc.
800 Hingham Street
Rockland, MA 02370

Network Security Assessment: From Vulnerability to Patch

Printed in Canada
1 2 3 4 5 6 7 8 9 0
ISBN-10: 1-59749-101-2
ISBN-13: 978-1-59749-101-3

Publisher: Andrew Williams   Page Layout and Art: Patricia Lupien
Technical Editor: Steve Manzuik and André Gold   Copy Editor: Audrey Doyle
Cover Designer: Michael Kavish   Indexer: Richard Carlson

Distributed by O'Reilly Media, Inc. in the United States and Canada.
For information on rights, translations, and bulk sales, contact Matt Pedersen, Director of Sales and Rights, at Syngress Publishing; email matt@syngress.com or fax to 781-681-3585.

Acknowledgments

Syngress would like to acknowledge the following people for their kindness and support in making this book possible.

Syngress books are now distributed in the United States and Canada by O'Reilly Media, Inc. The enthusiasm and work ethic at O'Reilly are incredible, and we would like to thank everyone there for their time and efforts to bring Syngress books to market: Tim O'Reilly, Laura Baldwin, Mark Brokering, Mike Leonard, Donna Selenko, Bonnie Sheehan, Cindy Davis, Grant Kikkert, Opol Matsutaro, Steve Hazelwood, Mark Wilson, Rick Brown, Tim Hinton, Kyle Hart, Sara Winge, Peter Pardo, Leslie Crandell, Regina Aggio Wilkinson, Pascal Honscher, Preston Paull, Susan Thompson, Bruce Stewart, Laura Schmier, Sue Willing, Mark Jacobsen, Betsy Waliszewski, Kathryn Barrett, John Chodacki, Rob Bullington, Kerry Beck, Karen Montgomery, and Patrick Dirden.

The incredibly hardworking team at Elsevier Science, including Jonathan Bunkell, Ian Seager, Duncan Enright, David Burton, Rosanna Ramacciotti, Robert Fairbrother, Miguel Sanchez, Klaus Beran, Emma Wyatt, Krista Leppiko, Marcel Koppes, Judy Chappell, Radek Janousek, Rosie Moss, David Lockley, Nicola Haden, Bill Kennedy, Martina Morris, Kai Wuerfl-Davidek, Christiane Leipersberger, Yvonne Grueneklee, Nadia Balavoine, and Chris Reinders for making certain that our vision remains worldwide in scope.

David Buckland, Marie Chieng, Lucy Chong, Leslie Lim, Audrey Gan, Pang Ai Hua, Joseph Chan, June Lim, and Siti Zuraidah Ahmad of Pansing Distributors for the enthusiasm with which they receive our books.

David Scott, Tricia Wilden, Marilla Burgess, Annette Scott, Andrew Swaffer, Stephen O'Donoghue, Bec Lowe, Mark Langley, and Anyo Geddes of Woodslane for distributing our books throughout Australia, New Zealand, Papua New Guinea, Fiji, Tonga, Solomon Islands, and the Cook Islands.

Lead Author
and Technical Editor

Steve Manzuik currently holds the position of Senior Manager, Security Research at Juniper Networks. He has more than 14 years of experience in the information technology and security industry, with a particular emphasis on operating systems and network devices. Prior to joining Juniper Networks, Steve was the Research Manager at eEye Digital Security and in 2001, he founded and was the technical lead for Entrench Technologies. Prior to Entrench, Steve was a manager in Ernst & Young's Security & Technology Solutions practice, where he was the solution line leader for the Canadian Penetration Testing Practice. Before joining Ernst & Young, he was a security analyst for a world wide group of white hat hackers and security researchers on BindView RAZOR Team.

Steve has co-authored *Hack Proofing Your Network, Second Edition* (Syngress Publishing, 1928994709). In addition, he has spoken at Defcon, Black Hat, Pacsec, and CERT conferences around the world and has been quoted in industry publications including CNET, CNN, InfoSecurity Magazine, Linux Security Magazine, Windows IT Pro and Windows Magazine.

Coauthor and Technical Editor

André Gold is currently the Director of Information Security at Continental Airlines, one of the world's largest and most successful commercial and freight transportation providers. André was appointed to this position by the company's former CIO, making him the first person to hold this post in the company's 50-year history. As the Director of Information Security, André has established a risk-based information security program based in part on increasing the security IQ of over 42,000 employees and protecting the over $2.5 billion continental.com property.

As an identified security practitioner, André has been featured in SC, Information Security, and CSO Magazine. André also presents at or participates in industry-related events. In 2006 André was named an Information Security 7 award winner in the retail sector, for his security contributions in the start-up and air transportation markets.

Before assuming his current role, André served as Technical Director of Internet and Network Services. In this role, he built and was responsible for Continental's infrastructure and continental.com property; a property which accounts for close to 25% of the company's revenue.

In his spare time, André is pursuing his MBA at Colorado State and has a BBA in Computer Information Systems from the University of Houston-Downtown. André was also a commissioned officer in the Army, receiving his commission from Wentworth Military Academy.

In addition to his position at Continental, André served on the Microsoft Chief Security Officer Council, the Skyteam Data Privacy and Security Subcommittee, Goldman Sachs' Security Council, as well as eEye Digital Security's and ConSentry Networks' Executive Advisory Councils.

Contributing Authors

Chris Gatford works for Pure Hacking Ltd. in Sydney, Australia as a Senior Security Consultant performing penetration tests for organizations all around the world. Chris has reviewed countless IT environments and has directed and been responsible for numerous security assessments for a variety of corporations and government departments.

Chris is an instructor for the Pure Hacking OPST course and in his previous role at Ernst & Young he was the lead instructor for eXtreme Hacking course. In both these roles Chris has taught the art of professional hacking to hundreds of students from global organizations.

Chris is a frequent speaker at many security related conferences (most recently presenting at AusCERT 2006). He is a member of several security professional organizations and is a Certified Information Systems Security Professional. More details and contact information is available from his homepage, www.penetrationtester.com and his current employer http://www.purehacking.com.

Ken Pfeil's IT and security experience spans over two decades with companies such as Microsoft, Dell, Avaya, Identix, BarnesandNoble.com, Merrill Lynch, Capital IQ, and Miradiant Global Network. While at Microsoft Ken coauthored Microsoft's "Best Practices for Enterprise Security" white paper series. Ken has contributed to many books including *Hack Proofing Your Network, Second Edition* (Syngress, 1928994709) and *Stealing the Network: How to Own the Box* (Syngress, 1931836876).

Bryan Cunningham (JD, Certified in NSA IAM, Top Secret security clearance) has extensive experience in information security, intelligence, and homeland security matters, both in senior U.S. Government posts and the private sector. Cunningham, now a corporate information and homeland security consultant and Principal at the Denver law firm of Morgan & Cunningham LLC, most recently served as Deputy Legal Adviser to National Security Advisor Condoleezza Rice. At the White House, Cunningham drafted key portions of the Homeland Security Act, and was deeply involved in the formation of the National Strategy to Secure Cyberspace, as well as numerous Presidential Directives and regulations relating to cybersecurity. He is a former senior CIA Officer, federal prosecutor, and founding co-chair of the ABA CyberSecurity Privacy Task Force, and, in January 2005, was awarded the National Intelligence Medal of Achievement for his work on information issues. Cunningham has been named to the National Academy of Science Committee on Biodefense Analysis and Countermeasures, and is a Senior Counselor at APCO Worldwide Consulting, as well as a member of the Markle Foundation Task Force on National Security in the Information Age. Cunningham counsels corporations on information security programs and other homeland security-related issues and, working with information security consultants, guides and supervises information security assessments and evaluations.

Contents

Foreword

I have been publicly involved with computer and software vulnerabilities in one form or another for more than a decade. In nonpublic capacities it seems that I have been involved with them, computer and otherwise, all my life. There were the early advisories that I published through the L0pht. There were reports that were sent to the government. There were offensive and defensive tools released, ranging from L0phtCrack to Anti-Sniff to SLINT, as well as private tools and tools for work only. Protecting high-profile networks, both large and small, was routine. Being tasked with breaking into well-defended enclaves was even more routine. But looking at any of these elements by themselves conveys little information. It was, and is, the understanding of the bigger picture (that is, how all the varying components interconnect from the technical bit level all the way to the business drivers and corporate attitude) that make the actual target. This remains the case irrespective of whether you are the attacker or defender.

Finding vulnerabilities was fun, largely because it was not well known what to look for. It was not always the case of people hiding information about how to find security flaws as much as it was that searching for vulnerabilities was a burgeoning field. Now there exists an almost overabundance of documents available online and in print dealing with general and specific verticals of vulnerabilities. But what does this information really tell readers in terms of the larger picture and how it relates to their specific real-world situations? How does this information enable people to do their jobs if they have the responsibility of a group within a company or perhaps an entire company itself?

What is the risk an attacker is willing to take in looking for a vulnerability? In many cases, where attackers can procure a copy of the software or operating system they are targeting and conduct their testing in their own environment, there is very little risk in searching for vulnerabilities. This scenario happens very frequently. However the real world can often differ from the lab. Perhaps it is not feasible for the attacker to replicate a particular environment because it is too elaborate or complex. Perhaps the target environment is not entirely known. In these cases what risks might people be willing to take to explore and experiment with live systems that are not theirs? What risks are involved not only in looking for unknown vulnerabilities within live external systems but also in attempting to exploit them? Does a system crash and draw attention to the attacker? Does the network become overly congested and prevent not only legitimate users but also the attacker from utilizing the services and resources contained within it?

How many and what types of opportunities for exploitation are provided to an attacker in a live environment? Are services and systems your organization offers available from anywhere at anytime? Are there sliding windows of opportunity during maintenance and rollover periods? Is the window of opportunity limited to the life cycle of software updates and revisions? Cost comes into play within the opportunity component as well. Some activities might be financially prohibitive, whereas others might be too expensive using time duration for development, delivery, and exploitation as the cost metric.

What is the motivation that drives the attacker to your environment? For some it is opportunistic, whereas for others, their motivation can be most definitely targeted. Perhaps the person has been tasked by a nation-state, competitor, or is moved to action based on a particular belief system. Or perhaps the person is simply bored, and it was your unlucky day.

This particular adversary modeling technique, also known as the ROM (Risk, Opportunity, and Motivation) model, can be very powerful.[1,2] It starts taking into account more components of adversary goals as well as applying existing real-world enclaves and environments to determine the chokepoints and activities that can be defended or witnessed. One of the benefits is that it does not look at a vulnerability without considering the environment, the goals of the adversary, the identification of the problem and environment that it exists within, and the management of the problem within the network and systems you might have been tasked to attack or defend.

Perhaps you already know how to look for vulnerabilities. Perhaps you are adept at testing them not only within artificial lab environments but also on

systems with complex interactions in the wild. Even modeling and understanding the adversaries that you are currently dealing with, as well as the many
varying types that in fact exist in the real world, are tasks that you feel comfortable with. What do you do to handle the risks that you know you are exposing
to the actors you have already defined and the ones you might have forgotten?
I have seen varying answers to varying situations. Some of which surprised me
at the time.

Take, for instance, a company of about 1,000 employees that was acquired
by a much larger organization. Shortly after this acquisition, the smaller company was told to provide unfettered access to a large business unit of the
acquiring organization. Upon a quick examination the lead security person
noticed that the network protection that the large business unit had in place to
prevent unauthorized access from the Internet at large was practically nonexis-
tent. The recommendation that was made was to not allow the business unit the
unfettered access it desired until it could improve its security posture at its
Internet access points. The rationale was that the recently acquired company's
security stance would be reduced to that of the lowest common denominator—in this case, the very porous defenses of the business unit requesting
access. This response turned out to be a naive one because of a lack of bigger
picture data (much like understanding a vulnerability on its own without
placing it into the constrains of an environment with potential attackers, operations that must be engaged in for the company to survive, adversaries with
varying goals, and costs of handling remediation efforts). As the lead security
person at the time, I had internalized a specific ROM model for the smaller
company and had not thought that the larger company might differ. As it
turned out the *correct* solution was to drop all the security filters and actions
that were preventing the business unit from attaining unfettered access. Why?
The business unit in question was the main money-maker for the larger company that had just completed the acquisition. The business unit made billions,
and, of course, in the act of making billions, the unit needed to take certain
risks. Although the risk of leaving its network relatively open and vulnerable
could arguably not be one the business unit entirely understood, it had mapped
out many others down to a very granular level. What the larger company had
determined was that it was willing to accept fraud and other losses of several
hundred million dollars per year. The small acquired company, in its totality of
revenue and holdings, was modeled into this and already accounted for.

Dropping security might enable the business unit to increase its profit tremendously while totally losing the smaller company through attack or compromise was an acceptable, and covered, possibility. Shortly after receiving this enlightenment, the security group provided all access, which is not to say that in place of the defenses that were removed there was not a sizable amount of monitoring gear created and deployed to ensure that vulnerabilities that were actively exploited would be quickly detected. Thus, it made sense to embrace the risk and embody it with the solution being to simply know as soon as possible when various inevitable breaches would occur.

When the authors of the book you have in your hands contacted me and explained what they were attempting to write, I was very pleased. I was unaware of any published books that attempted to cover the big picture in a meaningful way for people involved in varying real-world aspects of information assurance. The notion of explaining not only what a vulnerability in code might be but also how to find it—what tools are available to assist in discovering and testing it—understanding and classifying the environment you are protecting—how to manage and handle the vulnerabilities you know of and the ones you don't (but will potentially find out about in a none-to-pleasant way)—remediation and reconstitution of systems... well, if there had been widely available books covering these topics and written by well-known, knowledgeable people when I was starting out a long time ago, I would have consumed them ravenously.

Cheers,

.mudge (Peiter Zatko)
Technical Director, National Intelligence
Research and Applications division of BBN,
former advisory to the White House and Congress,
author of L0phtCrack,
and founder of @stake and Intrusic

Notes

1. John Lowry. "An Initial Foray into Understanding Adversary Planning and Courses of Action." In the proceedings of the DARPA Information Survivability Conference and Exposition (DIS-CEX II), Anaheim, CA (12-14 June 2001), vol. 1, pp. 123-133.

2. John Lowry, R. Valdez, P. Zatko, B. Wood, and D. Vukelich. "An Analytical Approach to Developing Observables for Novel Cyber Attacks and Exploitation." To be submitted for publication in the *Journal of the Intelligence Community Research and Development (JICRD)*.

## Chapter 1

Windows of Vulnerability

Solutions in this chapter:

- What Are Vulnerabilities?
- Understanding the Risks Posed by Vulnerabilities

☑ Summary

☑ Solutions Fast Track

☑ Frequently Asked Questions

Introduction

This book is not your typical information technology (IT) security book. Even though the authors of this book have technical backgrounds and have worked on such best-selling titles as Syngress' *Hack Proofing Your Network*, this book integrates the technical aspects of vulnerability management into the management of your business. Although it is important to be up on all the latest hacking methods, this knowledge is valuable only if you can tie the threats imposed by hackers to the risks these threats pose to your organization. This book will give you the tools to do just that.

Specifically, this chapter will address vulnerabilities and why they are important. We will also discuss a concept known as Windows of Vulnerability, and we will talk about how to determine the risk a given vulnerability poses to your environment.

What Are Vulnerabilities?

So, what are vulnerabilities? In the past, many people considered a vulnerability to be a software or hardware bug that a malicious individual could exploit. Over the years, however, the definition of *vulnerability* has evolved into a software or hardware bug *or misconfiguration* that a malicious individual can exploit. Patch management, configuration management, and security management all evolved from single disciplines, often competing with each other, into one IT problem known today as vulnerability management.

NOTE

Throughout this book, we will reference vulnerabilities by their CVE numbers. CVE stands for Common Vulnerabilities and Exposures, and a list of CVE numbers was created several years ago to help standardize vulnerability naming. Before this list was compiled, vendors called vulnerabilities by whatever names they came up with, making vulnerability tracking difficult and confusing. The CVE created a list of all vulnerabilities and assigned each one a CVE ID in the format *CVE-year-number*. Vendors have been encouraged to use CVE numbers when referencing vulnerabilities, a practice which has removed most of the confusion. More information on CVE numbers is available at http://cve.mitre.org.

On the surface, vulnerability management appears to be a simple task. Unfortunately, in most corporate networks, vulnerability management is difficult and complicated. A typical organization has custom applications, mobile users, and critical servers, all of which have diverse needs that cannot be simply secured and forgotten. Software vendors are still releasing insecure code, hardware vendors do not build security into their products, and systems administrators are left to clean up the mess. Add to this compliance regulations that make executives nervous, and you have a high-stress situation which is conducive to costly mistakes.

The complications surrounding vulnerability management create what is known as a Window of Vulnerability. Although this may sound like a clever play on words to draw attention to the most commonly run operating system, it is actually used in reference to the length of time a system is vulnerable to a given security flaw, configuration issue, or some other factor that reduces its overall security. There are two types of Windows of Vulnerability:

- **Unknown Window of Vulnerability** The time from when a vulnerability is discovered to when the system is patched.

- **Known Window of Vulnerability** The time from when a vendor releases a patch to when the system is patched.

Most organizations pay attention to the second type, Known Window of Vulnerability, but as you will see in later chapters, calculating the Unknown Window of Vulnerability is valuable when planning mitigation strategies.

NOTE

Many organizations offer, as a paid service, information on discovered vulnerabilities before vendor patches are available. Many larger enterprises see a value in such a service. If your organization is considering such a service, be sure to research the quality and quantity of vulnerabilities the service typically discovers, as such services are generally expensive.

Usually administrators use a table, such as the one shown in Table 1.1, to track when a vulnerability is reported and when the vendor patches it. You can use this table to calculate Unknown Windows of Vulnerability versus Known Windows of Vulnerability.

Table 1.1 Calculating Windows of Vulnerability

Vulnerability Name	Approximate Date Reported to Vendor	Date Vendor Released Patch	Time Delta	Date Patch Installed/Risk Mitigated
IE createtextrange Vulnerability (CVE-2006-1359)	2006-02-10	2006-04-11	60 days	
Sendmail Race Condition (CVE-2006-0058)	2006-01-01	2006-03-22	80 days	
WMF Vulnerability (CVE-2005-4560)	2005-12-27	2006-01-05	9 days	
QuickTime QTS Overflow (CVE-2005-4092)	2005-11-17	2006-01-10	54 days	
MediaPlayer BMP Overflow (CVE-2006-0006)	2005-10-17	2006-02-14	120 days	

Recently, a trend has emerged that adds another metric to be tracked. That metric is third-party vendors releasing unofficial patches, as shown in Table 1.2.

Table 1.2 Tracking Unofficial Third-Party Patches

Vulnerability Name	Approximate Date Reported to Vendor	Date Vendor Released Patch	Time Delta	Date Third-Party Patch Released	Time Delta	Date Patch Installed/Risk Mitigated
IE createtextrange Vulnerability (CVE-2006-1359)	2006-02-10	2006-04-11	60 days	2006-03-24	42 days	
WMF Vulnerability (CVE-2005-4560)	2005-12-27	2006-01-05	9 days	2005-12-31	4 days	

In this case, the second time delta is the time between the approximate date of report to the vendor (or public disclosure) and the release of the third-party patch. At the time of this writing (April 2006), there have been only two cases of a third-party patch being released. In both cases, the patch was well received by general users, so it is safe to assume that this trend will continue.

NOTE

Although some people welcome third-party patches, these patches have some limitations that organizations should consider. For instance, third-party patches are never superior to vendor-supplied patches. In addition, you should be able to easily remove any third-party patch you use once the vendor addresses an issue. Furthermore, third-party patches may not receive as much regression testing as vendor-supplied patches and could cause unwanted side effects. Organizations considering using a third-party patch should weigh these risks, consider the source, and take into account the true exposure a vulnerability presents to them.

The last metric in Table 1.2—Date Patch Installed/Risk Mitigated—will vary from organization to organization. You can use this final metric to calculate a third time delta based on either the notification to the vendor or the release of the public patch. The key here is to ensure that this final delta is as short as possible to minimize the total amount of time systems are vulnerable to flaws. As you read this book, you will see how implementing a proper vulnerability management plan can help you keep your overall risk to a minimum.

Before we get to implementing such a plan, yet another statistic is important to understand when planning a vulnerability management strategy. That statistic is the delta between either the time a vulnerability is reported to the vendor or the time the patch is released, and the time it takes for a working exploit to be released to the public. This statistic is important because the risk a vulnerability represents to an organization increases exponentially when working exploit code is available to the general public.

The timelines in Figure 1.1 represent some of the more serious vulnerabilities as well as all of the important data points concerning them.

Figure 1.1 Timeline of Serious Vulnerabilities

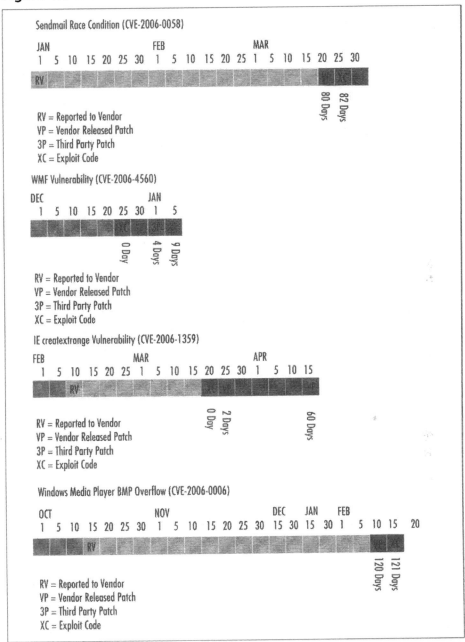

So, what does Figure 1.1 actually mean? As you can see, it illustrates the time between when a vendor became aware of an issue to when an issue was patched. Other data points are the date that the exploit code was released and the date a third-party patch was released. The figure helps show how long an organization can be vulnerable to an issue before it is even made aware of that issue. Once an organization becomes aware of an issue, its vulnerability to that issue extends until it can either patch the issue or mitigate it.

Most corporations are left at the mercy of the vendor and, in some cases, the person/organization that discovered the issue to make them aware that it exists. You can use a number of resources to remain up-to-date on security issues and their patches. For instance, most vendors offer patch and security issue mailing lists; also, multiple public mailing lists post issues. Table 1.3 is a list of security mailing lists and their relative usefulness.

Table 1.3 Security Mailing Lists

List Name	Web Site	Comments
Bugtraq	www.securityfocus.com/archive/1/description	This is one of the original security mailing lists. Traffic is high, but if an issue exists, it is almost always posted to this list.
VulnWatch	www.vulnwatch.org	This is comparable to Bugtraq, with the exception of the high volume of traffic, as it is not a general discussion list but a security issue announcement list only.
Full-Disclosure	https://lists.grok.org.uk/mailman/listinfo/full-disclosure	This is an unmoderated list. Traffic is extremely high and the list frequently goes off topic. You must have thick skin and a lot of time to filter e-mail.
Microsoft Security Bulletins	www.microsoft.com/technet/security/bulletin/notify.mspx	This is the Microsoft Security Bulletin list where you can be notified of issues concerning Microsoft products.
Apple Security Alerts	http://lists.apple.com/mailman/listinfo/security-announce	This is the Apple Computer Security Bulletin list.

Vendors become aware of vulnerabilities in many different ways. In an ideal world, the vendors themselves would find and fix all security issues before they ship their products, but the complexity of code combined with aggressive development cycles is conducive to development mistakes in the area of security. Usually an independent or commercial security researcher notifies vendors of vulnerabilities, and in some cases, vendors become aware of vulnerabilities at the same time the general public does, when they are disclosed without any prenotification.

Understanding the Risks Posed by Vulnerabilities

Regardless of how a vulnerability becomes public, the vulnerability poses a risk to an organization. The amount of risk the vulnerability presents depends on a number of factors:

- Vendor risk rating
- Number of affected systems within an organization
- Criticality of affected systems within an organization
- Exposure affected systems present to the organization

An organization can calculate risk in a number of ways. One of the more logical ways, at least at a higher level, is by using the following formula:

Risk = Vulnerability x Attacks x Threat x Exposure

where:

V = Vulnerability A measure of issues that are considered vulnerabilities. This measure is usually a function of a vulnerability assessment—for example, an audit conducted with Tenable Network Security's Nessus or eEye Digital Security's Retina.

A = Attacks A measure of actual attacks and dangers, which is typically a function of a host- or network-based intrusion detection/prevention tool—for example, eEye Digital Security's Blink or the open source network intrusion detection system, Snort. Organizations that do not have these tools in place can use public attack tracking services.

T = Threat A measure of lurking or impending danger. This is known as the threat climate, which comprises such factors as availability and ease of exploit.

E = Exposure An accounting of an organization's vulnerability to an attack, or how much periphery must be protected and how poorly it is being protected.

As you can see, two terms do not appear in this list: criticality and vendor risk rating. *Criticality* is a measure of how valuable an affected asset is to the organization if it is compromised. Some schools of thought place a lot of importance in this metric, perhaps too much importance, because if you consider a typical network, every system is interconnected to foster communication of various protocols. A system that is considered highly critical, by its very nature, is able to communicate with those that are not critical.

Penetration testers and even malicious attackers will typically attempt to compromise the lowest-hanging fruit first. These are the systems that are easy to compromise because an organization does not consider them critical enough to patch quickly. These systems then become staging points for further attacks on the internal infrastructure and the more critical systems. So, for example, if an organization's accounting systems are of the highest criticality, how do you rate all of the workstations that connect to these systems? If they are not equally critical, they could be left vulnerable and used as an attack vector against the truly critical accounting systems.

When dealing with patch management methodologies, which we will explain in depth later in this book, criticality becomes more of an issue, and it is definitely recommended to patch critical systems before noncritical ones, but in the case of calculating a risk rating, it is not as important as the other factors.

NOTE

A large banking institution has taken measures to place all financial audit systems on its own network and behind its own independent firewalls. Although segregating important systems is a good strategy, it does not take into account the fact that a large number of employees need to access this data. So, what you essentially have is a firewall acting as an expensive logging device, allowing a set of client machines through. Sure, the firewall protects against some threats, but if the threat is coming over an allowed communications channel, the firewall is not going to be of help. The real solution here is to put the entire department on its own segregated network and not allow any outside access to this network.

Vendor risk rating is typically an arbitrary rating assigned by the vendor with the vulnerable software. Although you should consider this measure, it is not as important as the preceding factors, which are environment specific.

NOTE

At the time of this writing, there was a lot of media attention surrounding what vendors were truly patching with patches. A presentation at the Black Hat Briefings Europe (www.blackhat.com) by one of this book's authors, Steve Manzuik, and a co-worker, Andre Protas, titled "Skeletons in Microsoft's Closet," highlighted a practice by all vendors, not just Microsoft, of silently fixing internally found vulnerabilities when releasing patches for publicly found vulnerabilities. In addition, various posts by other researchers on the technical mailing list Dailydave (www.immunitysec.com/mailman/listinfo/dailydave) highlighted other issues and their potential impact. Consider the impact this practice has on your internal threat assessment of a vulnerability. Can an organization know the true threat of a vulnerability if the vendor is not disclosing all potential issues?

Let's get back to our formula for measuring risk, and expand on it by looking at it in a different way. Those who have been in the information security industry for even the briefest amount of time probably recognize the classic analogy of a castle when referring to various protection mechanisms. Keeping with this analogy, let's use a castle that needs defending to better illustrate risk calculation.

You can view a computing asset—for example, a server—as a castle. Castle walls protect an inner sanctum containing gold. Armies are attempting to breach the castle walls and enter the inner sanctum to get the gold or disrupt the castle.

With this analogy, the following applies:

- **Exposure** How exposed the castle is to attack.

- **Periphery** A measure of the extent of the castle walls and the openings that can be attacked.

- **Lack of protection** A measure of how poorly this castle periphery is protected (by moats, guards, gates, etc.).

- **Threat** A measure of the enemy armies lurking on the hills surrounding the castle, who are priming for attack.

- **Attacks** A measure of the actual arrows and bombs and breach attempts on the walls and inner sanctum.

- **Vulnerabilities** A measure of how easy it is for the inner sanctum to be breached and used to gain access to the gold.

- Asset value/criticality A measure of how valuable and important the castle and inner sanctum are in terms of value (gold) and importance to the empire.

If each measure is given a binary number that is scaled between 1 and 5—1 being low and 5 being high—this method of risk calculation is very straightforward and simple. The higher the number, the higher the risk is to which the organization is exposed.

As an example, we'll discuss a fictional server environment in a popular Web hosting company consisting of systems vulnerable to the Sendmail Race Condition (CVE-2006-0058). In this case, Vulnerability would receive a score of 5 because of its impact on affected systems.

At the time of this writing, Attacks would receive a 2 based on the nature of the attack required to exploit this vulnerability and public reports of attacks exploiting this vulnerability. In addition, working exploit code is not available to the public.

Threat would receive a 4 based on the popularity of the company and the frequency with which it comes under attack.

Exposure in this case would receive a 5 because the service affected, Sendmail, is exposed to the Internet and is not easily protected.

Remember:

Risk = Vulnerability x Attacks x Threat x Exposure

So in this case:

Risk = 5 x 2 x 4 x 5

Risk = 200

The maximum risk will always be 625 and the minimum will always be 1. To further clarify this calculation let's look at the same environment but perform the calculation using the Windows Metafile (WMF) vulnerability (CVE-2005-4560).

As with the Sendmail vulnerability, Vulnerability in this case would receive a high score of 5 because it allows for remote code to be executed on affected systems.

At the time of this writing, Attacks would also receive a 5 because use of this vulnerability has been reported to be widespread and working exploit code is easily found on the Internet.

Threat for this vulnerability against this specific environment would actually receive the lowest score of 1 because this is a server environment running Sendmail. This vulnerability relies on users surfing to malicious Web sites to be effective, something that is not typically done from a server environment running Sendmail.

Exposure for this specific environment would also receive a 1. As stated earlier, Web browsing is not typically done from this environment.

Therefore:

Risk = 5 x 5 x 1 x 1

Risk = 25

If you take this same vulnerability but perform the calculation for an end-user environment that is constantly surfing the Internet, the calculation would look something like this:

Risk = 5 x 5 x 5 x 3

Risk = 375

We went to the trouble of explaining this based on two separate vulnerabilities multiple times to ensure that you understand that the risk score is completely dependant on the environment at risk. This also helps to illustrate how something such as a vendor risk rating does not really matter a heck of a lot to most organizations.

NOTE

Readers should check out the Common Vulnerability Scoring System (CVSS) for an alternate, vendor-agnostic, open standard of scoring vulnerabilities. CVSS is an attempt to solve the problem of multiple vendors having their own scoring system, which can cause confusion for IT security professionals trying to understand multiple systems.

Summary

This chapter covered the basic concepts of what a vulnerability is and how it can affect your environment. We talked about the different ways your network can be attacked and the different levels of exposure an organization has while waiting for patches. We looked briefly at some recent cases of third-party patches and some of the reasons to be wary of such things. We discussed the various free places to get security information but avoided talking about some of the pay vulnerability services, as we address those later in the book. Finally, we covered in great detail one way to calculate risk and determine an actual risk rating, as well as things to consider when securing systems, such as which systems communicate with each other. We also covered an alternate way to calculate risk, known as CVSS.

Solutions Fast Track

What Are Vulnerabilities?

☑ A vulnerability is a software or hardware bug or misconfiguration that a malicious individual can exploit.

☑ A vulnerability can be publicly disclosed before a vendor patch, or can even be used quietly by attackers. You can subscribe to a number of public mailing lists to keep up with disclosed vulnerabilities.

☑ An organization experiences multiple levels of risk to a vulnerability, depending on how the discoverer of the vulnerability deals with the information and how long it takes the vendor affected to issue a patch or workaround.

Understanding the Risks Posed by Vulnerabilities

☑ When determining risk, do not consider only the system that was affected. You need to consider all the systems connected to that system to understand the true risk.

☑ There are multiple ways to calculate the risk of a vulnerability. Use the one that best suits you and your environment.

Frequently Asked Questions

The following Frequently Asked Questions, answered by the authors of this book, are designed to both measure your understanding of the concepts presented in this chapter and to assist you with real-life implementation of these concepts. To have your questions about this chapter answered by the author, browse to **www.syngress.com/solutions** and click on the **"Ask the Author"** form.

Q: If a vulnerability has not been made public, there is no risk, right?

A: Not really. Just because you have not seen a vendor patch or a public report of an issue does not mean it does not exist. There have been cases of malicious individuals using unreported flaws to perform targeted attacks on organizations.

Q: How can vulnerability management help me defend against these unreported flaws?

A: Vulnerability management is not a panacea. It is only one part, albeit a very important part, of an organization's overall security posture. Only after an organization has addressed all known flaws can it effectively monitor for other attacks using unknown flaws.

Q: Can we standardize on CVSS rather than the method outlined in this book?

A: Sure. The method of calculating risk we presented in this book is one method used in various commercial products. CVSS is a great alternative and both methods have their own pros and cons.

## Chapter 2

Vulnerability Assessment 101

Solutions in this chapter:

- What Is a Vulnerability Assessment?
- Seeking Out Vulnerabilities
- Detecting Vulnerabilities via Security Technologies
- The Importance of Seeking Out Vulnerabilities

- ☑ Summary
- ☑ Solutions Fast Track
- ☑ Frequently Asked Questions

Introduction

Vulnerabilities exist; they always have and always will. Just think of the potential impact to the economy if vulnerabilities weren't present, at least in commercial-grade products. Would major organizations still invest in a security program? What sort of work would we be doing, if not security? As security practitioners and business leaders, we must realize that vulnerabilities are a part of life; a part of our consumption of technology. As such, we must practice due diligence in ensuring that vulnerabilities don't represent an undo liability to our organization, creating an unacceptable level of risk. This chapter focuses on what a vulnerability assessment is; traditional and alternative methods for discovering vulnerabilities; and the importance of seeking out vulnerabilities.

What Is a Vulnerability Assessment?

One might equate a vulnerability assessment (or VA) to a reconnaissance mission within the military. The purpose of the recon exercise is to go forth, into foreign territory, and ascertain weakness; vulnerabilities within the opposition. Upon completion of the exercise, military commanders should have greater insight and intelligence regarding their target(s); knowing its strengths as well as its weaknesses. Like reconnaissance missions, vulnerability assessments are security exercises that aid business leaders, security professionals, and hackers in identifying security liabilities within networks, applications, and systems.

In this section, we'll discuss the steps involved in conducting a vulnerability assessment: information gathering/discovery, enumeration, and detection. This section will provide an introductory view to vulnerability assessment. The next chapter will dive into the how-to and technical details associated with vulnerability assessments.

Step 1: Information Gathering/Discovery

Information gathering and discovery is the process an individual or group performs to ascertain the breath/scope of an assessment. The purpose of this step is to identify and determine the total number of systems and applications that will be assessed. Output of this step typically consists of host names,

Internet Protocol (IP) addresses, available port information, and possibly target contact information.

You can divide the information-gathering process into two components: nonintrusive and semi-intrusive efforts. *Nonintrusive efforts* reflect the public gathering of information regarding the target; the target is unaware of these activities. This includes *whois* queries to identify all of the domain names the target owns, as well as possible targets and IP address lookups via sites such as www.arin.net to identify IP address ranges associated with the target. Figure 2.1 shows a *whois* query against one of the IP addresses that hosts www.microsoft.com.

Figure 2.1 A whois Query

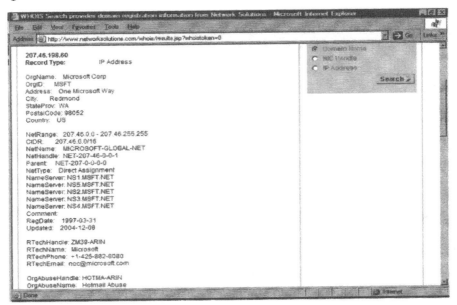

In Figure 2.1, we went to www.networksolutions.com/whois and conducted a *whois* query for 207.46.198.60, a Microsoft Web server. We determined the IP address by performing a domain name system (DNS) lookup, a process used to resolve an IP address to a domain name, against www.microsoft.com; another noninvasive information gathering technique.

By performing a *whois* query against the IP address, we were able to gather the following information:

- The company's physical address

- Contact information

- The IP address range used by the company

- DNS servers responsible for the domain

Having a better idea of the target footprint, we can proceed to discovering what systems and possible applications reside on the target network.

Tools & Traps...

Who What?

whois is a program that provides people with registered information regarding domain names and their registrants: for instance, the administrative contact, name servers, domain expiration, and so on. InterNIC maintains the *whois* database. Users can either leverage the *whois* tool on their local machine, if available, or visit www.internic.net to query for information.

Semi-intrusive efforts consist of nondisruptive communications calls between the attacker and target in an effort by the attacker to gain further information regarding the target's systems; the target can detect this. This communication usually consists of ping sweeps, to identify active hosts, and port scans, to ascertain what ports and, potentially, applications, reside on a given system. Utilizing Nmap software, we can quickly determine what hosts are available on a network, as shown in Figure 2.2.

Figure 2.2 An Nmap Ping Sweep

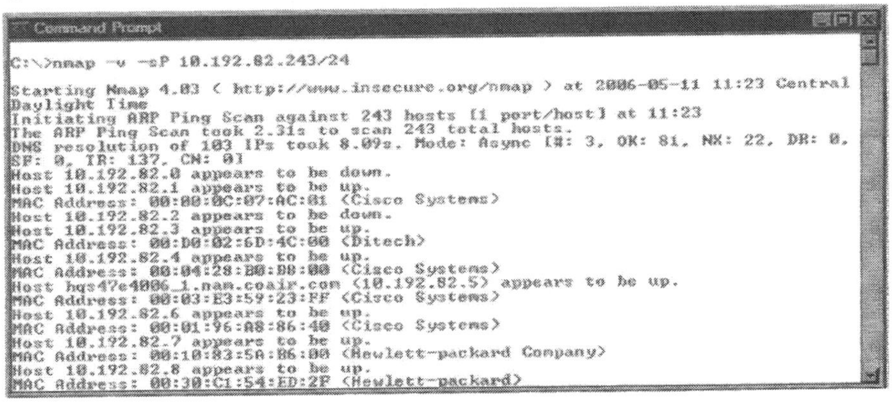

```
Command Prompt

C:\>nmap -v -sP 10.192.82.243/24

Starting Nmap 4.03 ( http://www.insecure.org/nmap ) at 2006-05-11 11:23 Central
Daylight Time
Initiating ARP Ping Scan against 243 hosts [1 port/host] at 11:23
The ARP Ping Scan took 2.31s to scan 243 total hosts.
DNS resolution of 103 IPs took 8.09s. Mode: Async [#: 3, OK: 81, NX: 22, DR: 0,
SF: 0, TR: 137, CN: 0]
Host 10.192.82.0 appears to be down.
Host 10.192.82.1 appears to be up.
MAC Address: 00:00:0C:07:AC:01 (Cisco Systems)
Host 10.192.82.2 appears to be down.
Host 10.192.82.3 appears to be up.
MAC Address: 00:D0:02:6D:4C:00 (Ditech)
Host 10.192.82.4 appears to be up.
MAC Address: 00:04:28:B0:D0:00 (Cisco Systems)
Host hqs47e4006_1.nam.coair.com (10.192.82.5) appears to be up.
MAC Address: 00:03:E3:59:23:FF (Cisco Systems)
Host 10.192.82.6 appears to be up.
MAC Address: 00:01:96:A8:86:40 (Cisco Systems)
Host 10.192.82.7 appears to be up.
MAC Address: 00:10:83:5A:B6:00 (Hewlett-packard Company)
Host 10.192.82.8 appears to be up.
MAC Address: 00:30:C1:54:ED:2F (Hewlett-packard)
```

Using the *-sP* (ping scan) switch within Nmap, we can conduct a ping sweep of the target network. This will help us determine what hosts are active and available. Once we've determined this, the information-gathering/discovery step is complete. It's now time to proceed to step 2, enumeration, and determine what operating systems and applications the target possesses.

Step 2: Enumeration

Enumeration is the process used to determine the target operating system—a process called *OS fingerprinting*—and the applications that reside on it. Upon determining the operating system, the next step is to substantiate the applications that reside on the host. Ports 0 through 1023 are considered *well-known ports*, or port numbers reserved for assignment by the Internet Corporation for Assigned Names and Numbers (ICANN).[1] Ports within this range are reserved for specific applications; for example, http is assigned port 80 and https (secure http) is assigned port 443. Though ports 0 through 1023 are reserved for specific applications, this does not preclude other applications from utilizing them.

Keeping with Nmap, we use its *-sV* (service/version info) switch to determine what applications are residing on what ports (see Figure 2.3).

Figure 2.3 Nmap Service Detection

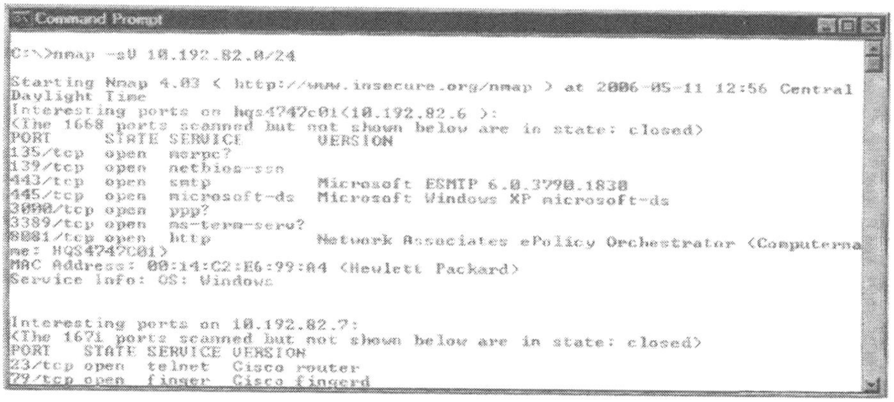

```
Command Prompt                                                    _ □ ×
C:\>nmap -sV 10.192.82.0/24

Starting Nmap 4.03 < http://www.insecure.org/nmap > at 2006-05-11 12:56 Central
Daylight Time
Interesting ports on hqs4747c01(10.192.82.6 ):
(The 1668 ports scanned but not shown below are in state: closed)
PORT     STATE SERVICE     VERSION
135/tcp  open  msrpc?
139/tcp  open  netbios-ssn
443/tcp  open  smtp         Microsoft ESMTP 6.0.3790.1830
445/tcp  open  microsoft-ds Microsoft Windows XP microsoft-ds
3890/tcp open  ppp?
3389/tcp open  ms-term-serv?
8081/tcp open  http         Network Associates ePolicy Orchestrator (Computerna
me: HQS4747C01)
MAC Address: 00:14:C2:E6:99:A4 (Hewlett Packard)
Service Info: OS: Windows

Interesting ports on 10.192.82.7:
(The 1671 ports scanned but not shown below are in state: closed)
PORT     STATE SERVICE VERSION
23/tcp  open  telnet  Cisco router
79/tcp  open  finger  Cisco fingerd
```

Notice anything interesting in Figure 2.3? Take a look at what service is running on tcp 443; it's Microsoft's Simple Mail Transfer Protocol (SMTP) service rather than a secure Web server, the reserved application for tcp 443.

Port enumeration plays a pivotal role in vulnerability assessment because it ensures that we map vulnerabilities to respective applications. Given Figure 2.3, if we were to assume the host in question was running a secure Web server rather than an e-mail server on port 443, it would have been highly unlikely that we would have been able to determine the host's vulnerabilities, negating future penetration possibilities. With the grunt work of information gathering and enumeration complete, it's now time to detect vulnerabilities on the target systems.

Step 3: Detection

Detection is the method used to determine whether a system or application is susceptible to attack (i.e., vulnerable). This step doesn't confirm that vulnerabilities exist; penetration tests do that. The detection process only reports the likelihood that vulnerabilities are present.

To detect vulnerabilities we'll need to utilize a vulnerability assessment tool such as Tenable Network Security's Nessus or eEye Digital Security's Retina. Neither tool is free, so we'll need to evaluate the cost or pursue open source alternatives prior to conducting this step.

Once we have procured a VA tool, we can continue the assessment, targeting the systems we've evaluated in steps 1 and 2 to determine whether they have any vulnerabilities. VA tools detect vulnerabilities by probing remote systems and comparing the systems' response to a set of good (expected) and bad (vulnerable) responses. If the VA tool receives what it considers a bad response it assumes the host is vulnerable.

Tools & Traps...

Assessment Complete?

In today's information age, vulnerability assessments are a must, but they are not the be-all and end-all. VAs need to be supported by an enterprise remediation strategy, and assessments should target not only Windows, UNIX, and Linux systems, but also all IP-connected devices and applications within your infrastructure.

Notes from the Underground...

Intrusive or Not Intrusive?

Vulnerability assessments, unlike good reconnaissance, can be intrusive. I recall walking into the office one morning, firing up e-mail, printing off an attachment, and walking over to the printer, only to hear, "You can print?" Unbeknownst to me, the vulnerability assessment I had launched the night before knocked out all the company's Hewlett-Packard direct cards and, ultimately, the printers. I was able to print because I was printing to the printer's Line Printer Remote (LPR) interface. After a little investigating, we found out that the firmware on the jet directs hadn't been upgraded in more than three years and simply port-pinging the jet directs rendered them unavailable. Who knew? Technically the printers weren't vulnerable, but their inability to handle port pings and our failure to include them in the company's remediation strategy caused some disruption.

Seeking Out Vulnerabilities

Identifying vulnerabilities across an enterprise is a major endeavor. We can't simply install a vulnerability scanner in selected locations and press Go. It doesn't work that way. It doesn't because today's enterprises consist of thousands of servers and tens of thousands of hosts connected via hundreds of network circuits with varying speeds. We simply can't get the required coverage within the desired timeframe. So what do we do? Do we stop conducting enterprise-level assessments knowing that 95 percent of all security breaches occur due to misconfigurations of systems or known vulnerabilities that have not been remediated? The answer, of course, is *no*. Enterprise-level assessments are still required. Instead of simply dropping scanners onto our networks, as done in years past, we should leverage our company's existing vulnerability management investment—its investment in security, patch, and configuration management technologies—and develop a hybrid approach to vulnerability assessment that takes advantage of the strength of each respective technology.

Detecting Vulnerabilities via Security Technologies

Traditionally when we wanted to ascertain system- or application-level vulnerabilities, we installed vulnerability assessment scanners throughout our enterprise. These scanners were responsible for detecting network hosts (information gathering), discovering available applications (enumeration), and ascertaining vulnerabilities (detection). VA scanners were typically network appliances running VA software or VA software running on a company-owned asset. Figures 2.4 and 2.5 represent a typical organization's VA infrastructure.

As you can see in Figures 2.3 and 2.4, in smaller networks, a single VA scanner may be sufficient for conducting the organization's vulnerability assessments. However, larger enterprises will require multiple VA scanners to support their assessment needs.

Figure 2.4 A Typical VA Scanner

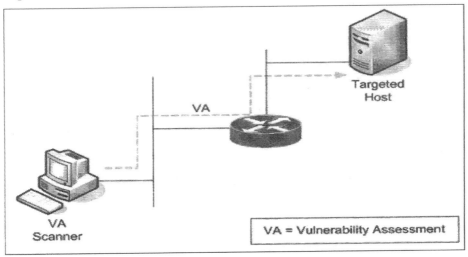

Figure 2.5 An Enterprise VA Deployment

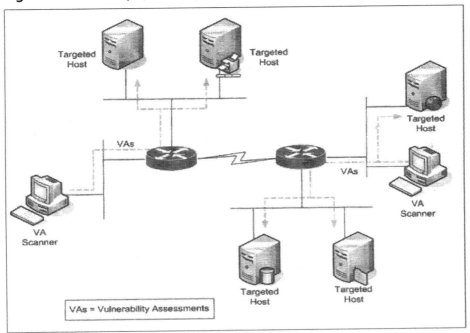

As you can imagine from Figure 2.5, traditional methods of gathering vulnerability assessment data could pose many challenges for large enterprises. Not only must an organization be concerned with managing the remediation infrastructure to address the discovered vulnerabilities, but it must also concern itself with the VA infrastructure used to ascertain these liabilities. Though traditional VA methodologies may pose some manageability and scalability challenges, they are often the only sure way to validate vulnerabilities exposed to a remote entity.

Deciphering VA Data Gathered by Security Technologies

Vulnerability assessment reports provide a lot of insightful information, as listed here and depicted in Figure 2.6:

- Duration of the assessment
- Number of machines scanned
- Vulnerabilities by severity
- List of all identified vulnerabilities
- Vulnerabilities per host

Figure 2.6 Vulnerability Analysis Results Using Retina

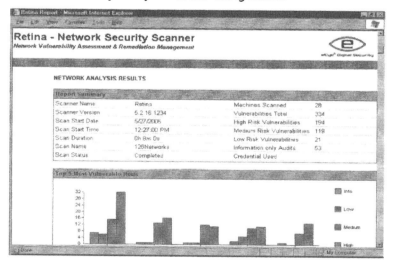

As a security analyst, manager, or business unit leader, you can quickly gauge your organization's susceptibility to known security vulnerabilities. In Figure 2.6, 334 vulnerabilities are present across 28 machines, 194 of which are considered high risk. In Figure 2.7, vulnerabilities are further broken down by risk, percentages, and average number of vulnerabilities by risk category per host.

Figure 2.7 Vulnerability Breakout

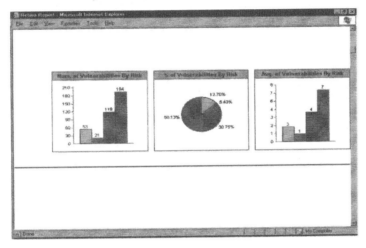

Analyzing the VA report further, we're able to discern what our most prominent vulnerabilities are, as reflected in Figure 2.8.

Figure 2.8 Top Vulnerabilities

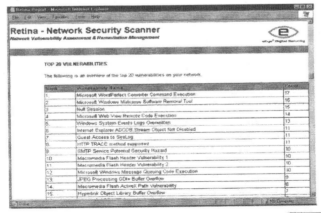

To a security practitioner and business professional, the chart in Figure 2.8 provides insightful and more reflective information regarding the true security posture of the organization. Figure 2.7 illustrated that more than 50 percent (194 out of 334) of the discovered vulnerabilities were of high risk. Figure 2.8 lists the top 20 vulnerabilities within the environment. Using these two figures, we can make risk determinations regarding the true security risk to the organization. By evaluating each vulnerability listed against its applicability to our organization, we can discern whether the vulnerabilities reported represent a benign (false) or malignant (real) threat to our organization. We can then decide whether our organization is operating at an elevated level of risk. How many vulnerabilities in Figure 2.8 would represent a benign (or questionable) threat to your organization? Table 2.1 shows 74 questionable vulnerabilities.

Table 2.1 Questionable Vulnerabilities

Vulnerability Description	Count
Microsoft Windows Malicious Software Removal Tool	15
Null Session Exposures	15
Windows System Events Logs Overwritten	13
Guest Access to Sys Instances	11
Macromedia Flash Header Vulnerability 1	10
Macromedia Flash Header Vulnerability 2	10
Total	**74**

These vulnerabilities are questionable or benign because they may not represent vulnerabilities within our organization. This means we have compensating controls to address the risk, or that as an organization, we've decided to accept the risk presented by the identified vulnerabilities.

Table 2.1 highlights the need for security and business professionals to know what represents a liability to an organization. Vulnerabilities are often deemed high or critical by software manufacturers, but that may not be accurate in terms of our own environments. Manufacturers and research companies are at the mercy of classifying vulnerability risk based on the lowest common denominator; the ultimate impact to an asset given no security or compensating controls.

Notes from the Underground…

Detect This

Vulnerability scanners are great at detecting known vulnerabilities and are pretty good at detecting configuration errors that represent vulnerabilities, but they, as well as most technologies, are inept at detecting 0 day (zero day) vulnerabilities, or vulnerabilities that haven't been released to the general public.

Accessing Vulnerabilities via Remediation (Patch) Technologies

Today all companies have remediation strategies and supported processes, and if they don't, they should. Most strategies outline how and when applications and systems are remediated. Prior to the past decade, these processes and supporting technologies focused on providing application stability—addressing things such as memory leaks—and application enrichment, adding new levels of functionality. The phrase, "if it ain't broke, don't fix it," was certainly the motto during this era.

Over the past 10 years, the remediation landscape has changed. Remediation efforts have gone from manual to automated processes, creating a new product industry. In addition, the primary objective and purpose of a remediation strategy is no longer to support application stability and enrichment, but to address application- and system-level vulnerabilities. In identifying this, remediation technology providers and patch management companies have added new interfaces within their products, allowing for a new and nontraditional way to identify vulnerabilities.

As we mentioned earlier, traditionally a company would have to roll out vulnerability assessment sensors to gather VA data. What if we haven't invested in VA technology or simply can't afford it? What should we do? Considering that most patching technologies keep a history of the systems and applications they've patched, we can simply leverage our remediation repository to help us assess the security state of our environment.

Extracting VA Data from Remediation Repositories

Many capable remediation solutions are available today. However, prior to selecting one, we should be cognizant of the scope of our remediation efforts. Are we simply concerned with Windows systems? Maybe we need to address UNIX, Linux, and possibly a mainframe environment, too. Whatever the solution, our selected technology should be able to provide us with VA information similar to what's presented in the following example.

The following two figures reflect VA reports that were generated via Microsoft's Systems Management Server (SMS). SMS refers to these figures as compliance reports, but we can also use the same information to infer vulnerability information. If we go to the SMS reporting home page, the screen in Figure 2.9 appears.

Figure 2.9 SMS Reporting Home Page

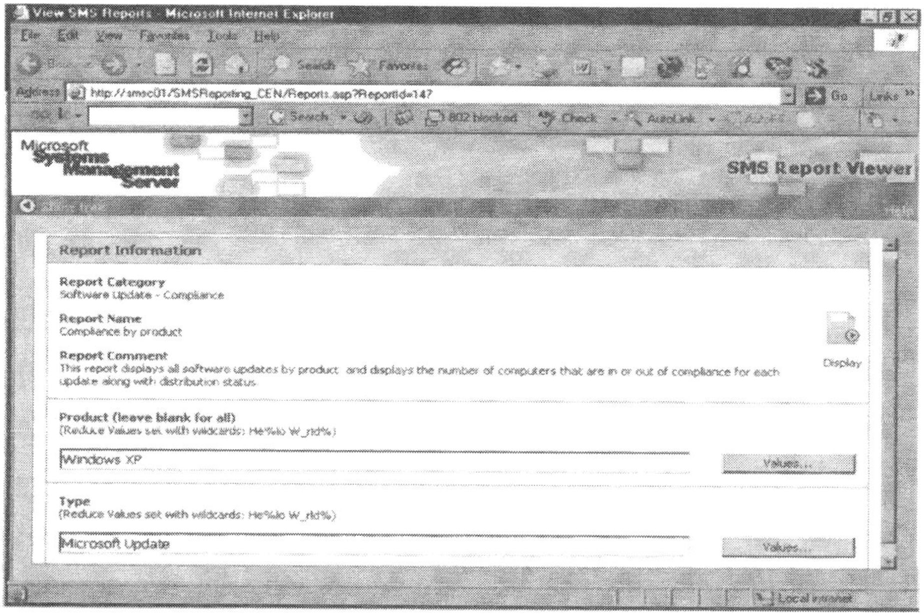

Upon accessing SMS' home page, we can generate compliance reports for operating systems, products, security bulletins, and so on. In Figure 2.9, we wanted to generate a compliance report for all Microsoft security updates on Windows XP hosts within our environment. The output of the report should reflect security patches and respective quantities that have been applied within our environment. Though SMS references Figure 2.10 as a compliance report, we also can use this report to determine vulnerabilities.

Figure 2.10 SMS Compliance Report

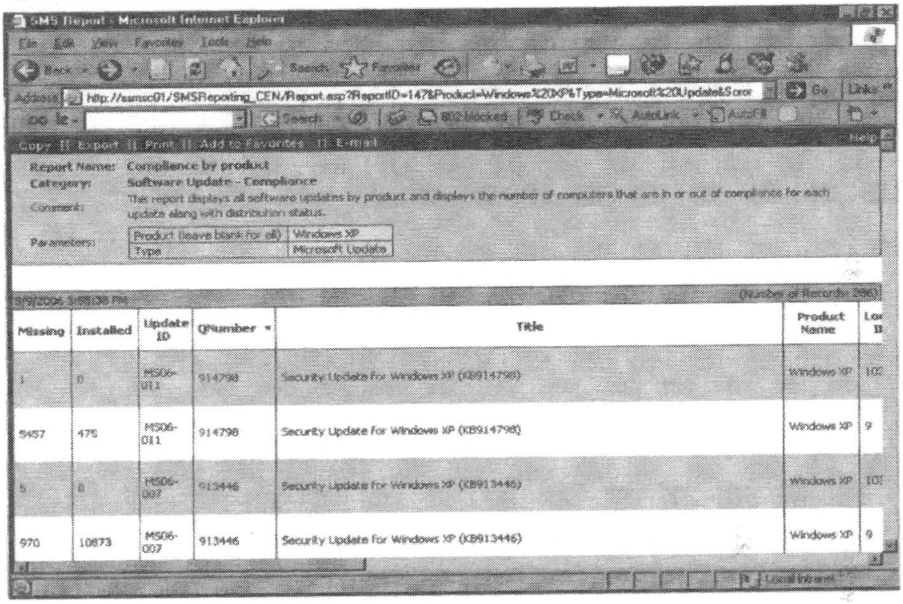

Regardless of whether we use SMS or another remediation solution, the purpose of the preceding illustration was not to showcase SMS, but to illustrate how we can leverage remediation environments to extract VA data. In Figure 2.10, 5,457 systems are missing MS06-011, QNumber 914798. If malware were developed against this bulletin, we could use reports such as that depicted in Figure 2.10 to help determine the level of risk to our organization.

Tools & Traps...

Remediation Caveat

Remediation technologies may scale better and provide more timely VA information than traditional vulnerability solutions, but they do not provide the hacker's perspective of an asset. Most remediation technologies query their database to ascertain whether a patching exercise was successful, negating consideration for compensating controls that may exist that would prevent the vulnerability from being exploited. Some also don't take into consideration whether a system has rebooted since it was last patched. A machine that has failed to reboot may still be vulnerable.

Leveraging Configuration Tools to Assess Vulnerabilities

Many corporations have invested in management/configuration tools. They often use these tools for fairly routine tasks, but we can extend them to extract vulnerability data from within our environments. Take, for example, Symantec's (formerly BindView's) bv-Control and bv-Admin products. Using both products, an organization could handle most of its daily Windows Active Directory operations. Conversely, we can also use these products to discover vulnerabilities within our organizations. To understand this better, let's take a look at a BindView deployment.

BindView's infrastructure has two key components (see Figure 2.11):

- **The BindView Information Server (BVIS)** The brain of the BindView technology.

- **The Query Engine** Handles query fulfillment and acquisition of requested data.

Figure 2.11 BindView Infrastructure

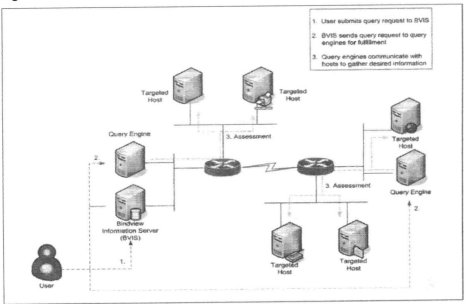

Leveraging our configuration management investment, we could (1) submit a query to the BVIS seeking to gather information regarding system patch levels. The BVIS would then (2) forward that request to the appropriate query engines and the query engines in turn would (3) gather the requested information. Figure 2.12 shows output of such an exercise.

We can leverage BindView reports such as the one in Figure 2.12 to assess the vulnerability risk posed by a single host or a collection of hosts within our enterprise.

There are a lot of similarities between traditional VA and configuration management technologies. Both require infrastructure and they go about acquiring vulnerability data in a similar fashion. There are some subtle, yet important, differences, though. Unlike traditional VA, configuration management technologies require administrative rights to fully assess a system. In addition, configuration management technologies are unaware of your entire enterprise and must be fed or extract system information from a repository such as Active Directory or a Network Information Service (NIS) domain.

Figure 2.12 BindView Output

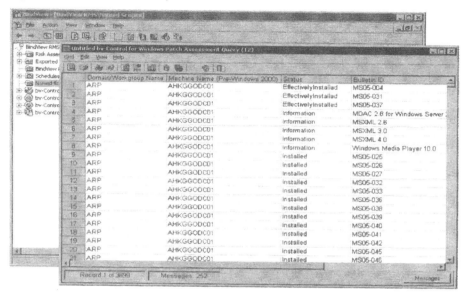

Though there are some shortcomings in leveraging configuration management technologies as the source of vulnerability data, as businesspeople we should leverage our existing investments and take advantage of the secondary and tertiary functions of our tools.

The Importance of Seeking Out Vulnerabilities

Seeking out vulnerabilities is important and is a vital part of an organization's information security program. Vulnerabilities present malicious users with an opportunity to gain unauthorized access to a system. Most everyone agrees with this. Whether organizations are due diligent in addressing this is another question. Many corporations do their part. Those that aren't may no longer have an option regarding this. Regulatory compliance, which we'll discuss later, as well as third parties, your business partners, are now mandating that companies conduct vulnerability assessments along with a plethora of other security requirements. Failure to seek out vulnerabilities and substantiate this to your business partner or a regulated body could spell a breach of contract and qualify as a termination of said contract.

Seeking out vulnerabilities is part of "Common Sense Security 101." Common Sense Security 101 refers to conducting security measures that make common sense; doing the things your customers and business partners would expect of you. It only makes sense to seek out vulnerabilities and integrate this process into your organization's information security program, given that more than 22,800 vulnerabilities have been released since 2003.

Looking Closer at the Numbers

The number of vulnerabilities that have been discovered and publicly disclosed has steadily increased since 2000. CERT, a federally funded research and development center operated by Carnegie Mellon University, has been maintaining reported vulnerability statistics since 1995. For the purpose of our efforts, we'll focus on reported vulnerability data since 2000. Vulnerability data prior to 2000 does not indicate the number of vulnerabilities that existed in commercial software. Furthermore, there wasn't as much emphasis on vulnerability research before 2000 as there is today. To illustrate this let's take a look at reported vulnerabilities from 1995 to 1999 (Table 2.2) and 2000 to 2005 (Table 2.3).

Table 2.2 Vulnerabilities Reported from 1995 to 1999*

Year	Vulnerabilities Reported
1995	171
1996	345
1997	311
1998	262
1999	417
Total	**1506**

*Numbers provided by CERT 2

Table 2.3 Vulnerabilities Reported Since 2000*

Year	Vulnerabilities Reported
2000	1,090
2001	2,437
2002	4,129
2003	3,784
2004	3,780
2005	5,990
Total	**21,210**

*Numbers provided by CERT [2]

From 1995 to 1999, only 1,506 vulnerabilities were publicly reported. In 2000 alone, 1,090 vulnerabilities were reported. Using 2000 as the base year, the period from which relative levels are measured, 2005 represents a more than 500 percent increase in the number of vulnerabilities reported annually. Figure 2.13 graphically displays this point.

Figure 2.13 Vulnerabilities Since 2000

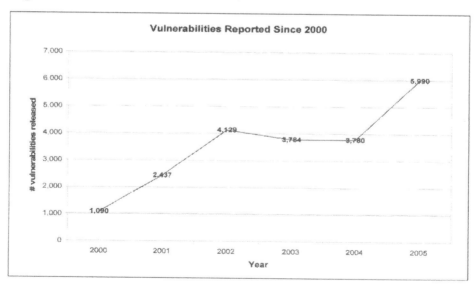

Having plotted the reported data since 2000, we can now use statistics to compare the number of expected vulnerabilities to the number of actual (reported) vulnerabilities between 2000 and 2005. To help us with that we'll use liner regression and we'll add a *best fit line* to Figure 2.14. The best fit line will plot an expected average of the reported vulnerabilities that we should have witnessed from 2000 to 2005 and will allow us to estimate reported vulnerabilities in future years.

Tools & Traps...

Best Fit Lines

Best fit line is a statistical term in regression analysis that describes minimizing the sum of the squares of the vertical distance between the actual Y values—reported vulnerabilities in our case—and the predicted values of Y, or estimated vulnerabilities. Confused? Me, too. No worries. Excel can handle the calculations for us. Simply input your data, graph it, and add a trend line, or best fit line, via the Chart menu.

Figure 2.14 Vulnerabilities with Best Fit Line

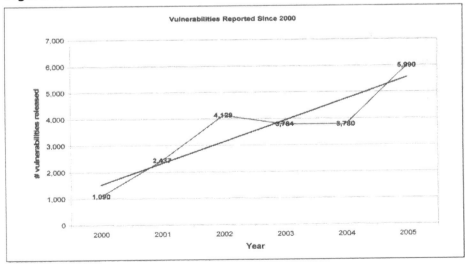

From Figure 2.14, we can infer that reported vulnerabilities will continue their upward trend, as they have since 2000. As we can see, the best fit line isn't an absolute measure of the number of vulnerabilities that is or will be reported, but it does help us estimate future reported vulnerabilities. How many reported vulnerabilities should we expect in 2006 and 2007? To help us to determine this we'll need the best fit line equation associated with Figure 2.14; the equation is generated via Excel (see Table 2.4).

Table 2.4 Best Fit Line Equation

Equation	$y = 805.26x + 716.6$
Values	**Description**
y	Estimated Number of Vulnerabilities for a Given Year
x	Time Period Estimating (e.g., 2000 = 1 , 2001 =2 , 2006 = 7)
805.26	Slope
716.6	y-intercept

Now let's compare the actual number of reported vulnerabilities from 2000 to 2005 to the estimated number of vulnerabilities for that same period and estimate the number of reported vulnerabilities for 2006 and 2007. To do this we'll replace x in the best fit line equation with the year and time period and compute the equation. Table 2.5 shows the results.

Table 2.5 Estimated Reported Vulnerabilities for 2006 and 2007

Year	Period	Reported Vulnerabilities	Estimated Vulnerabilities	Difference *
2000	1	1,090	1521.86	(432)
2001	2	2,437	2327.12	110
2002	3	4,129	3132.38	997
2003	4	3,784	3937.64	(154)
2004	5	3,780	4742.9	(963)
2005	6	5,990	5548.16	442
2006	7	?	6353.42	
2007	8	?	7158.68	

* Reported Vulnerabilities minus Estimated Vulnerabilities

Given the estimated reported vulnerabilities for 2006 and 2007—6,353 and 7,158, respectively—security practitioners, remediation teams, and business leaders alike should be busy drafting plans to address these future liabilities.

Though Microsoft recently bore the brunt of vulnerability news, independent of what operating systems and applications we run within our organizations all systems and applications are subject to vulnerabilities and will undoubtedly possess vulnerabilities throughout their life cycle. Figure 2.15 highlights the number of software vulnerabilities respective to their underlying operating system.

Figure 2.15 Software Vulnerabilities in 2005

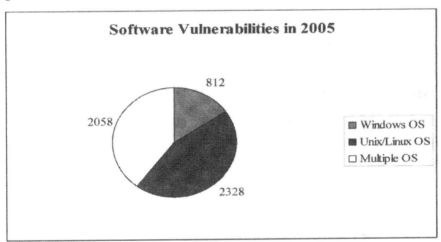

Vulnerabilities are a part of technology. Even if we're wrong on our 2006 and 2007 reported vulnerability estimates, vulnerabilities will continue to be present and will still require management. With the creation of new technologies such as Web services, as well as service-oriented architectures, new vulnerabilities and conduits of attack are bound to arise. Managing those vulnerabilities is not simply a technical challenge, but more important, is a business challenge, especially for organizations with limited resources.

Summary

As discussed in the previous chapter, single disciplines such as patch management, configuration management, and security management have evolved to support a function known as vulnerability management. Patch and configuration management technologies have traditionally supported nonsecurity-related initiatives, but nowadays they are primarily leveraged to detect and remediate security liabilities.

If we were conducting a vulnerability assessment five years ago, we would have installed VA software on a machine and conducted the exercise. Today we may query our system for a specific file and version number via our patching infrastructure or utilize remote configuration technologies to discern risk.

Are traditional VA methods antiquated? Of course not; traditional methods of vulnerability assessment still provide the most accurate level of vulnerability information, because VA doesn't require administrative rights, is capable of detecting all hosts residing within our network, and most important, provides us with the hacker perspective of our devices. In today's environment, though, a hybrid approach to vulnerability assessment that leverages security, patch, and configuration technologies will provide the greatest gains with optimal efficiency.

Solutions Fast Track

What Is a Vulnerability Assessment?

☑ Vulnerability assessments can be broken down into three steps: information gathering/discovery, enumeration, and detection.

☑ Information gathering is used to determine the breath of the assessment by gathering IP addresses, available port information, and possible contact information of the target.

☑ Enumeration validates the underlying operating system and running applications of the target.

☑ Detection determines what vulnerabilities exist.

Seeking Out Vulnerabilities

- ☑ There are multiple ways to discover vulnerabilities.

- ☑ Security technologies and VA tools can assess systems and applications for known vulnerabilities.

- ☑ Path management solutions can determine what systems haven't been patched and therefore pose a vulnerability to the company.

- ☑ Management/configuration tools can aid in seeking out vulnerabilities as well.

Importance of Seeking Out Vulnerabilities

- ☑ The number of reported vulnerabilities is on the rise.

- ☑ Vulnerabilities are present on every operating system.

Frequently Asked Questions

The following Frequently Asked Questions, answered by the authors of this book, are designed to both measure your understanding of the concepts presented in this chapter and to assist you with real-life implementation of these concepts. To have your questions about this chapter answered by the author, browse to **www.syngress.com/solutions** and click on the **"Ask the Author"** form.

Q: I conducted a vulnerability assessment against my system and it discovered nothing. Is it safe to assume my system is secure?

A: Absolutely not. Most VA tools evaluate a system for known vulnerabilities. Your systems/applications may still be vulnerable due to a vulnerability presented by a configuration error—for example, an open file share or a 0 day threat. A new breed of VA tools is trying to change this, though. Technologies from NT OBJECTives and Mu Security are using fuzzy logic and fault injection technology to detect unknown vulnerabilities. If the injection leads to a system exception, crash, or error, it can be determined that a vulnerability exists.

Q. How do I detect application vulnerabilities within internally developed, custom applications?

A: Custom applications tend to reside on commercial-grade systems. VA tools can assist in detecting underlying vulnerabilities in such systems. The best way to prevent vulnerabilities within internally developed applications is to ensure that security is embedded within your system's development life cycle (SDLC), and to practice secure coding. A byproduct of embedding security within the SDLC is the creation of application threat profiles. Threat profiles aid organizations in understanding the breath and depth of a vulnerability by mapping application dependencies, interfaces, supporting technology, and so on.

Q: Can I leverage network analysis tools to detect/discover vulnerabilities?

A: Absolutely. Network tools such as sniffers and profilers do a great job of mapping networks. A lot of times we assume that all of our Web servers are located within the data center, when in fact there may be Web servers running on user floors that are vulnerable because they aren't secured in the same fashion as our enterprise resources.

Q: Older systems and applications tend to be more secure than contemporary ones. Should I bother upgrading to the latest and greatest technology, knowing I'm going to have a vulnerability fight on my hands?

A: Companies should always assess the need for upgrades prior to making the investment. Regardless of whether you choose to stay with your existing system or upgrade, your vulnerability management strategy should address exposures to both environments. Furthermore, you'll eventually have to upgrade for one reason or another and vulnerabilities will forever be present. Our best advice is to assume the worst and plan for it.

Q: Can we really expect to see more vulnerabilities in the future?

A: The numbers don't lie. Keep in mind that these numbers reflect only reported vulnerabilities. Manufacturers are constantly fixing vulnerabilities, unbeknownst to us, and are not disclosing this. The numbers undoubtedly will increase, especially due to the advent and adoption of new technology.

PV27

## Chapter 3

Vulnerability Assessment Tools

Solutions in this chapter:

- Features of a Good Vulnerability Assessment Tool
- Using a Vulnerability Assessment Tool

☑ Summary

☑ Solutions Fast Track

☑ Frequently Asked Questions

Introduction

In the first few chapters of this book, we outlined the higher-level concepts of vulnerability management and vulnerability assessment. Chapter 2 in particular outlined the various methods for performing vulnerability assessments as well as the pros and cons of each method. In this chapter, we will explain and demonstrate the different tools available for performing vulnerability assessments. Our goal is not to recommend a specific tool, but rather to provide examples from the most common, industry-leading tools on the market today. Many years ago, when writing a similar chapter for the Syngress book *Hack Proofing Your Network*, I outlined a balance of open source and commercial tools. Since that time, the landscape has changed slightly, and one of the more popular open source tools has evolved into a commercial offering with a less-supported open source version remaining.

So how exactly do vulnerability assessment tools function? On a high level, a vulnerability assessment tool will probe a system for a specific condition that represents a vulnerability. In Chapter 1, we defined a vulnerability as a software or hardware bug or misconfiguration that a malicious individual can exploit, thereby impacting a system's confidentiality and/or integrity. It is the assessment tool's job to identify these bugs and misconfigurations.

Some tools operate by using an *agent*, which is a piece of software that must run on every system to be scanned; other tools operate without the use of agents, and some use a combination of the two configurations. The architecture of the scanning engines, agents, and systems will vary from product to product, but it is this architecture that affects overall scanning performance.

Features of a Good Vulnerability Assessment Tool

Before we get into specific tools and what they can and cannot do, let's discuss what makes a good vulnerability assessment tool. Regardless of the type of tool you are using, at a minimum a good tool should have the following features:

- **Low rate of false positives** One of the challenges that many vulnerability assessment tool developers face is that of false positives. A false positive occurs when the tool identifies an issue that does not actually exist, or wrongly identifies an existing issue as something else. Although it is debatable whether tools can completely avoid false positives, a high rate of false positives should be considered unacceptable. Later in this chapter, we will discuss in more detail why this can cause a problem on larger enterprise networks.

- **Zero false negatives** Probably the worse thing that a vulnerability assessment tool can do is not detect a vulnerability. This is typically referred to as a *false negative*. Not detecting a vulnerability not only leaves a system vulnerable, but also leaves the user of the vulnerability assessment tool with a false sense of security.

- **A concise and complete checks database** This is the one area of vulnerability assessment where vendors play what we refer to as a numbers game. One of the problems in the area of vulnerability assessment is the lack of standard naming conventions for vulnerabilities. This allows vendors to name and count issues however they want. For example, say vendor A claims its tool can scan for 1,400 issues and vendor B claims its tool can scan for 2,000 issues. Does this mean that vendor B's tool is actually checking for more issues, or is it simply counting issues in a different way? The Common Vulnerabilities and Exposures (CVE) database, created by Mitre Corp., has gone a long way toward solving this problem, but many vendors simply add the CVE references to their checks and continue to count them in their own way.

   For example, MS06-001–Vulnerability in Graphics Engine Could Allow Remote Code Execution (CVE-2005-4560) was a single vulnerability that was assigned a single CVE reference, CVE-2005-4560. But if you read the vendor advisory on the issue (www.microsoft. com/technet/security/Bulletin/MS06-001.mspx), you can see that the vulnerability affects seven different operating systems. So if you are a vulnerability scanning vendor, do you count this as one vulnerability check or seven? Obviously, there is a clear marketing reason to count this as seven vulnerability checks rather than one, which is what many vendors do. The best advice we can offer is to compare every tool being considered based on Mitre's CVE database (http://cve.mitre.org).

- **Credentialed checks** In the early days of vulnerability assessment tools, the concept of scanning a system with credentials was not really considered. Vendors marketed early tools as being capable of giving the outside "attackers' view" of a system. The reality is that threats to systems have always existed from both the outside and the inside, so having credentials on the system when scanning it helps detect these vulnerabilities. Furthermore, having credentials on a system allows for more accurate scan results, as you can more reliably check many issues by looking at the actual system settings or at such things as Registry keys and file versions. All of these types of checks require credentials.

- **Noncredentialed checks** Although credentialed checks are important for accuracy, noncredentialed checks are equally important to help show true remote threats. When performing a risk assessment on systems, it is important to take into account how the system can be compromised. Checks that return data without the use of credentials truly show what an attacker, who also would not have credentials, would be able to see. These checks are considerably more difficult for vulnerability assessment tool vendors to create, so this is a great metric to use when judging what software vendor to go with.

- **Low network traffic impact** Anyone who has been in the vulnerability assessment market for a long time has grown accustomed to running scans late at night, when network traffic is low, because of the impact that older vulnerability assessment tools had on network bandwidth. Over the years, most tools improved in efficiency and reliability, removing the requirement of scanning after hours. A good scanning tool will require bandwidth that is low enough to allow for scanning at any time on most networks. Typically environments with slow links will still want to wait until nonpeak times, to minimize network impact.

- **Minimal system impact** No matter what tool you use to perform your assessment, your scans may cause unexpected results on the systems being scanned. For example, printers with out-of-date firmware, out-of-date routers, and even certain older operating systems do not react well to being scanned.

- **Intuitive and customizable reporting engine** Vulnerability assessment is all about the data produced, meaning that the reporting capabilities of a vulnerability assessment product should be considered to be very important. A tool that has all of the preceding features implemented perfectly becomes less valuable if you cannot gather the data in an easily readable and presentable fashion.

- **Customizable checks** One complaint that we have always had and probably share with most IT professionals who perform a lot of vulnerability assessments is how many vulnerability assessment products leave the user at the mercy of the vendor in regard to what to check for. The ideal vulnerability assessment tool allows users to customize or even create new checks for issues that matter to their specific enterprise.

- **Enterprise scalability** All of the preceding features become useless quickly if the vulnerability assessment tool does not handle large enterprise networks well. Some of the best tools and some of the best ideas for tools are invalidated by the simple fact that the tool does not function well in an environment comprising multiple computers. So what does enterprise scalability mean exactly? This is more than just a marketing buzzword. To be truly scalable a VA tool must encompass all of the preceding features but also perform each of them in a way that takes into account the large amount of data that an enterprise network will return to the scanner. Typically, this is a lot easier said than done for most tools on the market today.

Although some vulnerability assessment tools will include additional features, any tool you consider using should have at least the features covered in the preceding list.

Now that you know some of the features to look for when deciding on a vulnerability assessment tool, let's take a look at how to use two of the more popular tools on the market.

Using a Vulnerability Assessment Tool

If you were to pick up your favorite IT industry magazine, you would easily find a handful of reviews of vulnerability assessment tools, all given good marks based on that magazine's criteria. Years ago, one of this book's authors even wrote such reviews for popular print and online publications. However, should you place all of your trust in magazine reviews when deciding which vulnerability assessment tool to use? One of the flaws in doing so is that you never really know what the full test criteria were. Did the reviewer scan a network of 10 systems or 100 systems? What if your network has 1,000 systems, or more? What if your network looks like the one in Figure 3.1? Would it be easy to get an accurate assessment of security threats in such a network?

Figure 3.1 A Large Network

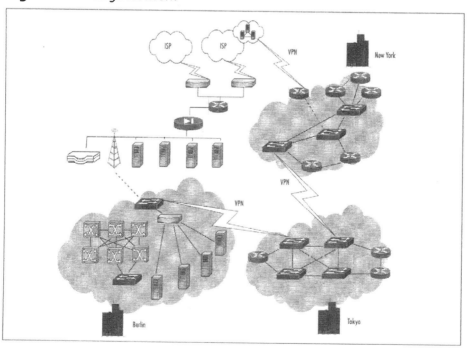

As you can see in Figure 3.1, vulnerability assessment is not as simple a process as loading the VA tool onto a system and feeding it a list of Internet Protocol (IP) addresses. To get a better feel for the process, in this section we will discuss how two popular vulnerability assessment tools work: the commercially available Retina from eEye Digital Security and the open source Nessus from Tenable Network Security. In the interest of full disclosure, the technical editor and lead author of this book, Steve Manzuik, works in the Research Department of eEye Digital Security.

NOTE

Although this section focuses on two of the more popular vulnerability assessment tools available today, a simple Google search for "Vulnerability Assessment Tool" yields millions of results.

Selecting a tool to use in your organization will not be an easy task, so hopefully this chapter will assist you in at least creating a short list of products to look at. There are many of Vulnerability Assessment Tools available today and each of them has their strengths and weaknesses. So let's get started with using the tools we selected for this book. Chapter 2 outlined a vulnerability assessment method; here we will attempt to match that method.

Step 1: Identify the Hosts on Your Network

As you may remember from Chapter 2, you cannot accurately judge how vulnerable your network is if you do not know about every device on your network. You can determine this information by performing what is usually called a *ping sweep* or *discovery scan*. Most tools will simply send an Internet Control Message Protocol (ICMP) ECHO (ping) packet to identify hosts on the network. If a system responds, it is alive; if a system does not respond, it is considered dead. Many tools will take things a step further and attempt to identify the remote operating system. Better tools, such as the examples we're using in this book, do more than a simple ICMP ECHO and give the user options. Figure 3.2 shows the options that Retina users have.

Figure 3.2 Retina Discovery Scan

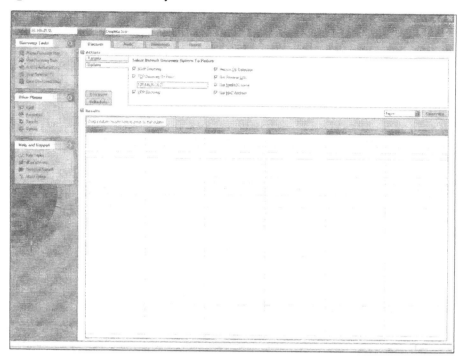

As you can see, Retina presents users with seven different check boxes that they can select, but only three of them relate to identifying live hosts on a network. It is important to know the difference between these options, how they work, and their potential impact on your network:

> **NOTE**
>
> Network Mapper (Nmap; **http://insecure.org/nmap/index.html**) is a great lightweight tool for quickly mapping a network. It is an open source tool that has been trusted and used since 1997, when the tool was first discussed in the Phrack Magazine article located at http://insecure.org/nmap/p51-11.txt.

- **ICMP Discovery** This is the simplest method of identifying systems on a network. An ICMP packet is also known as a ping packet. Although ICMP discovery is the most reliable way of identifying hosts, many IT professionals are taught to disable a system's (or switch's) ability to respond to ICMP as mitigation from unauthorized scans. Of course, although they're protecting against unauthorized ICMP scans, they have also effectively hidden their systems from legitimate scans as well.

- **TCP Discovery on Ports** This is a good way to identify hosts when ICMP might be disabled. Simply put, the Transmission Control Protocol (TCP) discovery method will attempt to connect to every IP address in the scan range on a specific port. If that port is open and listening for connections, the host will be considered alive. If none of the selected ports is alive and listening, the host will be considered dead.

- **UDP Discovery** This type of scan works a little differently. Although a TCP port scan looks for a response on an open port, a User Datagram Protocol (UDP) scan will actually look for closed ports. When a UDP scan hits a port that is closed, a specific error will be returned which proves that there is, in fact, a live system at that IP address.

You can use the preceding methods to detect that a host is alive. Once the host is detected as being alive, most vulnerability assessment tools will take things a step further by offering the following options:

- **Perform OS Detection** This is not a scan to identify hosts on a network, but rather an option that tells the tool to attempt to identify the remote operating system of the systems found to be alive. Different tools perform this step in multiple ways, each with their own degree of accuracy.

Are You Owned?

Operating Sytem Detection

Operating system detection tools can be, and have been, fooled in some cases. You can find a great, Nmap-specific paper on this subject at http://insecure.org/nmap/misc/defeat-nmap-osdetect.html. Essentially, the way to get past any operating system detection tool is to ensure that your operating systems report incorrect data back to the scanner. Although some see this as somewhat of a defensive measure, it does affect the reliability of your vulnerability assessment and you are best to not do this if you want accurate results from your scanners.

- **Get Reverse DNS** This option should be self-explanatory. It will simply match the IP address of live hosts to their domain name system (DNS) name. For example, the system at 155.212.56.73 has the DNS name of host73.155.212.56.conversant.net, which also happens to be the system hosting the Syngress Web site.

- **Get Netbios Name** This option should also be self-explanatory. It will cause the tool to map the NetBIOS names of each system being scanned to the IP address.

- **Get MAC Address** This option will map the network Media Access Control (MAC) address of each live system to the rest of the data collected.

Figure 3.3 shows the output of a Retina discovery scan performed on a smaller network, with sensitive information blacked out.

Figure 3.3 Retina Discovery Scan Results

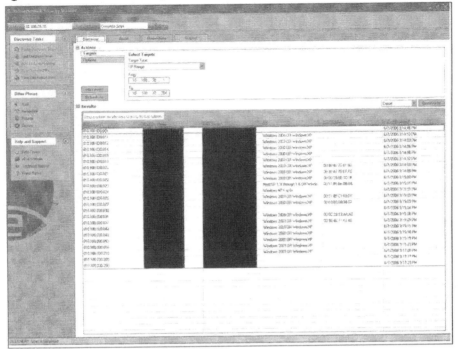

Step 2: Classify the Hosts into Asset Groups

We covered this step of the vulnerability assessment process in Chapter 2, but we'll review it here as well. By creating logical groups of hosts based on department or even physical location, you can more effectively approach scanning larger networks by section instead of trying to scan and deal with data from a mass scan. Take care to exclude any systems that you do not have permission to scan. Figure 3.4 shows the options you have for adding a group of hosts using Retina.

Figure 3.4 Adding to an Address Group in Retina

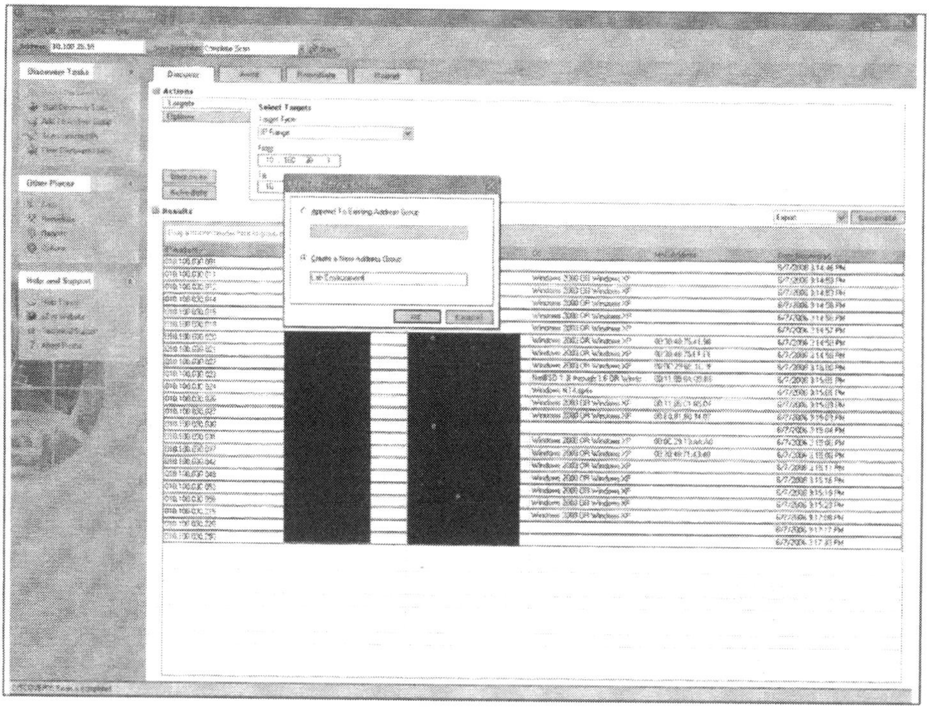

Step 3: Create an Audit Policy

For the most part, we recommend that all audits be used for initial scans. In some cases, you may not want to run certain audits, so you will want to exclude those audits. In Nessus, audits are called plug-ins (see Figure 3.5).

Figure 3.5 Nessus Plug-in Setup

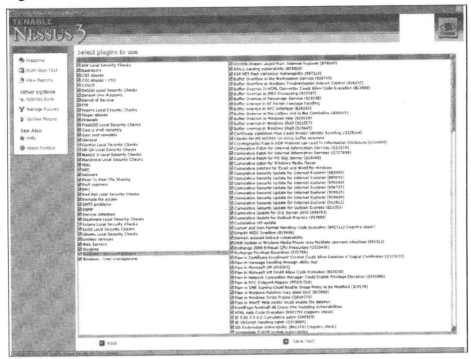

Retina, on the other hand, calls them audits, but the way you select them is similar to the approach you'd use in Nessus (see Figure 3.6).

Figure 3.6 Retina Audit Groups

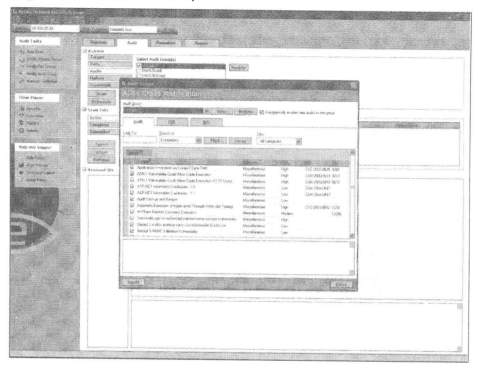

Step 4: Launch the Scan

This step is quite simple: Launch the scan and wait for your results (see Figure 3.7 and Figure 3.8).

Of course, scanning an enterprise network is not as easy; otherwise, you wouldn't need this book! In fact, you must consider and configure multiple additional options using these tools. One that we hinted at in the beginning of this chapter is whether to use credentials. Although the preceding examples do not use any credentials, entering various credentials for systems being scanned, especially at the domain level, can greatly improve the results the tools return. A number of other options are available, depending on the tool you use, but they are beyond the scope of this book, so we will leave them up to you, the reader, to explore.

Figure 3.7 Launching a Nessus Scan

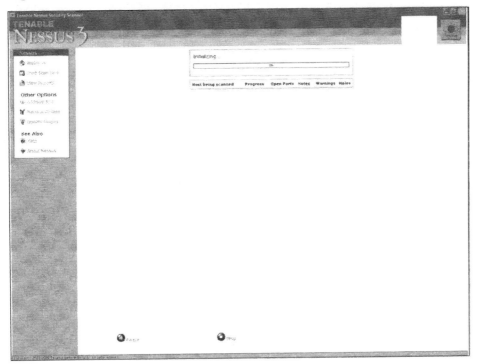

Step 5: Analyze the Reports

In a perfect world, these tools would produce a report that is completely perfect and accurate. In the real world, most vulnerability assessment tools make
their reporting customizable because no two users will want the same type of
report. Luckily most tools simply create a standard report in Hypertext
Markup Language (HTML) format, making customization very easy (see
Figure 3.9).

Figure 3.8 Launching a Retina Scan

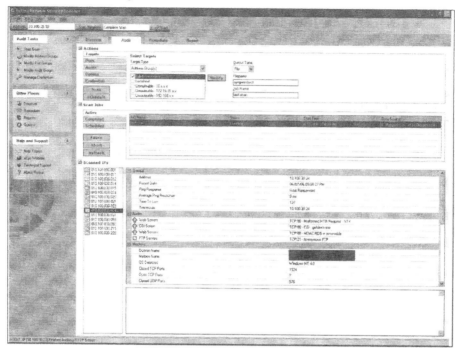

Figure 3.9 A Standard Report in Nessus

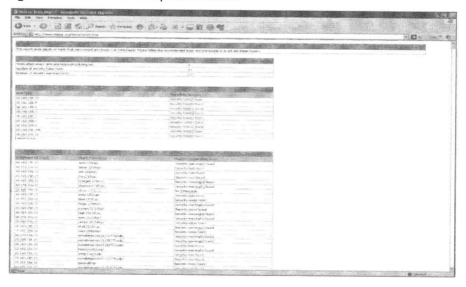

Step 6: Remediate Where Necessary

This step does not fit into this chapter of the book, but we thought we would include it here to simply give some hints as to what you will read in future chapters. The entire point of a vulnerability assessment tool is to identify vulnerabilities so that they can be remediated. Most vulnerability assessment tools will offer remediation advice, and although the tools discussed in this book have proven to be accurate, your mileage may vary. Therefore, we recommend that you carefully research all remediation plans before taking any action.

Summary

In this chapter, we discussed how two popular vulnerability assessment tools work. The real goal of this chapter was to give readers who may be new at performing vulnerability assessments an idea of what to expect, and more important, enough knowledge to successfully evaluate and select a tool that meets your organization's needs.

Solutions Fast Track

Features of a Good Vulnerability Assessment Tool

- ☑ Low rate of false positives
- ☑ Zero false negatives
- ☑ Concise and complete checks database
- ☑ Use of multiple credentials
- ☑ Use of no credentials for specific vulnerabilities
- ☑ Low network traffic impact
- ☑ Minimal system performance impact
- ☑ Intuitive and customizable reporting engine
- ☑ Customizable checks
- ☑ Enterprise scalability

Frequently Asked Questions

The following Frequently Asked Questions, answered by the authors of this book, are designed to both measure your understanding of the concepts presented in this chapter and to assist you with real-life implementation of these concepts. To have your questions about this chapter answered by the author, browse to **www.syngress.com/solutions** and click on the **"Ask the Author"** form.

Q: How would I know whether my vulnerability assessment tool has produced false negatives?

A: You wouldn't, unless you decided to double-check, which is a very good idea. To do this, set up a system on a test network and purposely do not install a patch for a vulnerability for which you know the scanner checks. Or, better yet, leave the system in a completely insecure state. Scan the system and make sure the scanner picks everything up. Fix the problems and scan again to verify. You might be surprised to see what your favorite tool misses.

Q: I am trying to decide which vulnerability assessment tool to use, but I am confused. One vendor claims its product checks for more issues than competing products, but another vendor says its product will check for the same things. How can I tell which product checks for more issues?

A: The short answer is to ask both vendors to provide you a list of their checks, cross-referenced to CVE entries. The long answer is to assess what vulnerabilities are important to you and then get a list based on CVE entries. For example, one vendor may claim to scan for every known Red Hat Linux vulnerability, but your organization does not run Linux, let alone Red Hat, so this should not be an evaluation factor.

Q: I read the list of what a good tool should have, but every tool claims to have these features. How do you really tell the difference?

A: Most tool vendors will offer at least a 30-day trial version of their product. Your best bet is to take them up on that offer and actually use each tool and decide which one works best for you. Never trust a magazine review, or even a book, for that matter, that says one tool is better than others, because this is purely a subjective opinion. Test the tools to decide which works best for you and meets the needs of your organization.

## Chapter 4

Vulnerability Assessment: Step One

Solutions in this chapter:

- Know Your Network
- Classifying Your Assets
- I Thought This Was a Vulnerability Assessment Chapter

- ☑ Summary
- ☑ Solutions Fast Track
- ☑ Frequently Asked Questions

Introduction

This chapter will begin our discussion of developing a vulnerability assessment (VA) methodology, by outlining the first steps to performing a proper vulnerability assessment. A vulnerability assessment is different from a penetration test in that typically you perform a VA with broad knowledge of the environment you are testing; as you will learn in an upcoming chapter, a pen test is typically more in-depth and focused. The purpose of a vulnerability assessment, as we previously discussed, is to take a broad snapshot of an environment that shows exposures to known vulnerabilities and configuration issues. Note the wording in that last sentence: *known vulnerabilities and configuration issues*. If your goal is to find new vulnerabilities, a VA tool will not help you.

If we, the authors of this book, have done our jobs correctly, you will be able to use what you'll learn in these chapters to create your own vulnerability assessment methodology.

The first two chapters of this book demonstrated the importance of vulnerability management, what vulnerabilities are, and what they mean to an organization. In Chapter 2, we discussed at a high level the basics of vulnerability assessment. In this chapter, we will provide examples of how to perform a vulnerability assessment. Whether your network is small or large, the basic VA framework is the same, but in some cases, the tools you can use differ. We will point out variances that may occur depending on the size of your network, as well the different tools you can use.

Performing a vulnerability assessment is only one step in developing a vulnerability management framework, but it is a very important step. You can perform a vulnerability assessment either internally or externally. In Chapter 2, we discussed how to identify external network hosts, using various tools on the Internet as well as Nmap. In this chapter, we will go into more detail regarding use of Nmap and commercial tools to scan systems once you have identified the network range you are assessing.

We will assume that you are performing your vulnerability assessment under optimal conditions: in other words, that you have actual knowledge of the network you are assessing. By *knowledge* I am referring only to the Internet Protocol (IP) range(s) that your network is configured to use.

Know Your Network

You cannot perform an effective vulnerability assessment if you do not know exactly what is on your network. I have lost count of the number of times I have been brought in to perform an assessment based on a network diagram that the IT manager thought was correct, yet I ended up identifying multiple systems on the network that he either forgot about or didn't know existed. The simplest way to address this is to scan your entire network to identify hosts. As we discussed in Chapter 3, you can accomplish this in a number of different ways; we will review the steps here.

For a smaller network, it is very easy to perform an Nmap scan of your address space. Nmap is an extremely efficient tool. Figure 4.1 shows Nmap for Windows running.

Figure 4.1 Nmap for Windows

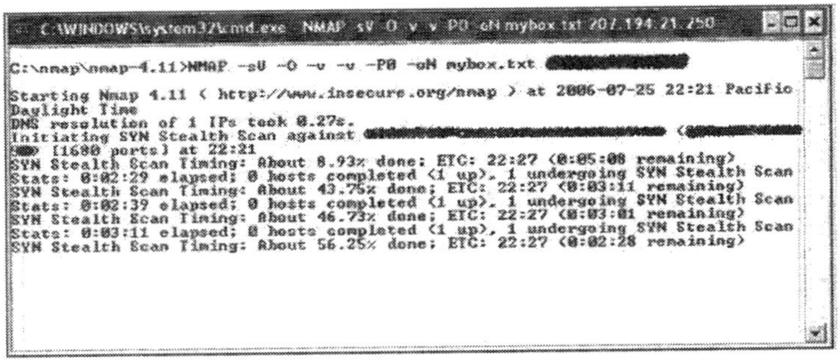

As you can see in Figure 4.1, I used the following Nmap syntax to scan my systems:

```
#NMAP -sV -O -v -v -P0 -oN network.txt <network address range>
```

This is a rather generic example, and I highly recommend that you review the Nmap documentation for alternate, more efficient ways to scan for hosts on a network. The key here, however, is that you scan across your entire network range, not just the systems that you know exist.

NOTE

Over the years, we have seen various devices, operating systems, and services crash when hit with Nmap or other scans. Typically, you will find that IT managers exclude these things from scan ranges to prevent them from crashing. What these IT managers are doing, however, is excluding systems that are so out-of-date that they are probably the most attractive target to an attacker. In today's environments, there is no good reason for a system to crash when it receives network traffic from a scanner. Systems that do should be replaced with something more robust, as the system's crashing is, in fact, a denial of service (DoS). Ignoring the problem will not make it go away, nor will it increase your overall security posture.

In the preceding line of code, *-sV* tells Nmap to probe open ports and write back listening service version information. You can also control how Nmap performs this with the following:

--version-intensity <level> Set from 0 (light) to 9 (try all probes).

--version-light Limit to most likely probes (intensity 2).

--version-all Try every single probe (intensity 9).

--version-trace Show detailed version scan activity (for debugging).

-O tells Nmap to perform operating system detection on each host. You can customize how aggressive Nmap performs this with the following:

--osscan-limit Limit operating system detection to promising targets.

--osscan-guess Guess operating system more aggressively.

-v sets the verbosity level of the Nmap output. Using it twice sets it to maximum verbosity.

-P0 tells Nmap to skip the host discovery and assume that all hosts are online and attempt a port scan. This is important to identify hosts that do not respond to ping packets.

-oN network.txt tells Nmap to output all the results into a text file named network.txt. You can also have Nmap output the scan in XML format, which can be helpful if you are trying to use this tool on a larger network.

<network address range> is the IP address range of your network. Again, I cannot stress enough that you need to make sure you are including the entire IP range you are using, even if you are sure that sections of it are empty. Sometimes you will find systems you forgot about, or worse, that you never knew about.

NOTE

Documentation, more information, and the latest versions of Nmap are available at www.insecure.org/nmap.

As I alluded to earlier, Nmap is a great tool if your network is small enough that you can manage the data or if your IT guys have the time and ability to parse through all of the data it returns. An important part of vulnerability management is asset classification, which is difficult to do by hand, and therefore, makes Nmap not the greatest option for larger organizations. In fact, I would argue that if you have more than 50 systems to assess, Nmap is not your best option.

If you are attempting to perform a large assessment, simply using Nmap will not scale, so this is where commercial tools come in. These tools will allow you to create asset groups of hosts which will help you perform a better risk assessment. For example, some people find it helpful to organize systems by physical location or even by organizational department.

In the preceding chapter, we talked about two commercial tools: Tenable Network Security's Nessus and eEye Digital Security's Retina. Both of these tools perform the same function as Nmap, but they represent the data in a way that allows for easier asset classification. Both vendors offer enterprise management consoles that can take asset classification one step further for more complex networks. As a quick review from Chapter 3, Figure 4.2 shows what the discovery scan looks like in Retina.

Figure 4.2 A Discovery Scan in eEye Digital Security's Retina

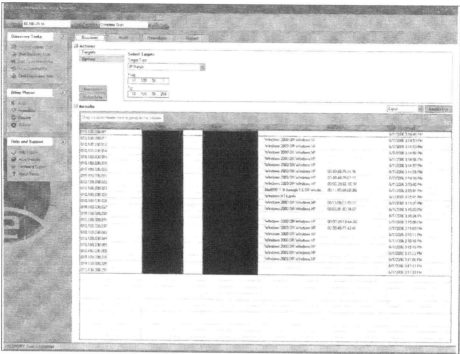

In this case, the tool is scanning an entire network range for systems that are alive—in other words, the system either is responding to a ping, or an Internet Control Message Protocol (ICMP) packet, or has services listening for connections. As you may know, many administrators will typically disable a system's ability to respond to a ping packet, as this used to be a good way to thwart basic port scanning software. Of course, port scanning software and vulnerability assessment software have both advanced to the point where disabling ICMP responses does not effectively hide a system, although it does dramatically slow down the scanning software.

Once your scan is complete, you should have a list of the systems on the network, their corresponding IP addresses, the names of the system, and hopefully the operating systems they are running. Depending on your software, you may even have the Media Access Control (MAC) address of the systems, which some people like to keep track of. This data may be helpful later for other things, including forensics, systems management, and system tracking.

It is a good idea to track down systems for which you don't have operating system data, and fill in that information. Most vulnerability assessment tools should be able to detect most mainstream operating systems, but nondefault system configuration, customized applications, and nonstandard operating systems may present problems.

> **NOTE**
>
> If you find that Nmap does not identify some of your systems, you should consider sending the fingerprint to the Nmap development team for them to integrate into their fingerprint database. The plus side of doing this is that most commercial products use portions of Nmap in their technologies, which means you are indirectly helping vendors keep their tools up-to-date as well. You can submit fingerprint information at www.insecure.org/cgi-bin/nmap-submit.cgi.

Once you have a complete list of systems on your network, it is a good idea to go through the time-consuming task of verifying the data the tool found. In a perfect world, you would be able to skip this step, but when it comes to vulnerability assessment you are better off being safe than sorry. Missing one machine can mean the difference between keeping a hacker out of your network and letting one in. Ensure that you have the following data for each machine:

- **IP address** This seems pretty obvious at first, but note that some systems may have multiple IP addresses. Be sure to identify which systems are *multihomed* and have multiple IP addresses. In some cases, these systems may even communicate on multiple networks.

- **MAC address** As alluded to earlier, this isn't essential to your vulnerability assessment, but it is nice to have data points on all systems for various reasons.

- **Operating system** This one is obvious. Because so much of vulnerability management is centered on patch and configuration management, you need to track the operating systems of all of your machines. You should include printers, routers, and other network devices.

- **Operating system patch level** Every vulnerability assessment tool should be able to give you this data point.

- **Services (Web, database, mail, etc.)** Having a list of what services each system is supposed to be offering to users is essential when considering a secure configuration. You should review all systems and turn off any services that are not required.

- **Software installed** This should comprise a complete list of all authorized software installed on the system. You can use a tool such as Microsoft's Systems Management Server (SMS) to inventory the complete system and then cross-reference that inventory with a list of what is authorized. The concept of authorized software is not just a licensing concern, but also a security concern, as the patch level and overall security of an unauthorized package would be relative unknowns to IT.

The last bullet item is one that I find a lot of people seem to overlook. With all the attention on operating systems—particularly Microsoft operating systems—over the years, everyone seems to have forgotten about applications. Recently this has become more apparent, as we have seen a major increase in application-level vulnerabilities. So while corporations have concentrated on their operating systems, they have left themselves open to application attacks. Luckily, most good vulnerability assessment tools have kept up on application as well as operating system vulnerabilities.

NOTE

There is a distinct difference between a vulnerability assessment and an application audit. The typical vulnerability assessment will check common applications for patch levels and misconfigurations, and an application audit is typically more in-depth and includes testing for issues for which most vulnerability assessment tools cannot test.

Once you have a list of all systems on your network, you are ready to start organizing your assets into logical groups for easier management. This is the first step of an asset classification exercise that will, in the long run, make managing your systems much easier. If I were to perform a vulnerability assessment on my employer's network, I would organize my assets into the following generic groups:

- North America
  - Operations
  - Sales
  - Marketing
  - Engineering
- Europe
  - Operations
  - Sales
  - Marketing
  - Engineering
- Global Outsourced

You can structure your own groups in whatever way is easiest for you. Just remember that for larger networks, organizing your groups will facilitate asset classification.

By performing asset classification, you are assigning a value to an asset in order to organize it according to its sensitivity to loss or disclosure. Once you do this, you can better target your information security efforts to protect more sensitive systems on the network. Of course, you do all of this in the context of your network architecture and existing security controls.

Figure 4.3 Creating Asset Groups in Retina

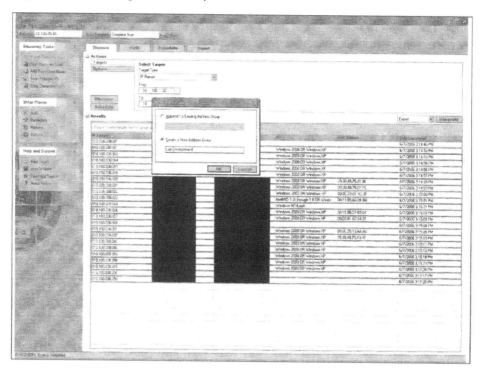

One thing many organizations still seem to overlook, especially when doing asset classification, is the network architecture and which systems can "talk" on the network to other systems. For example, you may have a group of systems that is perceived as low risk but may connect directly to higher-risk systems. Therefore, lax security on the low-risk systems may, in fact, expose an attack vector on the higher-risk systems.

Classifying Your Assets

In Chapter 1, we discussed the concept of risk ratings and how organizations calculate the risk they are exposed to. In doing so, we presented the following formula:

Risk = Vulnerability * Attacks * Threat * Exposure

While this is a good way to calculate the risk an asset is exposed to, it is not a good way to calculate the value or the classification of an asset itself. ISO 17799 states:

"The organization should be in a position to understand what information assets it holds, and to manage their security appropriately.

This section contains the following sub-sections:

5.1 Accountability for assets - an inventory of information assets (IT hardware, software, data, system documentation, storage media and ICT services) should be maintained. The inventory should record ownership and location of the assets. All [information] assets should be accounted for and have a nominated owner. An inventory of information assets (IT hardware, software, data, system documentation, storage media and ICT services) should be maintained. The inventory should record ownership and location of the assets, and owners should identify acceptable uses.

5.2 Information classification - information should be classified and labeled accordingly."

While the preceding statement is about as vague and helpful as Section 404 of the Sarbanes-Oxley Act of 2002 (SOX; see Chapter 10), we will attempt to give you some actual ideas and direction regarding what it takes to perform the boring and often long task of truly classifying your assets. As we said earlier, asset classification is the art of assigning a value to an asset so that you can organize it according to its sensitivity to loss or disclosure. How exactly do you determine this? For small organizations this step is typically quite easy. For larger organizations this task can be very time consuming.

The major steps required for asset classification and control are as follows:

- **Identifying the assets** For this step, you need to identify what assets are critical to your business. The easy way to do this is to think about what systems, data, and software are essential for the business to function. In addition, you should consider any assets that contain critical or confidential information.

- You can classify assets into four categories: information assets, software assets, physical assets, and services. *Information assets* include every piece of information inside your organization. This can include databases, customer information, data files, operations and support procedures, archived information, and continuity plans. Identifying all of the information assets in your organization is typically the hardest and most time-consuming step, as this is difficult to automate with tools.

- *Software assets* comprise system and application software that your organization has purchased or in some cases developed in-house. Take care in this step to identify which software assets are custom developed or are no longer available for purchase.

- *Physical assets* comprise the computing hardware, storage media, and even printers in your organization. You can use Nmap to classify these assets, as long as all the devices are using Transmission Control Protocol/Internet Protocol (TCP/IP).

- *Services* are sometimes overlooked, but this category should include anything that your organization has outsourced or is provided by a third party, such as data centers and phone systems.

Are You 0wned?

Printers Are Threats

Despite the various research projects presented in public forums on the ways to use devices such as printers as an attack platform, many organizations fail to include these in their vulnerability management strategy. Most network-aware printers allow for File Transfer Protocol (FTP), Hypertext Transfer Protocol (HTTP), and in some cases, Telnet communications, which can allow an attacker the ability to leverage the printer and the limited storage on the printer in an attack.

- **Identifying who is accountable for the assets** It would be impossible for any IT employee or manager to be able to identify the criticality of an asset, especially when the IT resources do not work with all of computing assets on a daily basis. What is critical to IT may not necessarily be critical to the business. This is why every asset needs to have an asset owner. The asset owner needs to be intimately familiar with the asset he is assigned to. The folks in the IT department are ultimately the ones who manage most of the assets, but they should not be the owners of those assets.

- **Preparing a schema for information classification** When preparing a schema for asset classification, the criteria you use could include the following:

  - **Confidentiality** Can the information be freely distributed, or do we need to restrict it to certain identified individuals?

  - **Value** What is the asset's value? Is it a high-value item and, therefore, costly to replace, or is it a low-value item?

  - **Time** Is the information time sensitive? Will its confidentiality status change after some time?

  - **Access rights** Who will have access to the asset?

  - **Destruction** How long will the information be stored? How can it be destroyed, if necessary?

You need to evaluate each asset against the preceding criteria and classify it for easy identification. For instance, you can define confidentiality in terms of the following:

- **Confidential** The access is restricted to a specific list of people. These could be company plans, secret manufacturing processes, formulas, and so on.

- **Internal only** The access is restricted to internal employees only. These could be customer databases, manufacturing procedures, and so on.

- **Shared** The resources are shared within groups or with people outside of the organization. This could be operational information and contact information, such as the organization's internal telephone book, to be shared with business partners and agents.

- **Unclassified** The resources are publicly accessible. This could include the company sales brochure and other publicity material.

Similarly, you can define value based on whether the asset is of high, medium, or low value. In such cases, you should prepare a detailed explanation, giving your reasons for this classification. For instance, a critical component costing a few rupees may be a very high-value item, as it is not easily available and could stop the production of a high-cost item.

You should define access rights for individuals as well as groups. Who is cleared to access confidential information in the organization? And who decides on the access rights? Logically, the asset owner will decide on access rights.

Destruction should be a scheduled and controlled activity. The information the company no longer needs but which could still be useful to competitors should be destroyed as per a predetermined schedule and method—depending on the confidentiality classification. For information recorded on hard disk, mere deletion of files does not obliterate them. A more stringent procedure such as multiple overwriting may be needed.

Classification schema should lead to a structure that you can implement. It should be simple to understand and identify.

I Thought This Was a Vulnerability Assessment Chapter

Asset classification is a necessary evil that all information security managers need to perform as part of their jobs. And performing asset classification as well as vulnerability assessment all boils down to one thing: Knowing Your Network.

So let's jump back to the beginning of this chapter, where we talked about creating asset groups. While some organizations find it easier to simply group assets by physical or even logical location, when you are dealing with a large-scale vulnerability management process it is far more efficient to break the generic asset groupings into smaller subsets so that you can complete more focused vulnerability assessments. To use my network example earlier in this chapter, we started with the following:

- North America
  - Operations
  - Sales
  - Marketing
  - Engineering
- Europe
  - Operations
  - Sales
  - Marketing
  - Engineering
- Global Outsourced

After conducting an asset classification exercise, my generic groups would expand into the following:

- North America
  - Operations Confidential
  - Sales Confidential
  - Marketing Confidential
  - Engineering Confidential

  - Operations Internal Only
  - Sales Internal Only
  - Marketing Internal Only
  - Engineering Internal Only

- Operations
- Sales
- Marketing
- Engineering
  - Europe
    - Operations Confidential
    - Sales Confidential
    - Marketing Confidential
    - Engineering Confidential

    - Operations Internal Only
    - Sales Internal Only
    - Marketing Internal Only
    - Engineering Internal Only

    - Operations
    - Sales
    - Marketing
    - Engineering
  - Global Outsourced

As you can see, anything below the Internal Only Classification is grouped together. You will also notice that I prefer to keep a separate asset group for any asset that is outsourced, because typically there are contractual requirements regarding outsource agreements when it comes to vulnerability assessment and pen testing. In some cases, you may even want to add a "special cases" group comprising an asset group of systems that have special requirements that need to be met before, during, or after a vulnerability assessment is performed on them. Before doing this, however, you should review my note earlier in this chapter about excluding certain systems from your tests.

By grouping your assets in this way, you gain multiple advantages when it comes to security. First, you can schedule your tests based on the criticality of the assets. For example, I know of multiple organizations that schedule internal vulnerability assessments at regular time intervals. In fact, I recommend that you schedule scanning of confidential and internal assets more often than other assets.

Leaving the geographic groupings in place also allows you to accommodate potential bandwidth limitations of scanning remote systems. For example, one financial organization I worked with during my consulting days had a number of branch offices in remote locations connected with slow links. By grouping their assets geographically, I was able to easily schedule the scans of these remote offices to take place during nonbusiness hours to limit the impact on the network. In addition, larger organizations find it very helpful to deploy distributed scanners that report back to a single reporting host.

This is why I recommend you use Nmap to identify assets only if you are running a small network. Commercial tools really shine when it comes to performing this task, and although some manual intervention is still necessary, having a tool that allows you to enter and track each group is essential.

Summary

In this chapter, we discussed how to identify assets on a network using both Nmap and commercial tools. We discussed ISO 17799 and asset classification and explained why they are important to vulnerability management. At this point, you should have a good idea of what you have on your network, what it does, and how important it is to your business. The next chapter will take us into the really fun stuff: actually scanning systems and identifying vulnerabilities.

Solutions Fast Track

Know Your Network

- ☑ Scan your entire network to identify hosts using Nmap for smaller networks and Nmap in conjunction with commercial tools for larger networks.

- ☑ Once you have completed your scans, you must verify that the scan results are valid.

Classifying Your Assets

- ☑ The major steps required for asset classification and control are: Identifying the assets, identifying who is accountable for the assets, and preparing a schema for information classification.

- ☑ You should regularly destroy unnecessary information and data, sot that it can not be used

Frequently Asked Questions

The following Frequently Asked Questions, answered by the authors of this book, are designed to both measure your understanding of the concepts presented in this chapter and to assist you with real-life implementation of these concepts. To have your questions about this chapter answered by the author, browse to **www.syngress.com/solutions** and click on the **"Ask the Author"** form.

Q: How do I determine the ranges to perform asset inventory against?

A: Before beginning discussion of how to correct internal security issues in your most sensitive environments, you need to determine what you have and where you are most vulnerable. Every location at which your organization hosts sensitive data will have different profiles that you will need to take into account when developing solutions for securing them.

Q: What is the goal of asset inventory?

A: The goal of asset inventory is to understand and identity corporate assets for each identified business operation. This will allow you to create security zones for security assessment, based on the classification and prioritization of the hosts and networks.

Q: Are there scripts to automate the process of host discovery?

A: Yes. Mark Wolfgang (www.moonpie.org) has created a script called discover.pl that is very useful for enumerating live hosts as well as services running on them. The script is fast and can chew through a Class C in a few minutes.

Chapter 5

Vulnerability Assessment: Step Two

Solutions in this chapter:

- An Effective Scanning Program
- Scanning Your Network
- When to Scan

☑ Summary

☑ Solutions Fast Track

☑ Frequently Asked Questions

Introduction

In the preceding chapter, we talked about the boring but necessary first steps of conducting a vulnerability assessment. This chapter will expand on that and move into the more enjoyable steps of actually identifying and confirming vulnerable systems. This is a appropriate topic, because now is the perfect time to demonstrate why a good VA program is required: as we were putting together this chapter, the information technology (IT) world was scrambling to deal with a new form of malware that was exploiting an issue with the Microsoft Windows Server Service. Although some organizations were on high alert and their IT staff were being worked to death dealing with this threat, other organizations were calm and in a business-as-usual mindset because they had a proper vulnerability assessment (VA) methodology in place.

In this case—and really in any case where a new threat is exploited in the wild—just by following the steps outlined in the preceding chapter an organization would already have a list of systems that it needs to check for the existence of a threat, as well as a list of systems which it should not waste time checking. This chapter will take you through the steps of scanning not only for specific threats, but also for every known vulnerability in existence.

One thing to remember when performing any vulnerability assessment, or even a penetration test, for that matter, is that you are conducting a point-in-time assessment. To borrow from a famous Bruce Schneier quote: Vulnerability management is a journey, not a destination. This means that you cannot perform a vulnerability assessment only once and forget about it. You must check your networks constantly.

An Effective Scanning Program

So, how often should you be scanning your networks? Unfortunately, that question is not easy to answer, and the answer depends on your organization. We will, however, attempt to provide you with some general guidelines based on our experiences with various organizations.

There are essentially three different reasons you would want to perform a vulnerability assessment:

1. A new threat becomes evident and you want to verify that your systems are not vulnerable or identify systems that are vulnerable.

2. A vendor releases a patch or a number of patches and you want to verify that your systems are patched and are not vulnerable, or some other event causes wide-scale changes to your environment.

3. You want a point-in-time assessment of your current security posture and a list of vulnerabilities affecting your organization.

NOTE

A few years ago, a large financial institution solicited consulting organizations to provide bids on performing a quarterly vulnerability assessment on its entire network. The vendors attempting to win the bid did not know that the organization was selecting not one vendor for the work, but four different vendors. The organization's idea was to use two different vendors every quarter, and then correlate and compare their results. This would ensure not only that each vendor was performing a thorough job, but also that the organization requesting the work would receive a complete picture from two different perspectives. This institution still has this practice in place today, and it works well. This may or may not be the correct way for your organization to handle this task, but it might be worth investigating.

The first reason in the preceding list—a new threat becomes evident and you want to verify that your systems are not vulnerable or identify systems that are vulnerable—has become very necessary recently. As stated earlier, at the time of this writing, many IT departments were battling a new form of malware that was leveraging a known and patched vulnerability. In addition, we have seen multiple vulnerabilities released without vendor patches. This, of course, leads to the question, "How can a mostly reactive VA tool help with 0 day vulnerabilities?" A good VA tool can, in fact, help you with this, but not in the easy and direct way that many vendors may want you to believe. As you may remember from Chapter 3, one feature of a good VA tool is its capability to report back (sometimes referred to as *write-back*) the software versions of key operating system components. So, in the case of an Internet Explorer 0 day vulnerability, although you won't be able to detect the specific vulnerability, you will be able to detect what version of Internet Explorer your systems are running and cross-reference that to what versions are vulnerable to the specific 0 day vulnerability.

The second reason you may want to run a vulnerability assessment is to either double-check that all systems have been patched for a vulnerability, or obtain a list of systems that require a patch. This is a great way to verify that your patch management software actually did its job and rolled out the patches. So, for example, if a vendor such as Microsoft releases patches on the second Tuesday of every month and your patch management methodology states that all patches will be rolled out by the following Tuesday, on Wednesday it would be a great idea to run a vulnerability scan to identify any systems that were missed. In addition, if some other event, such as a software roll-out project or a new hardware implementation, causes a major change to your environment, you will want to verify that all systems are up-to-date and are not vulnerable.

The last and probably most common use of a VA tool is to take point-in-time snapshots of your overall network security posture. A good tool will also baseline each snapshot and provide you with a differential report, allowing for clear and concise trending of how well your organization is handling vulnerabilities. A typical organization will implement a program to use a VA tool in this fashion at a set interval.

At this point, you may be wondering what scanning program is best for your organization. Every organization is different and has its own policies, so we can't tell you in this book exactly what you should do, but hopefully the information we present will give you enough insight to determine your organization's needs.

Scanning Your Network

In the preceding chapter, we talked about identifying hosts on your network as well as classifying those hosts. Now we move on to the fun stuff and actually start scanning systems and identifying vulnerabilities. Regardless of what tool you are using, by now you should have a list of every system on your network that is communicating using the Transmission Control

Protocol/Internet Protocol (TCP/IP). If you followed the advice we gave in the preceding chapter, you have also organized these systems in a logical way as well as given each group, or subset of groups, a classification. You did this based on the assumption that you would want to more consistently scan resources containing higher-risk data.

If you remember, we created the following groups:

- North America
  - Operations Confidential
  - Sales Confidential
  - Marketing Confidential
  - Engineering Confidential

  - Operations Internal Only
  - Sales Internal Only
  - Marketing Internal Only
  - Engineering Internal Only

  - Operations
  - Sales
  - Marketing
  - Engineering
- Europe
  - Operations Confidential
  - Sales Confidential
  - Marketing Confidential
  - Engineering Confidential

- Operations Internal Only

- Sales Internal Only

- Marketing Internal Only

- Engineering Internal Only

- Operations

- Sales

- Marketing

- Engineering

- Global Outsourced

For the sake of not boring you, we will concentrate on only one asset group, North America, when explaining the following steps. Obviously, you will want to repeat each step for every asset group. One nice feature of almost all VA products is the fact that they have built-in scheduling features that allow you to automate redundant tasks. We will address this a bit more, later in the book. For the following examples, we used eEye Digital Security's Retina, simply because one of the authors was recently employed at the company and we had a license handy, but the same concepts exist, or at least should exist, for all VA tools. Figure 5.1 shows the creation of specific asset groups. We had to black out the host names and domain name system names because we collected all of this data from a live network.

Table 5.1 lists the asset groups we created which fall in line with our original asset classification.

Figure 5.1 Creating Asset Groups

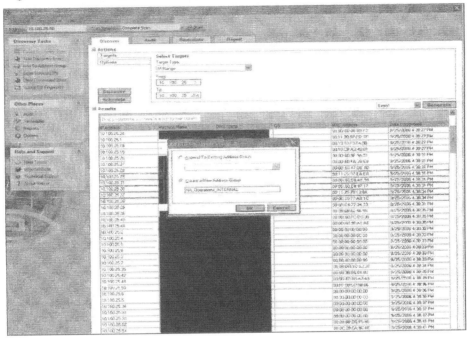

Table 5.1 Asset Group Names and Descriptions

Group Name	Description
NA_Operations_CONFIDENTIAL	North America Operations–Confidential Data Systems
NA_Operations_INTERNAL	North America Operations–Internal Data Systems
NA_Operations	North America Operations–Other Systems
NA_Sales_CONFIDENTIAL	North America Sales–Confidential Data Systems
NA_Sales_INTERNAL	North America Sales–Internal Data Systems
NA_Sales	North America Sales–Other Systems
NA_Marketing_CONFIDENTIAL	North America Marketing–Confidential Systems

Continued

Table 5.1 continued Asset Group Names and Descriptions

Group Name	Description
NA_Marketing_INTERNAL Systems	North America Marketing–Internal Data
NA_Marketing	North America Marketing–Other Systems
NA_Engineering_CONFIDENTIAL Data Systems	North America Engineering–Confidential
NA_Engineering_INTERNAL Systems	North America Engineering–Internal Data
NA_Engineering	North America Engineering–Other Systems

The group names we created are self-explanatory. As your network grows, you will find that the more self-explanatory your group names are, the easier it will be to recall which systems are in which groups. Clearly, if we had listed every asset group in Table 5.1, the table would be much larger, but hopefully the more abbreviated version we provided gets the point across.

The next step is to actually run scans against hosts. Obviously, as part of your vulnerability management strategy, you would schedule scans to run in set intervals. We discussed this a little bit in Chapter 4 as well. At a minimum, your organization should scan all hosts, concentrating on the Confidential and Internal Only hosts first, after every patching cycle. As you will learn while you read this book, there is a definite connection between patch management and vulnerability assessment.

When you are performing your scans, you may choose to scan either by asset classification (i.e., all confidential asset groups first, all internal asset groups next, etc.), or by operational area (i.e., all Operations groups first, all Sales groups next, etc.). We recommend that you concentrate on the higher-risk systems—the Confidential and Internal Only groups—from each organizational group, because despite improvements by vendors to increase the performance of their scanner engines, scanning large networks still takes time, and the longer it takes to identify and deal with vulnerable systems, the larger the window of vulnerability will be.

In Figure 5.2, we are scanning all confidential asset groups first. One step we did not address here (but which we will get to) is what to scan for. For this initial step, we are assuming that you have not performed a vulnerability assessment in the past, so to create a baseline you will need to scan for every possible vulnerability. The final chapter of this book will tie everything together and offer a complete plan that not only covers this step, but also takes into account every other aspect, including patch management and vulnerability remediation.

Figure 5.2 Scanning All Confidential Asset Groups First

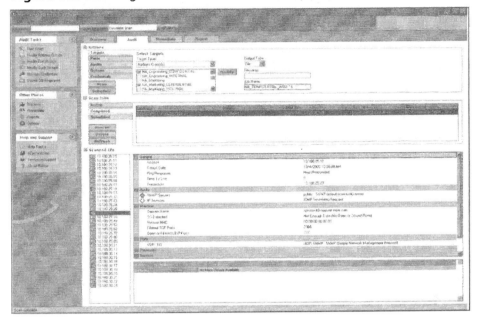

It is also important to note that in Figure 5.2, we are not supplying user credentials to the scanner product because we are scanning a production network. As we discussed earlier in the book, you will see different scan results based on whether you supply credentials; Table 5.2 provides a quick review of that earlier discussion.

Table 5.2 Scanning with and without Credentials

Option	What It Does	Benefits	Problems
Scan without credentials	The scanner will attempt to audit the target system without authenticating to that system with any user rights.	This gives you the "hacker's" view of a system, as the typical attacker would not have credentials.	Scanning in this manner will not identify the patch level of the system or vulnerabilities that a user with credentials could leverage.
Scan with credentials	The scanner will use administrator-level credentials to connect to the target system and audit Registry entries, files, and other configuration options.	This gives a more complete scan of the system and allows the scanner the capability to check for vulnerabilities in things such as client-side software as well as configuration issues that equate to vulnerabilities.	Some feel that this does not give a true hacker's view of a system. Although this is a true statement, getting the true hacker's view of a system and actually securing a system are two different things.

As you can see in Table 5.2, there is a definite advantage to using credentials over not using credentials. One nice thing about most VA tools is that even if you do use credentials, the noncredentialed checks will (or at least should) run without credentials, so you essentially get the best of both worlds.

Now that we have run the scan we are presented with an overview of what the scanner found to be vulnerable, along with a list of the vulnerabilities (see Figure 5.3). As you will remember from Chapter 3, a good VA tool offers a wide range of reporting options.

Figure 5.3 Network Analysis Results

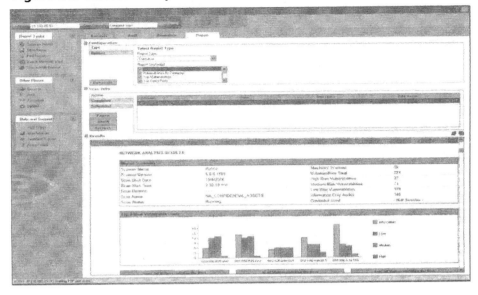

Figure 5.4 Security Management Console for Managing Large Amounts of Vulnerability Information

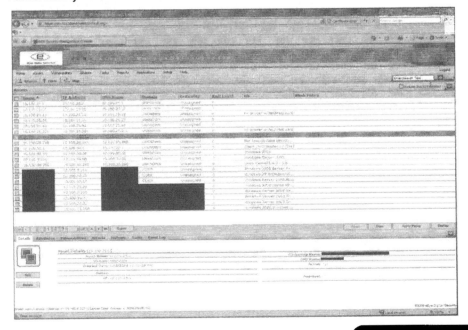

In addition, some products offer an enterprise console for managing large amounts of vulnerability information across an enterprise. Figure 5.4 shows an example.

When to Scan

By now, it should be obvious how easy it is to scan a network for vulnerabilities. But it might not be obvious when or how often you should conduct a scan. In this section, we will discuss how to determine optimal timing of your vulnerability scanning program.

Earlier in this chapter we discussed the three different scenarios that should be considered triggers for the need to run a vulnerability assessment. As a reminder, we will repeat them here:

■ A new threat becomes evident and you want to verify that your systems are not vulnerable or identify systems that are vulnerable.

■ A vendor releases a patch or a number of patches and you want to verify that your systems are patched and are not vulnerable, or some other event causes wide-scale changes to your environment.

■ You want a point-in-time assessment of your current security posture and a list of vulnerabilities affecting your organization.

This list should not only give you an idea of why you would want to scan your systems, but also allow you to infer when to scan, and even how to do it. When we showed an example of how to run a simple scan in this chapter, we simply left all audits enabled. This meant that our scanner checked our network for every potential vulnerability, which also meant that our scan took longer to complete.

One of the battles every VA vendor fights on a constant basis when developing products is scan performance versus scan completeness. The more you are auditing for, the longer your scans will take. The typical goal of most vendors is to get as much coverage with audits as possible, while still allowing scans to run in a relatively quick manner. That being said, to scan a Class B network for all possible vulnerabilities can take multiple days, regardless of what product you are using.

Because of the amount of time it takes to conduct a complete scan, and because of how frequently one of the three triggers that should cause a scan occurs, it is impractical to try to scan for every vulnerability every time you run a scan. With that in mind, we suggest the scan schedule shown in Table 5.3.

WARNING

Many IT organizations, even large ones, get trapped into reacting constantly to the monthly Patch Tuesday schedule that Microsoft uses. Although it makes perfect sense to release patches monthly on a set schedule, one unintentional side effect is that those responsible for patching and systems security become so focused on Microsoft's Patch Tuesday that they fail to plan and sometimes fail to notice when other vendors, most of which do not follow a set schedule, release an important patch. This actually assists in shifting the attack surface from one that has been operating system (and core application) specific to one that is more client side specific because other third-party applications are less likely to be patched.

Table 5.3 Suggested Scan Schedule

Trigger	When to Scan	What to Scan For
A new threat becomes evident and you want to verify that your systems are not vulnerable or identify systems that are vulnerable.	This is a reactive scan issue that you need to deal with when you are made aware of the threat. In this case, you will want to assess which assets on your network are most exposed to the threat and begin scanning those first, moving down the list to systems less at risk.	Performance and accuracy are important in this type of scan. You will want to scan for only a specific threat in order to create a comprehensive list of systems that you should reconfigure or patch to defend against the issue. Note that in some cases, this will be a 0 day threat, so you may be able to scan for only specific

Continued

Table 5.3 continued Suggested Scan Schedule

Trigger	When to Scan	What to Scan For
		operating systems or software versions and not the actual vulnerability itself. But this is purely product dependant and something to consider when choosing what VA tool to use.
A vendor releases a patch or a number of patches and you want to verify that your systems are patched and are not vulnerable. Some other event causes wide-scale changes to your environment.	As you will learn when you get to the chapters on vulnerability remediation and patch management, it is very difficult for an organization, especially a large one, to test and roll out a patch quickly. So for this scan event trigger you will need to coordinate with your patching process for the exact timing. It makes sense to schedule your vulnerability assessment for the evening after all patches have been rolled out. This will help you get a list of all systems that, for whatever reason, were not patched.	Usually a good VA vendor will have released audits for new issues the same day it releases a patch. Scan for just these vulnerabilities, starting with your highest-risk asset group. Note that in some cases, you can scan for both the presence of the patch (a credentialed scan) and the remote exploitability of the issue (a noncredentialed scan). When possible, it is a good idea to do both, because sometimes a patch can fail during installation in a way that fools the VA tool.
You want a point-in-time assessment of your current security posture and a list of vulnerabilities affecting your organization.	This scan trigger is the most predictable and easiest to plan for. Scheduling this depends solely on how often your environment changes.	In this case, you will want to scan for every potential vulnerability that your scanning tool can detect. This will allow you to find systems that, for whatever

Continued

Table 5.3 continued Suggested Scan Schedule

Trigger	When to Scan	What to Scan For
	Most organizations will do an enterprisewide vulnerability scan once per quarter, and sometimes more often, such as once every two months, in order to detect changes.	reason, are not up to patch or secure configuration levels. This full scan will also allow you to track the progress being made by those who are responsible for securing machines. For example, if a group of systems is vulnerable to something the first time you run a scan, by the second time the issues should have been fixed. This is also the time to generate a baseline to report against each scan cycle in order to prove that your vulnerability management program is in fact working.

Summary

In this chapter, we covered the actual scanning of systems for vulnerabilities and discussed the reasons why you would want to perform a scan. We outlined each reason in detail, and although there may be others that we did not list, we did cover the most common ones. We looked at one scanning tool in particular—eEye Digital Security's Retina—and discussed how it works as well as what types of reports you can create with it. Finally, we provided a sample scanning schedule that should have given you some clear guidelines as to when you should be scanning your network and what you should be scanning for.

This chapter should have provided you with the basic framework to plan your own VA schedule which will dramatically help you to improve your organization's security posture.

Solutions Fast Track

An Effective Scanning Program

- ☑ A credentialed vulnerability scanning tool allows you to check for things such as Registry key settings and file versions which would be unavailable to a noncredentialed scanner.

- ☑ Not using credentials gives a "hacker's" view of your systems, but does not give full coverage.

Scanning Your Network

- ☑ You should save your reports after each scan and compare them in order to monitor your progress in ensuring the security of your organization.

- ☑ By scanning for every vulnerability once every so often, while performing point-in-time scans for specific vulnerabilities, you get optimal coverage and optimal performance.

When to Scan

- ☑ You should scan when a new threat becomes evident and you want to verify that your systems are not vulnerable or identify systems that are vulnerable.

- ☑ You should scan when a vendor releases a patch or a number of patches and you want to verify that your systems are patched and are not vulnerable, or some other event causes wide-scale changes to your environment.

- ☑ You should scan when you want a point-in-time assessment of your current security posture and a list of vulnerabilities affecting your organization.

Frequently Asked Questions

The following Frequently Asked Questions, answered by the authors of this book, are designed to both measure your understanding of the concepts presented in this chapter and to assist you with real-life implementation of these concepts. To have your questions about this chapter answered by the author, browse to **www.syngress.com/solutions** and click on the **"Ask the Author"** form.

Q: When I run a vulnerability scan I do not get any results back from my product. Does this mean that my systems are all completely secure?

A: Before you make the assumption that you have achieved complete security, which is impossible by the way, make sure you ran your scans *with* credentials as most scanners are limited in what they can pick up without credentials.

Q: Why do my scans take hours to complete when I am only scanning one Class C network?

A: You have probably set options in your scanning program that add time to the overall process. Things like password grinding, and full port scans can dramatically increase the time to do scans.

Q: This chapter talks a lot about commercial products. Budget is tight so what free products are out there than can help me?

A: The best free scanner on the market is still Nessus. That being said, if you have a large network, you will find it very time consuming to scan it with the stand alone free version. As valuable as those budget dollars are, you will want to look at purchasing a scanner that has enterprise type features.

Q: How long should Vulnerability Assessment reports be retained in my organization?

A: We recommend at least a year so that you can easily compare them and show progress but check with normal company policy on record retention to be sure.

Q: I don't have permission to run any type of vulnerability scans on my network should I do so anyways to help justify the budget to properly deal with our security?

A: Absolutely! That is if you want to find yourself unemployed and potentially accused of "hacking" your companies network. Never, ever run any type of security scanning tool without explicit permission to do so. No matter how good your intentions.

Chapter 6

Going Further

Solutions in this chapter:

- Types of Penetration Tests
- Scenario: An Internal Network Attack
- Penetration Testing
- Vulnerability Assessment versus a Penetration Test
- Internal versus External

☑ Summary

☑ Solutions Fast Track

☑ Frequently Asked Questions

Introduction

Vulnerability assessment (VA) represents a key element of an organization's information security program. A VA highlights an organization's security liabilities and helps asset owners, security managers, and business leaders determine information security risk. VAs only report vulnerabilities, though. They don't substantiate that vulnerabilities actually exist; penetration tests do that.

The past few chapters discussed the tools, methodologies, and concepts that go into VA. This chapter assimilates that information and continues with penetration testing. We'll discuss the two types of penetration (pen) tests, walk through a pen test, cover the differences between VAs and pen tests, and discuss the pros and cons of conducting penetration tests from within versus externally to our corporate network.

Types of Penetration Tests

Penetration testing is the process of evaluating the security posture of a computer system, network, or application (assets). The process involves analyzing assets for any weaknesses, configuration flaws, or vulnerabilities. The analysis is carried out from the perspective of a potential attacker and leverages exploitation of known and possibly unknown security vulnerabilities.

There are two types of penetration tests: black box and white box tests. Black box testing assumes no prior knowledge of the environment to be tested and the testers must first determine the location and extent of the assets before commencing their analysis. At the other end of the spectrum, white box testing provides the testers with complete knowledge of the environment to be tested; often including network diagrams, source code and Internet Protocol (IP) addressing information. As one might assume, there are many shades of gray too.

Black box testing is what we often associate with penetrating testing. Black box testing is usually carried out by a malicious attacker, sometimes a trusted third party, seeking to gain unauthorized access to an asset. To accomplish this a black box tester may leverage known and unknown, 0 day, security vulnerabilities to penetrate a host. The purpose and intent of a black box tester vary. If a nefarious attacker is conducting the exercise, the attacker could seek unauthorized access for:

- **Staging** Staging future attacks. Attackers often like to exploit assets via intermediary sources. This aids in concealing their identity.

- **Information disclosure** Unearthing sensitive data on a system. Data could include password files, credit card numbers, company propriety information, and so on.

- **Bots** Attackers could seek to convert an exploited asset into a bot. The attackers could then use the exploited system to carry out programmatic requests such as spamming or denial of service (DoS) attacks on their behalf.

Notes from the Underground...

Bots

Bots, also called *zombies*, are compromised computers that are used to create DoS or spam attacks, among other things. These computers are typically compromised via a vulnerability or malicious piece of software and wait for commands from the person in control of the bot.

There are no rules of engagement or restrictions for black box testing, unless a third party is conducting the attack. Everything from cross-site scripting, SQL injection, and even DoS attacks is fair game. Some exploits can render a system unavailable. To the malicious attacker this is a moot point.

There are rules of engagement for white box testing. We might expect this, considering the fact that white box testers are usually organizations and contracted third parties. For an organization, discovering and validating vulnerabilities is important, but maintaining an asset's availability during a penetration test is vital too. Because of this, organizations tend to place the following restrictions on penetration tests:

- **Scheduled** Tests need to be scheduled and coordinated during off-peak hours to minimize the impact to the business.

- **Authorized** Tests need to be approved by the security team as well as the asset/business owner.

- **Limited** Exploits that render the system unavailable are typically excluded. Unknown, 0 day, vulnerabilities are not tested either; organizations typically don't have access to this information and corresponding exploits.

Like vulnerability assessments, penetration tests are a key element of an organization's information security program. Penetration tests not only determine an asset's security liability to the organization, but they also:

- **Validate information security programs** Independent, third-party assessments of an organization's environment can validate the strengths and weaknesses of a company's information security program.

- **Substantiate product liability** Pen tests conducted against technologies an organization consumes enable a company to determine the security liability of the technology prior to procurement.

- **Confirm security controls** Most organizations practice *defense in-depth strategies*, or the layering of security technologies to protect an asset. Pen tests can aid in identifying weak spots within this strategy.

- **Support Internet Audits (IAs)** Due to an onset of new federal and industry regulations, IA departments are under pressure to substantiate their organization's information security programs. IA departments are exercising their resolve in ensuring that their organizations are practicing due diligence in protecting their corporate assets. For all organizations, penetration tests are part of this due diligence equation.

Scenario: An Internal Network Attack

We've conducted a vulnerability assessment and believe an asset is vulnerable, but what's the true liability of that asset to our organization? Depending on how we've discovered the vulnerability—via security, remediation, or configuration technologies—the asset may or may not pose a liability to our organization. To determine the asset's true risk to the organization we'll expand upon our VA efforts and conduct a pen test.

Penetration tests can be sourced externally or internally to a company's network. External pen tests provide the outsider's perspective of an asset, and internal pen tests illustrate the asset's susceptibility to insider attacks. We'll further discuss the differences between external and internal tests later in this chapter. For now, we'll focus on internal penetration testing.

To aid our pen test discussion we'll walk through an internal penetration test against a front-end Web server and a supporting database server. The Web server in our example supports the company's e-commerce initiatives, and the database houses customer records. The purpose of the pen test is to determine whether we can gain unauthorized access to the customer data that's housed within the database. To do this we'll conduct a direct attack against the database server. If we're unsuccessful in penetrating the database server, we'll attempt to compromise the Web server and see whether we can use it as a conduit to the database server and, ultimately, the customer records. Table 6.1 and Figure 6.1 depict the landscape of the internal network.

Client Network

Following is the list of assets that comprised the client's network.

- 1 Internet facing router
- 2 Internal routers
- 1 Intrusion Prevention System (IPS)
- 2 Web servers
- 1 Database server
- 1 Application server

Table 6.1 Target Systems

#	Host	IP Address	Operating System	Open Ports
1	Web	10.192.144.54	?	?
2	Database	10.192.146.34	?	?

Figure 6.1 Client Network Diagram

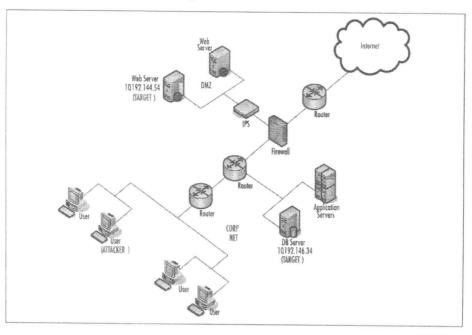

Whether we're conducting an internal or an external penetration test the process is the same. We must:

- **Gather information** Determine the available hosts, their underlying operating system, and running services.

- **Detect vulnerabilities** Assess the systems for vulnerabilities.

- **Attack and penetrate** Leverage the vulnerabilities we've discovered in the previous step to attack and penetrate the host(s); gain unauthorized access.

To assist us with our penetration test we'll use:

- Nmap 4.03 from www.insecure.org/nmap for information gathering

- Retina 5.0 from eEye Digital Security for vulnerability assessment

- Core Impact 5.1 from Core Security for attack and penetration

Step 1: Information Gathering

First things first: We must get a lay of the land. We need to obtain as much information as possible about the assets in question: the database server and Web server. We already know their IP addresses, but we need additional information regarding the hosts. We need to know:

- **Operating systems** Determining the underlying operating systems will aid us in assessing the assets for vulnerabilities. Some applications run on only certain operating systems—for example, Microsoft SQL does not run on UNIX. Based on this it would be pointless to assess a UNIX host for Microsoft SQL vulnerabilities knowing that UNIX is not a Microsoft SQL-supported platform.

- **Open ports** Discover open (listening) ports on the hosts. Open ports will provide insight into the services running on the systems.

- **Running applications/services** Enumerate the applications/services running on the hosts. In our scenario, we'll be attacking a Web server and a database server, but what other applications are running on these hosts? The Web and database services may be secure, but other applications could possess vulnerabilities that we could leverage to gain unauthorized access to the systems.

Since this attack is being sourced from within the client's network, we'll begin our assessment by actively fingerprinting the systems, seeking to discover their operating systems, and then determine open (listening) ports on the Web and database servers. Upon determining the open ports, we'll attempt to identify the services/applications running on each system.

> **NOTE**
>
> *OS fingerprinting*, also called TCP/IP stack fingerprinting, is the process of determining the identity of a remote operating system by analyzing packets received from that host. There are two types of OS fingerprinting: active and passive. Passive OS fingerprinting identifies the remote operating system by *sniffing* (capturing) packets exchanged

between the source and remote systems. Active OS fingerprinting is the process of sending packets to a host and interpreting the response or lack thereof from that host.

Operating System Detection

In order to determine the operating system, or to conduct a pen test, for that matter, we must be able to establish IP connectivity to the Web and database servers. Simply pinging the hosts could validate connectivity. Ping tends to be blocked by most corporate firewalls, so we'll need a utility that's not solely predicated on ICMP to validate connectivity and ultimately determine the underlying operating systems. For this, we'll utilize Nmap; specifically, Nmap version 4.03.

Nmap is a great freeware utility that can aid us in gathering information. It will help us determine the availability of our targets and the ports the systems expose, and enumerate the applications/services running on the systems.

To determine the Web and database servers' availability we'll use Nmap's *–sP* (ping scan) switch. This command will help us identify whether we have IP connectivity to the target hosts from our position within the internal network. Upon executing the command (see Figure 6.2), we can see that connectivity does indeed exist between us and the target systems, and that the corporate firewall isn't blocking ICMP after all. If the firewall was blocking ICMP, we could have leveraged the *–P0* (treat all hosts as online) switch to determine connectivity. This command attempts to make a Transmission Control Protocol (TCP) connection, a socket connection, to well-known ports on the systems to establish connectivity.

Upon determining IP connectivity to our targets, our next step is to determine their underlying operating systems. For this, we'll utilize Nmap's *–O* (enable operating system detection) switch. Figure 6.3 illustrates the output of that command. The actual command is *namp –O 10.192.144.54 10.192.146.34. TCP/IP fingerprint was removed from Figure 6.3*

Figure 6.2 Nmap Ping Scan Command

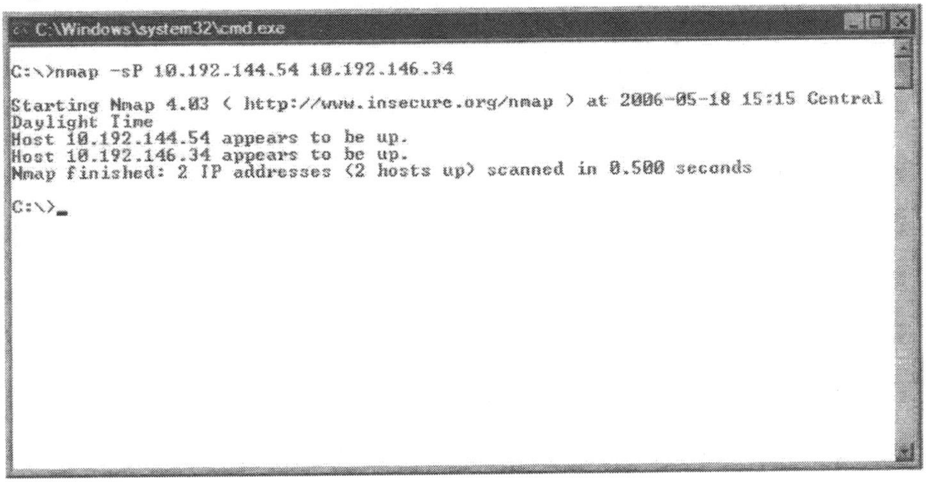

Figure 6.3 Nmap Operating System Detection Command

```
Starting Nmap 4.03 ( http://www.insecure.org/nmap ) at 2006-05-18 16:01
Central Daylight Time
Interesting ports on 10.192.144.54:
(The 1664 ports scanned but not shown below are in state: closed)
PORT        STATE SERVICE
135/tcp     open  msrpc
139/tcp     open  netbios-ssn
443/tcp     open  https
445/tcp     open  microsoft-ds
1043/tcp    open  boinc-client
2105/tcp    open  eklogin
2301/tcp    open  compaqdiag
3372/tcp    open  msdtc
3389/tcp    open  ms-term-serv
49400/tcp open  compaqdiag
No exact OS matches for host (If you know what OS is running on it, see
http://www.insecure.org/cgi-bin/nmap-submit.cgi).

Interesting ports on 10.192.146.34:
(The 1665 ports scanned but not shown below are in state: closed)
PORT        STATE SERVICE
```

```
111/tcp   open   rpcbind
135/tcp   open   msrpc
139/tcp   open   netbios-ssn
445/tcp   open   microsoft-ds
1433/tcp  open   ms-sql-s
3389/tcp  open   ms-term-serv
4125/tcp  open   rww
4987/tcp  open   maybeveritas
5555/tcp  open   freeciv
No exact OS matches for host (If you know what OS is running on it, see
http://www.insecure.org/cgi-bin/nmap-submit.cgi).

Nmap finished: 2 IP addresses (2 hosts up) scanned in 13.038 seconds
```

Leveraging the −O switch within Nmap we were unable to ascertain the operating system of the Web and database servers. Referring back to Figure 6.3 Nmap reported "No exact OS matches for the host". We could infer the operating system based upon the ports Nmap discovered. In Figure 6.3, Nmap detected that *tcp 139, netbios-ssn, tcp 445*, and *microsoft-ds* were open on the Web and database servers. Considering that *netbios-ssn* and *microsoft-ds* are specific to the Windows operating systems we could deduce that both the Web and database servers are running a version of Windows.

Discovering Open Ports and Enumerating

In the preceding section, we leveraged Nmap to validate connectivity and accessibility to the Web and database servers (targets). Upon discovering that we had IP connectivity, we then inferred the underlying operating system of each system based on the output that Nmap provided. Having garnered these two pieces of information, it's now time to discover the available (open) ports on each host and the applications or services running on each system. Remember, enumerating an asset will allow us to accurately assess it for vulnerabilities.

The Nmap −O switch gave us insight into the available services on each host. Though the intent of the switch is to determine the operating system, it also provided available port and service information. The command didn't provide us with the version number of each identified service, though. Considering that different versions of a respective application may contain different vulnerabilities, we'll leverage Nmap's −s*V* (server detection) switch to provide the version number or description of each enumerated service. Figure 6.4 recants the open port information from Figure 6.3 and displays the version or description of each running service. Take a look at the *Service Info:* attribute of each host too.

Figure 6.4 Nmap Service Detection Command

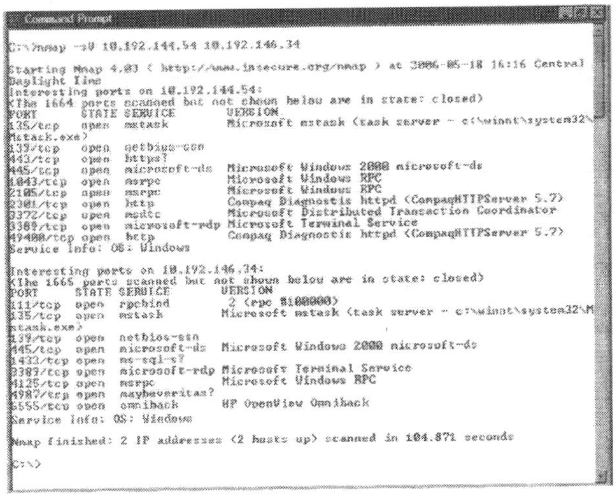

Via the −s*V* switch, we're able to determine the version number or description of each listening service. The −s*V* switch also provided further insight into each system's underlying operating system. Recall that when we attempted to detect the operating system via the −*O* switch, Nmap reported "No exact OS matches for host". We still don't have an exact operating system match, but we're able to now validate that the targets are running a version of the Windows operating system. When using the −*O* switch Nmap leveraged Transmission Control Protocol/Internet Protocol (TCP/IP) stack fingerprinting to deduce the underlying operating system. This command doesn't take into account the running services, like the −s*V* command does. By utilizing the −s*V* command, we can better determine the operating system based on the running applications on the targets.

For operating system detection and enumeration, we utilized multiple Nmap commands. We did this for illustration purposes only and to aid in the discussion of information gathering. To garner the same level of information we could have leveraged Nmap's −A (enable operating system and version detection) switch. Figure 6.5 illustrates the output of this command; *the TCP/IP fingerprints were removed from Figure 6.5.*

Figure 6.5 Nmap Operating System and Version Detection

```
Starting Nmap 4.03 ( http://www.insecure.org/nmap ) at 2006-05-19 00:03
Central Daylight Time
Interesting ports on 10.192.144.54:
(The 1664 ports scanned but not shown below are in state: closed)
PORT        STATE SERVICE       VERSION
135/tcp     open  mstask        Microsoft mstask (task server -
c:\winnt\system32\Mstask.exe)
139/tcp     open  netbios-ssn
443/tcp     open  https?
445/tcp     open  microsoft-ds  Microsoft Windows 2000 microsoft-ds
1043/tcp    open  msrpc         Microsoft Windows RPC
2105/tcp    open  msrpc         Microsoft Windows RPC
2301/tcp    open  http          Compaq Diagnostis httpd (CompaqHTTPServer 5.7)
3372/tcp    open  msdtc         Microsoft Distributed Transaction Coordinator
3389/tcp    open  microsoft-rdp Microsoft Terminal Service
49400/tcp open  http          Compaq Diagnostis httpd (CompaqHTTPServer 5.7)
No exact OS matches for host (If you know what OS is running on it, see
http://www.insecure.org/cgi-  bin/nmap-submit.cgi).


Service Info: OS: Windows


Interesting ports on 10.192.146.34:
(The 1665 ports scanned but not shown below are in state: closed)
PORT        STATE SERVICE       VERSION
111/tcp     open  rpcbind        2 (rpc #100000)
135/tcp     open  mstask        Microsoft mstask (task server -
c:\winnt\system32\Mstask.exe)
139/tcp     open  netbios-ssn
445/tcp     open  microsoft-ds  Microsoft Windows 2000 microsoft-ds
1433/tcp open  ms-sql-s?
3389/tcp open  microsoft-rdp Microsoft Terminal Service
4125/tcp open  msrpc         Microsoft Windows RPC
4987/tcp open  maybeveritas?
```

```
5555/tcp open  omniback       HP OpenView Omniback

Service Info: OS: Windows

Nmap finished: 2 IP addresses (2 hosts up) scanned in 116.968 seconds
```

As reflected in Figure 6.5, the −*A* command provides the same level of information we collected via the −*O* and −*sV* switches. In streamlining the information-gathering process, we could have combined the operating system detection and application enumeration processes by running Nmap with the −*A* switch.

Having determined the underlying operating systems and running services on each host, we've successfully completed step 1 of the penetration test, information gathering. It's now time to proceed to step 2, vulnerability detection. In step 2, we'll seek to identify any application or system-level vulnerabilities that we can later leverage in step 3, attack and penetration, to exploit the Web and database servers. Before we continue, let's organize the data we gathered via Nmap and update our System Information Table. Table 6.2 represents the updated System Information Table.

Table 6.2 Updated System Information with Nmap Results

#	Host	IP Address	Operating System	Open Ports
1	Web	10.192.144.54	Windows	135/tcp open mstask 139/tcp open netbios-ssn 443/tcp open https? 445/tcp open microsoft-ds 1043/tcp open msrpc 2105/tcp open msrpc 2301/tcp open http 3372/tcp open msdtc 3389/tcp open microsoft-rdp 49400/tcp open http

Continued

Table 6.2 Updated System Information with Nmap Results

#	Host	IP Address	Operating System	Open Ports
2	Database	10.192.146.34	Windows	111/tcp open rpcbind 135/tcp open mstask 139/tcp open netbios-ssn 445/tcp open microsoft-ds 1433/tcp open ms-sql-s? 3389/tcp open microsoft-rdp 4125/tcp open msrpc 4987/tcp open maybeveritas? 5555/tcp open omniback

Step 2: Determine Vulnerabilities

Having complete step 1, information gathering, we now need to assess the Web and database servers for vulnerabilities. To do this we'll need to switch tools. Nmap aided in the information-gathering process, but it's not a vulnerability assessment tool; its strengths reside in the information-gathering arena. To detect vulnerabilities we need a vulnerability assessment utility. Several VA tools are on the market, but for our purposes, we'll utilize Retina 5.0 from eEye Digital Security. Table 6.3 includes a partial list of the vulnerability scanners on the market today.

Table 6.3 List of VA Scanners

Company	Product	URL
eEye Digital Security	Retina	www.eeye.com
Tenable Network Security	Nessus	www.nessus.org
Internet Security Systems (ISS)	Internet Scanner	www.iss.net

Setting Up the VA

Within Retina, we need to create a scan job. The scan job will define the parameters of our vulnerability assessment. As per the Retina User Guide, these parameters include:

- **Hosts** Hosts to be assessed

- **Ports** TCP and User Datagram Protocol (UDP) ports that are included in the assessment

- **Audits** Vulnerabilities the hosts are evaluated against

- **Options** Attributes such as operating system detection, reverse domain name system (DNS) query, and so on

- **Credentials** Account information, if any, used to remotely connect to a system

The following steps will guide us through setting up a scan job within retina.

1. Upon launching Retina, select the **Audit** tab from the **Retina** interface. Figure 6.6 shows the Audit interface.

Figure 6.6 Retina Audit Interface

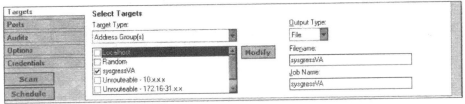

2. Next, select the **Targets** tab and create an Address Group associated with the Web and database servers by selecting the **Modify** button on the Targets tab.

3. After creating the Address Group, supply a Filename and Job Name to the scan and select the **Ports** tab. The **Filename** and **Job Name** parameters are simply descriptors for the scan. Selecting the Ports tab displays Figure 6.7.

Figure 6.7 Retina Ports Interface

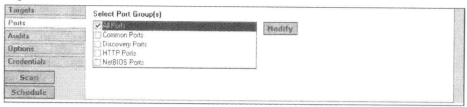

For our purposes, select **All Ports**. We're doing this to ensure that we don't miss any applications or services that could be running on an uncommon or frequently used port. If we were conducting a vulnerability assessment against our enterprise, we would need to reduce the number of ports evaluated to improve the audit speed and performance. Accessing every host against more than 65,000 ports could prove to be quite time consuming. Since we're evaluating only two hosts, this isn't an issue for use. Following are descriptions for the various Port Group options:

- **All Ports** Scans on all ports

- **Common Ports** Scans common application ports such as TCP port80 for web servers and TCP port 25 for email servers

- **Discovery Ports** Scans those ports used in Discover.

- **HTTP Ports** Scans ports 80 and 443

- **NetBIOS Ports** Scans ports 135, 139, and 445

4. After selecting All Ports, continue to the **Audits** tab and check **All Audits**. Figure 6.8 displays Retina's default audit selection. Recall that audits determine which known vulnerabilities our hosts will be evaluated against.

Figure 6.8 Retina Audit Groups

We've decided to evaluate the Web and database servers against all the vulnerabilities within the Retina database. Once again, if this were an enterprise assessment, we'd want to scope this. Since we're evaluating only two hosts, we'll select **All Audits** to unearth all possible system and application-level vulnerabilities.

5. Next we'll define the options of the scan by selecting the **Options** tab. These options include:

   ■ Perform OS Detection

   ■ Get Reverse DNS

   ■ Get NetBIOS Name

   ■ Get MAC Address

   ■ Perform Traceroute

   ■ Enable Connect Scan Connect to the target port and complete a full three-way handshake (SYN, SYN/ACK, and ACK).

   ■ Enable Force Scan

   ■ Perform the Various NetBIOS Enumerations

   For our scan, we select **Perform OS Detection, Enable Connect Scan Mode**, and **Perform the Various NetBIOS Enumerations**. Notice that we're repeating some of the same efforts we conducted in the information-gathering phase. Unfortunately, Retina can't utilize the information gathered via Nmap. Because of this, we'll need to repeat these exercises to accurately detect the vulnerabilities present on the Web and database servers. We could have leveraged Retina to begin with. We instead utilized Nmap for its robust operating system detection and enumeration options.

6. Having finalized our options, and because we're not leveraging credentials within this scan, we select the **Scan** button shown on the left-hand side in Figure 6.8 to initiate the vulnerability assessment.

Interpreting the VA Results

Once the vulnerability assessment is complete, we analyze the results to see whether any vulnerabilities were discovered on the Web and database servers. Remember that the goal of the penetration test is to see whether we can gain unauthorized access to customer records housed on the database. Ideally we'd like to discover a vulnerability on the database server and use it as an avenue into the system. If a vulnerability isn't present on the database server, we'll look to exploit the Web server in an attempt to gain access to the customer records. Figure 6.9 contains the output of our vulnerability assessment. Table 6.4 is our System Information Table, updated to include the Retina data.

Figure 6.9 Retina Vulnerability Output

```
eEye Digital Security


Retina Network Security Scanner
Network Vulnerability Assessment & Remediation Management


Summary Report


10.192.146.34
- - - - - - - - - - - - - - - - - - - - - - - - - - - - - - - - - - - - - -


General10.192.146.34 (Machine Informaiton - DB Server)
- - - - - - - - - - - - - - - - - - - - - - - - - - - - - - - - - - - - - -


Machine Name: N/A
NetBIOS Domain: N/A
DNS Name:
IP Address:    10.192.146.34
MAC Address:   N/A
Traceroute:
Time to Live: 125
Ping:  Host Responded
Open TCP Ports:     N/A
Open UDP Ports:     N/A
Operating System:    Windows 2000
```

```
---------------------------------------------
```

Audits 10.192.146.34   **(Vulnerability Detail)**

```
---------------------------------------------
```

Limited Null Session

Risk Level: Low
BugtraqID: 494
CVE: CVE-2000-1200

DCOM Enabled

Risk Level: Medium
BugtraqID: N/A
CVE: CAN-1999-0658
No Remote Registry Access Available

Risk Level: Information
BugtraqID: N/A
CVE: N/A

TCP:3389 - Terminal Services enabled

Risk Level: Low
BugtraqID: N/A
CVE: N/A

Microsoft Windows Non-Default User Service

Risk Level: Information
BugtraqID: N/A
CVE: N/A

ICMP Timestamp Request

Risk Level: Low
BugtraqID: N/A
CVE: CVE-1999-0524

```
------------------------------------------

Ports  10.192.146.34        (Open Ports)

------------------------------------------


111    :    TCP    :    Open   :    SUNRPC - SUN Remote Procedure Call
135    :    TCP    :    Open   :    RPC-LOCATOR - RPC (Remote
Procedure Call) Location Service
139    :    TCP    :    Open   :    NETBIOS-SSN - NETBIOS Session
Service
445    :    TCP    :    Open   :    MICROSOFT-DS - Microsoft-DS
1433   :    TCP    :    Open   :    MS-SQL-S - Microsoft-SQL-Server
3389   :    TCP    :    Open   :    MS RDP (Remote Desktop Protocol) /
Terminal Services
4987   :    TCP    :    Open   :    Unknown Port
5250   :    TCP    :    Open   :    Unknown Port
5555   :    TCP    :    Open   :    ServeMe
10204  :    TCP    :    Open   :    CA License Client/Server


--------------------------------------------------------------------


10.192.144.54

------------------------------------------


General10.192.144.54 (Machine information - Web Server)

------------------------------------------


Machine Name: N/A
NetBIOS Domain:      N/A
DNS Name:
IP Address:   10.192.144.54
MAC Address:  N/A
Traceroute.
Time to Live: 125
Ping:  Host Responded
Open TCP Ports:      N/A
Open UDP Ports:      N/A
```

```
Operating System:    N/A
------------------------------------------
Audits 10.192.144.54      (Vulnerability Detail)
------------------------------------------


TCP:2301 - JetPhoto Server "Name" And "Page" Variables Cross Site Scripting

Risk Level:    Low
BugtraqID:    N/A
CVE:    N/A


DCOM Enabled

Risk Level:    Medium
BugtraqID:    N/A
CVE:    CAN-1999-0658


Microsoft MSDTC and COM+ Buffer Overflow (902400) - Remote

Risk Level:    High
BugtraqID:    15056,15057
CVE:    CAN-2005-1979,CAN-2005-2119,CAN-2005-1978


TCP:3389 - Terminal Services enabled

Risk Level:    Low
BugtraqID:    N/A
CVE:    N/A


TCP:2967 - Norton AntiVirus Corporate Edition (managed service) detected

Risk Level:    Information
BugtraqID:    N/A
CVE:    N/A


ICMP Timestamp Request

Risk Level:    Low
BugtraqID:    N/A
```

```
CVE:    CVE-1999-0524


No Remote Registry Access Available


Risk Level:    Information
BugtraqID:     N/A
CVE:   N/A

-------------------------------------------


Ports  10.192.144.54        (Open Ports)

-------------------------------------------


135    :       TCP    :       Open   :       RPC-LOCATOR - RPC (Remote
Procedure Call) Location Service
139    :       TCP    :       Open   :       NETBIOS-SSN - NETBIOS Session
Service
443    :       TCP    :       Open   :       HTTPS - HTTPS (Hyper Text Transfer
Protocol Secure) - SSL (Secure Socket Layer)
445    :       TCP    :       Open   :       MICROSOFT-DS - Microsoft-DS
1065   :       TCP    :       Open   :       HP OpenView
2103   :       TCP    :       Open   :       ZEPHYR-CLT - Zephyr Serv-HM
Conncetion
2105   :       TCP    :       Open   :       EKLOGIN - Kerberos (v4) Encrypted
RLogin
2301   :       TCP    :       Open   :       CIM - Compaq Insight Manager
3389   :       TCP    :       Open   :       MS RDP (Remote Desktop Protocol) /
Terminal Services
```

Table 6.4 Summary of Retina Output

#	Host	IP Address	Operating System	Open Ports	Vulnerabilities/ Severity
1	Web	10.192.144.54	Windows 2000	135/tcp 139/tcp 443/tcp 445/tcp 1043/tcp 2105/tcp 2301/tcp	JetPhoto (Low) DCOM (Medium) MSDTC (High) TS (Low) Norton (Low) ICMP(Low)

Continued

Table 6.4 continued Summary of Retina Output

#	Host	IP Address	Operating System	Open Ports	Vulnerabilities/ Severity
				3372/tcp	
				3389/tcp	
				49400/tcp	
2	Database	10.192.146.34	Windows 2000	111/tcp	Null Session (Low)
				135/tcp	DCOM (Medium)
				139/tcp	TS (Low)
				445/tcp	ICMP (Low)
				1433/tcp	
				3389/tcp	
				4125/tcp	
				4987/tcp	
				5555/tcp	

Referring to Table 6.4 we notice that the database doesn't contain a high-level vulnerability that we can exploit to gain unauthorized access to it. The highest-level vulnerability it possesses is associated with Microsoft Distributed Component Object Model (DCOM) being enabled, which really doesn't represent a vulnerability. The Web server, on the other hand, does possess a high-level vulnerability. It's susceptible to a Microsoft Distributed Transaction Coordinator (MSDTC) and Component Object Model (COM)+ buffer overflow. In an effort to gain access to the customer records, we'll need to first exploit the Web server. If we're successful, we'll attempt to leverage the Web server to gain access to the database.

Penetration Testing

Penetration tests utilize the vulnerabilities discovered during a VA to *exploit*, or gain unauthorized access to, targeted systems. Whereas a vulnerability assessment identifies security holes within a system or application, a penetration test takes advantage of these weaknesses to gain unauthorized system-level access.

Having reported and detected the vulnerabilities present on the Web and database servers, it's now time to exploit, attack, and penetrate these weaknesses. To aid us we'll leverage Core Impact 5.1 from Core Security.

Additional penetration tools include Dave Aitel's Canvas and Metasploit. You can also find free vulnerability exploits at www.packetstormsecurity.org and www.securityfocus.com/bid.

Step 3: Attack and Penetrate

In our scenario, we discovered a high-level vulnerability on the Web server. We will now attempt to exploit this vulnerability to gain unauthorized access to the system. To do this we'll:

1. Upload the data we obtained during steps 1 and 2, information gathering and vulnerability assessment, into Core Impact (Impact).

2. Execute Impact's Attack and Penetration Module to attack and exploit the Web server.

3. Leverage the Web server to gain access to the database.

Uploading Our Data

Upon launching and configuring a workspace within Impact, we're presented with the window shown in Figure 6.10. This is the interface we'll leverage to conduct our attack.

Figure 6.10 Impact Interface

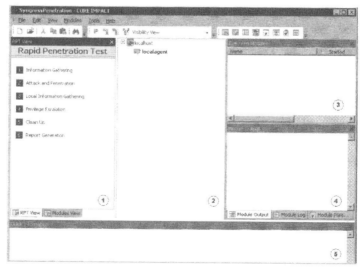

Here's an explanation of the different parts of the Impact user interface, as explained in the Core Impact User Guide

1. **The Modules panel** Provides access to Impact modules. Modules are the actions, such as information gathering, attacking, sniffing, and so on, that we can perform on the network or against a host.

2. **The Entity View panel** Displays information about our targets. This panel initially contains only an entry for the local host (the machine on which Impact is running). As we attack and exploit systems, they, too, are added to the Entity View panel.

3. **The Executed Modules panel** Displays information about each module or action that was performed during the penetration test.

4. **The Executed Module Info panel** Displays information about the currently selected module or action in the Executed Modules panel.

5. **The Quick Information panel** Displays information about the currently selected item in the console. For example, if we select a module, the panel displays module documentation. If we select a host, the panel displays information about that host.

To upload our data into Impact we select the **Modules View** tab within the **Modules** panel. We then expand the **Import-Export** module. Figure 6.11 shows the available import-export options for Impact.

As shown in Figure 6.11, Impact has import modules for Nmap and Retina; the two tools we utilized during steps 1 and 2 of our penetration test. To streamline our penetration efforts we'll upload the data we previously collected. To upload the data we simply click on the corresponding module and follow the instructions. Figure 6.12 depicts the Nmap interface.

Figure 6.11 Impact Import-Export Module

Figure 6.12 Impact Nmap Import Interface

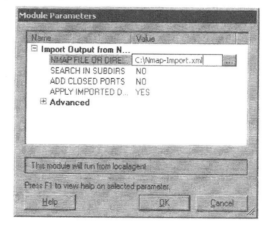

We generate the Nmap file value referenced in Figure 6.12 by appending the −oX (<*filename*>) tag to the Nmap commands we executed earlier during the information-gathering phase. When we append these arguments, Nmap will output the results to an XML file.

Upon uploading the Nmap and Retina data into Impact, our Entity View panel is updated with the following:

- The IP addresses of the Web and database servers
- Open ports on both systems
- Vulnerabilities discovered during the VA

Once we have both of these systems defined within the entity view, we can proceed to the attack and penetration phase of our test. Figure 6.13 reflects the updated entity view.

Figure 6.13 Updated Entity View

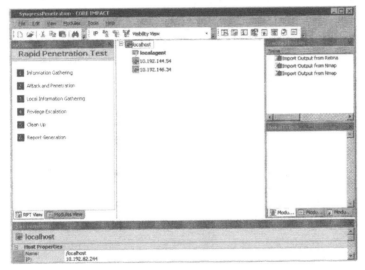

Attack and Penetrate

Based on the vulnerabilities previously discovered, we know we must first exploit, or penetrate, the Web server if we hope to gain access to the customer records. We need to do this because there were no identified vulnerabilities on the database server.

To exploit the Web server we could either selectively, or manually, run Impact exploits against the Web server, or we could leverage Impact's Attack and Penetration Wizard to exploit the host. The Attack and Penetration

Wizard will compare the Web server's vulnerabilities and open ports against exploit modules within Impact and attempt to automatically exploit the system.

To invoke the Attack and Penetration Wizard click on the **RPT View** tab within the **Modules** panel and select **Attack and Penetration**. Upon doing so, Figure 6.14 appears.

Figure 6.14 Attack and Penetration Wizard

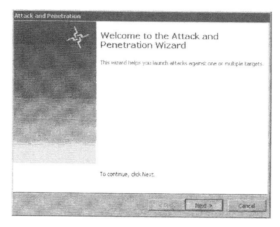

Click **Next**, and the screen in Figure 6.15 appears. Here we define the system we want to attack; the Web server in our scenario.

Figure 6.15 Target Selection

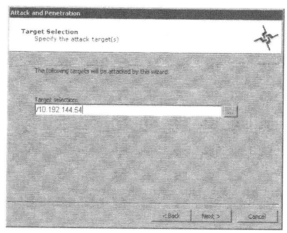

In an effort to maintain system stability, we will not run any exploits that might render the system unavailable (see Figure 6.16).

Figure 6.16 Exploit Selection

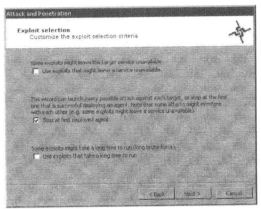

After clicking **Next**, we assume the remaining default settings and allow Impact to begin its attack on the Web server. We can follow the status of the attack by viewing the attack modules within the Executed Modules panel. Following the attack, we see that Impact is able to penetrate the Web server via the MSRPC UMPNPMGR exploit (see Figure 6.17), and loads a level 0 agent on the system. If we had our speakers on during the attack, we would have heard Impact announce "New Agent Deployed."

Figure 6.17 Module Output

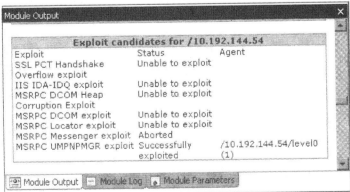

Notice that Impact exploited the remote Web server via the MSRPC UMPNPMGR vulnerability and not via a DCOM-related one. This is because we configured Impact to stop its attack upon successfully deploying its first agent. Although we provided Impact with VA data, Impact attacked, or ran exploits against, the system based upon the Web server's open ports and vulnerabilities.

NOTE

Within Impact, a level 0 agent provides basic shell access to the remote system supporting a finite number of commands. A level 1 agent is an administrator or root equivalent agent that has the ability to do anything and everything on the remote system. Communication calls between the Impact operator and the level 1 agent are also secure, but they are not with a level 0 agent.

Having gained unauthorized access to the Web server, we now need to determine the context, or identity, under which we're operating. By connecting to the level 0 agent and launching a mini-shell, we execute the *whoami* command to determine the identity we've assumed. Figure 6.18 highlights the output of the *whoami* command.

Figure 6.18 whoami command

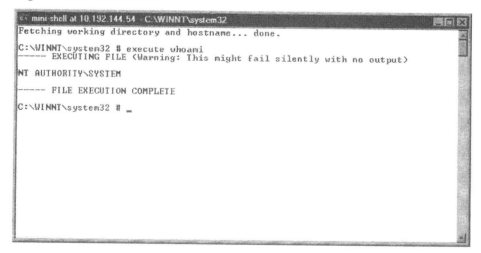

The *whoami* command displays the identity of the logged-in user. In Figure 6.18, we've determined we're operating under the context of Authority\System; a Windows built-in administrative equivalent account. Via Impact, we've gained unauthorized administrative access to the Web server. We'll now upgrade to a level 1 agent. Upgrading to a level 1 agent will provide us with a rich mini-shell and allow us to execute command-line arguments as though we are at the Web server's console. Figure 6.19 reflects an updated entity module containing the level 1 agent.

Figure 6.19 Entity Module: Level 1 Agent

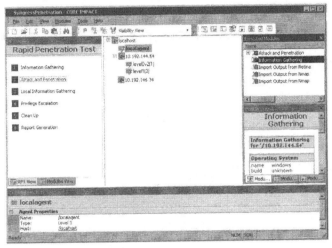

Having established a level 1 agent on the Web server, we now have several options regarding attacking the database server and ultimately gaining access to the customer records. We could:

- **Source attacks from the Web server** Since the database supports the Web server, the firewall between the two systems may contain a more liberal set of firewall rules. If this were the case, we could repeat steps 1 and 2, information gathering and VA, sourcing these efforts from the Web server. Doing so may provide insight into vulnerabilities that were undetectable from our position within the network.

- **Install software on the Web server** We could install a packet driver, remote control software, and so on. Doing so may allow us to discover credentials that are leveraged by the Web server to access the database.

- **Search the Web server for information** We could search the Web server for information. Such a search may disclose proprietary company data or other sensitive data housed on the system, or enable us to access credentials to other resources.

Searching the Web Server for Information

Of the aforementioned options, searching the Web server for information is the easiest to conduct and the hardest to detect. If we installed a remote piece of software on the Web server, its antivirus program may detect and quarantine that software, and sound an alarm concerning this. Sourcing our penetration efforts from the Web server is a viable option, but it requires that we restart our penetration efforts from scratch. Looking back at our System Information Table will provide further insight as to why this is the best option (see Table 6.5).

Table 6.5 System Information Table

#	Host	IP Address	Operating System	Open Ports	Vulnerabilities/ Severity
1	Web	10.192.144.54	Windows 2000	135/tcp 139/tcp 443/tcp 445/tcp 1043/tcp 2105/tcp 2301/tcp 3372/tcp 3389/tcp 49400/tcp	JetPhoto (Low) DCOM (Medium) MSDTC (High) TS (Low) Norton (Low) ICMP (Low)

Continued

Table 6.5 continued System Information Table

#	Host	IP Address	Operating System	Open Ports	Vulnerabilities/ Severity
2	Database	10.192.146.34	Windows 2000	111/tcp 135/tcp 139/tcp 445/tcp 1433/tcp 3389/tcp 4125/tcp 4987/tcp 5555/tcp	Null Session (Low) DCOM (Medium) TS (Low) ICMP (Low)

In Table 6.5, we've highlighted two key attributes. On the Web server, we've highlighted the operating system and on the database we've highlighted the open port, TCP 1433. This tells us two things:

1. The Web server is more than likely running Microsoft Internet Information Server (IIS) 5.0. IIS 5.0 runs only on Windows 2000.

2. If we're able to detect database credentials on the Web server, we can use our position from within the network to connect to the database server for TCP 1433, the Microsoft SQL default port.

Discovering Web Services

Until now, we've discovered no information to validate that the Web server is indeed a Web server. Looking at Table 6.5, you can see that TCP port 80 is not referenced as an open port. This could be due to a variety of reasons. Considering that this is the client's e-commerce Web server, it's highly unlikely that the client changed the system's default port; doing so would require the client to inform its customers as to what the new port is, and this simply doesn't scale. More than likely the client has filtered the port, via its firewall, from its internal clients. To determine this we'll leverage our Impact mini-shell and dump all of the TCP port 80 connections to the Web server (see Figure 6.20), to ascertain whether the server is indeed accepting Web connections. We'll use the *netstat* command for this purpose; *netstat* is used to display protocol statistics and current TCP/IP connections. From Figure 6.20, we can confirm that the Web server is indeed accepting TCP connections on port 80.

Figure 6.20 Web Server Detection

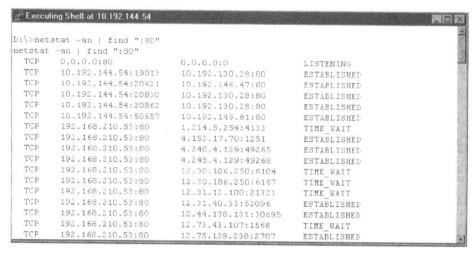

We then confirm that the client is running IIS via the *iisreset /status* command (see Figure 6.21), which is unique to IIS.

Figure 6.21 iisreset /status Command

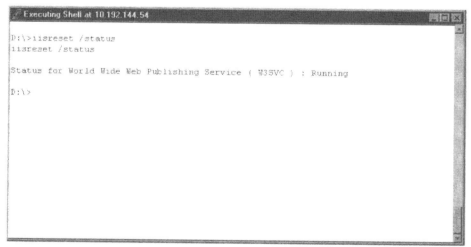

Having validated the existence of a Web server, it's now time to unearth access credentials to the database. To do this we consider:

- Both the Web and the database servers are running Windows 2000.

- The Web server supports the client's e-commerce initiatives.

- Active Server Pages (ASP) is the primary method to support dynamic Web content on Windows 2000 and IIS.

- Active data objects (ADO) and Object Linking and Embedding Data Base (OLE DB) are the predominant application program interfaces (APIs) used to connect to a database from a Web server.

Maintaining access to our mini-shell we search the Web server for all .asp files that contain "sqloledb." These files contain access credentials to databases. Hopefully we'll find at least one file that references the customer database. Figure 6.22 contains the output of our search.

Figure 6.22 findstr Output

Well, well, well. Look at what we've found. Leveraging the *findstr* command within Windows we're able to uncover a connection string and credentials to the customer database. Figure 6.23 highlights the output from Figure 6.22 that references the customer database.

Figure 6.23 SQL Credentials

```
WebServ\wwwroot\companyabc.com \Search.asp:                              m
objECD.ConnectionString = "Data Source=10.192.146.34;Initial Catalog=customer ;
User ID= Engine; Password=bkeng10; Provider=SQLOLEDB;"
```

At this point, there's no need to continue our attack from the Web server. Having garnered user credentials to the database and with the database, TCP 1433, being available to us from our attack position, we can simply connect to the database from our local machine. To connect to the database we'll use Microsoft's SQL Query Analyzer and the credentials from Figure 6.23. Upon connecting, we're presented with the screen shown in Figure 6.24.

Figure 6.24 Query Analyzer Connection

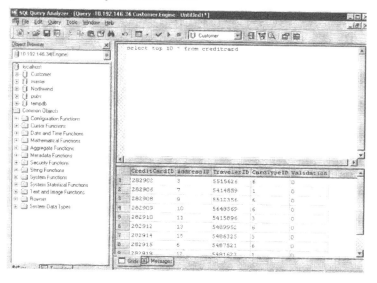

As we can see by viewing the available databases within Figure 6.24, the customer database represents the only user-created database; the rest of the databases are installed by default with Microsoft SQL. Expanding **Customer** we locate a table titled "creditcard." Upon querying the creditcard table, selecting its 10 top records, we uncover customer data. Now it's only a matter of joining the fields within the creditcard table and the rest of the tables within the customer database to assemble the complete customer record. At this point, we have accomplished our objective. We have accessed customer records. The penetration test is over.

Vulnerability Assessment versus a Penetration Test

After walking through a vulnerability assessment and a penetration test, we might think penetration tests are the way to go. Penetration tests do substantiate the vulnerabilities unearthed during an assessment. In some situations, penetration tests are necessary. In others, they simply aren't reasonable or practical.

Penetration tests are great for a small or targeted collection of assets; for example, network perimeters, third-party peering points, and internal financial or human resources systems. Unfortunately, penetration tests do not scale when we get into the hundreds, thousands, tens of thousands, and hundreds of thousands of systems which comprise major enterprise environments. Comparatively speaking, vulnerability assessments do scale. Not only do they scale, but also they are cheaper in terms of both time and resources, and they give us a more exhaustive view of security liabilities across our enterprise.

Tips for Deciding between Conducting a VA or a Penetration Test

If you are undecided as to whether to conduct a vulnerability assessment or a penetration test, here are some tips to help facilitate your decision.

You should conduct a vulnerability assessment when:

- **Time is a constraint** Penetration tests can be very time consuming, depending on the number of assets we are evaluating and the number of vulnerabilities that are present on any given host. Imagine how long a penetration test would take against 100 or perhaps 1,000 hosts. On most occasions, we're not interested in whether a vulnerability can be exploited, for we may have compensating controls to mitigate the exploitation, but we would still like to know whether the vulnerability appears to exist. Though a vulnerability may not be exploitable today, this may not hold true for tomorrow. Many times vulnerabilities are re-released with new attack vectors allowing for

new conduits of exploitation. Think we've seen the last re-release of a
Microsoft Remote Procedure Call (RPC) vulnerability?

- **Cost is an issue** Not only do penetration tests require substantially
  more time, but they also cost more to conduct. In many instances,
  companies have to contract out penetration work, for they simply do
  not have the expertise on staff. Most organizations today, though, are
  fairly adept at conducting vulnerability assessments; especially given
  the number of VA products on the market.

- **Validating** Want to know the success of that latest service pack
  push? Run a VA against the hosts in question. Systems often remain
  vulnerable after patches have been deployed, simply because the
  machines haven't been rebooted. VAs are great at identifying this.
  Let's compare our VA reports against the remediation team's reports.
  We may find ourselves asking, "So, fellows, are we sure those
  machines were patched?"

- **Trending** How have we done at managing vulnerabilities across our
  enterprise today as compared to yesterday, last month, or perhaps last
  year? Sure, the number of vulnerabilities is increasing and the
  window between disclosure and exploit is shrinking, but trending
  vulnerabilities across our enterprise can provide valuable insight into
  our organization's remediation and change control processes.

You should conduct a penetration test when:

- **You have a limited number of assets** Penetration tests are very
  practical against a small number of hosts—for example, the company's
  financial or accounting systems. Where a vulnerability assessment
  attempts to identify all weaknesses, a penetration test simply seeks to
  exploit any one of the N number of vulnerabilities on a given
  system. Attempting to exploit all vulnerabilities is usually pointless. It
  doesn't matter whether the front door or back window of our house
  is unlocked; a thief can effectively use either of these avenues as an
  entry point into our home.

- **Confirmation is needed** We conduct a VA and find five high-level vulnerabilities on a system. Is that system truly vulnerable? Can an unauthorized entity compromise that system? The only true way to substantiate this is to conduct a penetration test. If we can leverage one of the identified vulnerabilities to gain access to the system, someone else can too.

- **You are fiscally flexible** Penetration tests are typically outsourced to a company's information technology (IT) provider, an external auditor, or a third party. Outsourcing the work validates the organization's security posture, supports the company's security program, and is required by most regulations. Outsourcing application development and support services may have their cost benefits, but outsourcing penetration testing can be quite expensive.

- **Time is not of the essence** What takes longer, hacking five systems or conducting a vulnerability assessment against those same five systems? Who said there was no such thing as a stupid question? Penetration tests depend on vulnerability information, so naturally, they take longer to conduct. If we want to confirm that the identified vulnerabilities exist and time is on our side, penetration tests are the way to go.

Internal versus External

We can conduct vulnerability and penetration assessments either from within our network or external to it. An internal assessment will expose vulnerabilities that employees, contractors, third parties, or anyone else that has access to our internal network can exploit. An external assessment gives us a view of our security liabilities as seen by customers, competitors, business partners, and hackers.

To further distinguish internal and external assessments and the value proposition of each, let's look at a typical network, as shown in Figure 6.25.

Figure 6.25 A Typical Network

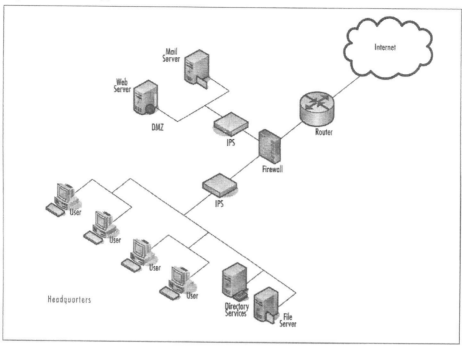

In Figure 6.25, as in most organizations, a firewall represents the first line of defense against outside threats. Some organizations also enable firewall capabilities on their edge, Internet router. Behind the firewall and before the corporate network resides the company's *DMZ*; a hardened and semitrusted portion of the company's network used to host Web, e-mail, and other Internet services. Behind the DMZ, separated by yet another firewall, resides the corporate network where end users and enterprise services live.

Given Figure 6.25, if we were to conduct an internal assessment—say, against the Directory Services server—we would, in essence, be evaluating the security posture of that respective host and the applications that reside on it. If that server possessed vulnerabilities, any one of the four illustrated users could attempt to exploit, penetrate, and gain unauthorized access to the system without transversing any security infrastructure. Though many organizations have implemented firewalls, IPSes, and other types of security infrastructure within their corporate network, these devices do not protect the vast majority of internal systems. Because of this, an organization should develop a comprehensive vulnerability assessment process that identifies all vulnerabilities on all network-connected devices.

Conversely, if we were external to the network depicted in Figure 6.25 and conducted an assessment—say, against the company's Web or e-mail server—our assessment would transverse multiple layers of security; a firewall followed by an intrusion prevention device. In this scenario, exploitation of a vulnerability is more difficult, for we have to successfully pass through both the company's firewall and IPS devices.

Organizations should routinely conduct both internal and external assessments. External assessments are great at testing and measuring a company's defense-in-depth strategy and provide valuable insight into what an entity, foreign to the company's network, may be able to gain access to. Internal assessments aid organizations in identifying process, change control, configuration, and remediation weaknesses for assets, when evaluated from this perspective, typically are not protected by security infrastructure. Even if they are, it's usually not to the same extent to which DMZ assets are protected.

Internal assessments are also good at identifying vulnerabilities that internal users can exploit. Remember that the internal threat is just as great, if not greater than, the external threat. We never know when an employee or contractor may attempt to sabotage or break into an internal system, while it's pretty safe to assume that this activity is constantly occurring from sources outside our organization's network.

Summary

As mentioned at the beginning of this chapter, vulnerability assessments and penetration tests are valuable components of a company's information security program. However, before conducting either test, we should identify what we're trying to accomplish. Are we attempting to validate that a vulnerability exists? Perhaps we would like to know whether an outsider can gain unprivileged access to our system. Still yet, we may simply want to know the success of our last remediation push.

Vulnerability assessments and penetration tests can provide answers to these questions. Both have their strengths, as well as relative weaknesses, depending on our ultimate objective. A wise man once said, proper prior planning prevents piss-poor performance. We should heed that advice when deciding whether to conduct a pen test when all we need is VA data. There's nothing like attempting to exploit a thousand machines when all we want to know is whether they are vulnerable.

Solutions Fast Track

Types of Penetration Tests

☑ Black box testing assumes no prior knowledge of the environment to be tested.

☑ White box testing provides the testers with complete knowledge of the environment to be tested.

Who conducts Pen Test?

☑ Organizations conduct pen tests in support of their information security program

☑ 3rd Parties conduct pen test to substantiate an organization's compliance requirements

☑ Malicious attackers conduct pen test in an effort to exploit systems for nefarious reasons

Penetration Testing Involves

- ☑ Information Gathering—Determining the depth and breath of the evaluation

- ☑ Vulnerability Assessment—Assessing systems and applications for vulnerabilities

- ☑ Attack and Penetration—exploiting a system via an identified vulnerability

Value of VA vs Pen Test

- ☑ Vulnerability Assessments are quicker, more cost effective, and can be conducted against a larger set of assets

- ☑ Penetration tests determine the true liability of an asset.

Frequently Asked Questions

The following Frequently Asked Questions, answered by the authors of this book, are designed to both measure your understanding of the concepts presented in this chapter and to assist you with real-life implementation of these concepts. To have your questions about this chapter answered by the author, browse to **www.syngress.com/solutions** and click on the **"Ask the Author"** form.

Q: Do I need to use a commercial-grade pen test tool to conduct a thorough assessment of my environment?

A: Attackers typically don't. Neither do you. You can certainly download exploits off the Internet and compile them yourself. This will require some knowledge of C and, perhaps, C++.

Q: Is there any benefit to having a third party conduct a black box penetration test against my organization?

A: Of course. By doing so, you may discover ingress points into your environment that you didn't know existed.

Q: In the scenario described in this chapter, we conducted a pen test from within a network. Is there really value in launching a pen test from here?

A: Absolutely. In this day and age, network boundaries are shrinking. Many organizations have established business-to-business circuits with their partners. Sourcing pen tests from within your network will reveal what your business partner has access to. Plus, theft via insiders is a major concern these days.

## Chapter 7

Vulnerability Management

Solutions in this chapter:

- The Vulnerability Management Plan
- The Six Stages of Vulnerability Management
- Governance (What the Auditors Want to Know)
- Measuring the Performance of a Vulnerability Management Program
- Common Problems with Vulnerability Management

- ☑ Summary
- ☑ Solutions Fast Track
- ☑ Frequently Asked Questions

Introduction

Back in the good old days, the typical approach to vulnerability management was to have the security group identify threats and then "toss" them to information technology (IT) administrators for remediation. As the number of security threats mounted over the years, this casual approach was no longer viable. In previous chapters, we discussed vulnerability discovery through the use of vulnerability assessment (VA) scanners, patch management, and configuration management tools. However, vulnerability management requires more than just the use of one of these previously mentioned tools.

Vulnerability management is best defined as the overall process of managing the risk presented to an enterprise due to vulnerabilities, whether they are software or hardware related. Vulnerability management ties directly into vulnerability discovery and vulnerability assessment in many ways, and depends greatly on the patch management process as well.

Vulnerability management also includes the grouping of security practices and processes which assist in managing security liabilities, allowing you to integrate vulnerability management into existing information security and IT workflows.

This chapter outlines the building blocks of a vulnerability management program and discusses what's necessary to maintain an effective program.

> **NOTE**
>
> Don't assume that large enterprises solve the vulnerability management problem simply by throwing people at it. Regardless of an organization's size, you can't address vulnerability management by adding more people to the team. For example, one large international corporation created a team of more than fifty people dedicated to vulnerability management and patch deployment. Despite having labs dedicated to testing patches and fixes, the company still couldn't keep up with the tide of work, primarily because of poor and undocumented processes.

The Vulnerability Management Plan

As with any plan, unless it's documented, receives appropriate sponsorship, and is effectively communicated, it's probably not very attainable. The same holds true for a vulnerability management plan. You must document the plan's goals, objectives, and success criteria. To help the plan along, you also must receive executive buy-in and sponsorship if you hope for the plan to be effective. Without senior management support, the ability to enforce vulnerability management policies, processes, and practices is forever hampered.

NOTE

Historically, vulnerability assessment has been viewed as a technology or IT problem, and not an organizational or risk management problem.

In an effort to garner senior management buy-in, your vulnerability management plan must be measurable and mapped to organizational risk as well as IT risk. By doing this, you can change senior management's predisposition regarding vulnerability management and get them to understand that this is a business issue and not solely an IT matter.

Planning a vulnerability management program is no different from planning for any other project or program. As mentioned earlier, the plan should clearly articulate its intent and relevance to the business. If you have not established a vulnerability management program, the following five steps can help you in this endeavor:

1. Gain an understanding of your organization's tolerance and appetite for risk.

2. Define acceptable levels of risk and timeframes in which elevated levels of risk are to be remediated.

3. Establish asset and vulnerability classifications. Understanding which assets are important to the business and coming up with a vulnerability classification system will increase the effectiveness and efficiency of your vulnerability management program.

4. Assign roles and responsibilities. Identify and document asset owners, custodians, and the entity responsible for an asset's remediation.

5. Finally, develop a method for measuring the program's success. If you can't measure it, you can't attest that the organization is operating within or at an acceptable level of risk.

A well-thought-out and vetted vulnerability management plan will receive input from various business units and all levels of management from within the company. This is especially true when developing a vulnerability management plan for the first time, as information about security is shared across multiple layers of the organization in an attempt to map information security to business risk.

The Six Stages
of Vulnerability Management

Establishing a vulnerability management plan is pretty straightforward, but the devil is in the details of your environment. As mentioned earlier, vulnerability management comprises the identification, assessment, remediation, and monitoring of software and hardware vulnerabilities. In total, a vulnerability management plan consists of six stages, as shown in Figure 7.1.

Figure 7.1 Stages of a Vulnerability Management Plan

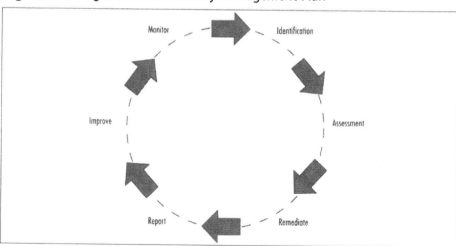

Stage One: Identify

The critical first step in vulnerability management is to identify, check, and track all the information assets attached to your network. Establishing an asset inventory is the first port of call for understanding the "vulnerability terrain." Maintaining an accurate asset database often is unattainable for many companies; however, without an accurate asset inventory, a vulnerability management plan will be severely hampered and possibly doomed to failure. The accuracy of your inventory impacts your ability to know which security alerts are applicable to your environment.

NOTE

Inevitably, you'll forget about some of the technologies in place at your organization, only to stumble across them years later, littering the dark corners of your data centers and closets. Typically, such technologies include machines in development labs, nomadic home/work machines, machines hidden behind a network address translator device, vendor-maintained devices, fax machines, printers, and many other rogue and network-aware devices.

Other, more obscure examples include production machinery (factory robots), supervisory control and data acquisition devices, and medical equipment. These devices are just as susceptible to vulnerabilities as mainstream technologies are (sometimes they're even more susceptible). Don't discount them!

The types of technologies that you have implemented within your organization map directly back to the types of vulnerabilities present in your environment. Leveraging an accurate asset inventory will help you to ensure that only applicable vulnerability information is processed or considered within your environment.

If you don't already possess an up-to-date asset database, you should leverage the following best practices before creating one:

- Establish a single point of authority for the inventory.

- Identify and document the assets' owners and custodians.

- Establish a process to update the asset management system via inputs and outputs from the change management process.

- Use an asset numbering scheme and consistent abbreviations and notations when entering data.

- Validate the inventory at least annually to ensure its accuracy.

- Ensure that the classification of each asset is recorded (refer to Chapter 1 for asset classification guidance).

- Ensure that the inventory database is extensible, because you might add additional information to the asset record down the road (for example, the last day and time that the asset was assessed for vulnerabilities).

Stage Two: Assess

Having established the list of assets to be assessed, you can now turn your attention to assessing your corporate assets for vulnerabilities. As part of the assessment, you must classify as well as identify the level of criticality each discovered vulnerability represents. Categorizing a vulnerability as having a high, medium, or low level of severity will help you to prioritize your remediation efforts later.

Vulnerability identification is the cornerstone of the vulnerability management process, and we covered it in more detail in Chapter 2. As noted in that chapter, you should make scanning and remediation a priority. You should first assess your highly sensitive, mission-critical systems and line-of-business systems, followed by the rest of the assets within your organization. How you prioritize the remaining assets is subjective, and each company does it differently. You may choose to scan the testing and development environments first, for they represent the organization's next generation of corporate assets, or you could elect to scan all employee desktops. Once again, this is up to you, but you should make sure that whatever process you choose reflects which assets are most important to your organization.

- Before performing your vulnerability assessment, keep these best practices in mind:

- Begin your assessment with the output from your asset inventory system.

- Ensure that you have the authorization to conduct an assessment, and follow appropriate company protocol during the assessment.

- Test new scanners and new vulnerability checks in a lab to identify any false positives, false negatives, and potential service disruptions prior to the assessment.

- Document the assessment methodology. This ensures that the assessment process is consistent and repeatable across the organization.

Stage Three: Remediate

Remediation is a key part of every vulnerability management program. We will cover remediation in more detail in Chapter 9, but it's important to highlight some of the key aspects of it here because it's so integral to your vulnerability management plan.

In the remediation stage, you develop your strategy for remediating the vulnerabilities you've discovered within your environment. This course of action reflects of a combination of technologies, processes, policies, and training. Because vulnerabilities impact the entire organization, this step will typically include multiple business groups. Depending on the breadth of exposure and presented risk, all business units within an organization may hold a level of remediation responsibility and accountability.

To ensure that your remediation efforts are repeatable and sustainable, you should formalize your remediation process. As part of formalizing these efforts, you should also ensure that the organization's most critical assets receive priority. By doing this, you can establish a systematic method by which vulnerabilities are remediated within the organization.

Before remediating any vulnerabilities, you should keep these best practices in mind:

- Consider utilizing a tool or suite of tools that can notify asset owners and custodians of vulnerabilities present on their systems. Otherwise, your teams will have to spend time sending out notification e-mails to users.

- Specific remediation goals may vary based on the criticality of the system. Focus on the highest-risk vulnerabilities present on your most critical assets. For example, some organizations may rely heavily on Web presence as a source of revenue (for instance, an online auction site, an online retail site, etc.). For such organizations, their Internet infrastructure (Web server, applications, back-end systems, and network devices) may have the highest priority.

- Track and measure remediation efforts. You can break out this process by individual, team, or division, depending on whom within your organization is responsible for remediation. Tracking remediation efforts in this manner allows you to analyze efforts, measure them for effectiveness, and track them against agreed-upon goals.

- Work with business units in advance to determine acceptable levels of risks. Get the business units to agree on remediation time frames and have them acknowledge the risks of not remediating vulnerabilities in a timely manner. Having business units sign off on risk helps champion the seriousness of vulnerability management.

Stage Four: Report

As with anything, especially anything within the realm of security, you must be able to attest to the level of effort you've put forth. Vulnerability management reporting provides you with this level of attestation for your vulnerability management program. It also helps you to communicate the importance of vulnerability management throughout the organization. Without such reports, it would be hard to assess the organization's security posture and associated level of risk. Reporting also provides that gap analysis between what is fixed and what needs to be fixed, and you can use it as the tangible asset given to management to measure the success and failure rates of your vulnerability management program.

You can perform the reporting step before the remediation step, but performing it after the remediation step allows you to report on the quick wins. You can use this to demonstrate to management that actions are being taken to mitigate organizational liabilities.

There is a challenge, however, of in balancing vulnerability management reporting against remediation efforts. Without the proper information at the beginning of your program (quantifiably fiscal information and vulnerability statistics), it is difficult to bring vulnerability management full circle. Many organizations, especially those with little or no documentation, will also have problems connecting the right people with the correct vulnerability management reports. When people and assets are aligned, reporting helps you to hold business units and departments accountable for patching and fixing vulnerable hosts; provided you don't have a centralized remediation team.

When you are ready to create your reports, keep these best practices in mind:

- Determine which reports are relevant to your organization's respective lines of business.

- Determine which reports indicate the risk present within the environment.

- Focus your reports on the highest risk vulnerabilities associated with the most critical assets first.

Stage Five: Improve

Whether you've just established your vulnerability management program or have had one for some time, your program probably can stand a little improvement. As part of improving and enhancing your vulnerability management program, you should review the wealth of data collected from each preceding stage and look for opportunities to modify your organization's security policies, practices, or procedures to improve your program's effectiveness and, more important, reduce organizational risk.

Common areas to improve include:

- **Asset management process.** As mentioned previously, most organizations struggle to maintain an up-to-date asset inventory database. However, maintaining such a database is critical to any vulnerability management program and organizations should strive to accomplish this. In populating your database, you need to decide which assets belong in it and which ones don't. Does an asset you own, but out-source from a monitoring and management perspective, belong in the database? Some companies incorporate these assets into their asset management systems. If you follow this practice, and the asset does become a corporate-managed asset, you need to ensure that its information is input into your corporate database.

- **Configuration management process.** From time to time, organizations change the tools they use to manage their environments. When such a change occurs in your organization, you need to ensure that your previous tool set is removed from all supported systems and that the system documentation referencing the tools is updated. Doing this has a twofold effect: you reduce your attack surface on your assets because you're removing a tool you no longer need that may possess existing or future vulnerabilities, and you potentially ensure the integrity of your asset management system if you are leveraging your management tool to populate your asset database.

- **Assessment process.** Tools used to discover vulnerabilities have changed over the years (accelerated by recent acquisitions and mergers within the security space), and may become less effective and require replacement over time. Because of this, you should pay attention to the process and technology you use to discover vulnerabilities within your environment. As mentioned in Chapter 2, you can leverage configuration, remediation, and security technologies to aid in assessing systems and applications for vulnerabilities. Over time, you may need to rethink and adjust how you leverage these tools for assessment purposes, though.

Stage Six: Monitor

This step involves ascertaining applicable vulnerabilities against your organization's assets. To be effective, monitoring efforts should be proactive. As a regular course of business, security staff should track vulnerabilities through security advisories and vulnerability information sources.

Monitoring consists of more than simply checking security newswires for the latest vulnerabilities and exploits, though. It also entails evaluating security information to determine its applicability within your organization based upon your technology usage and any underlying compensating controls. Evaluating adequate protection and compensating controls, as they relate to the applicability of a vulnerability, is a very time-consuming and potentially arduous task, but it's a vital part of any vulnerability management program.

In Chapter 1, we identified resources of vulnerability information. All vendors of commercial vulnerability management tools embed this information within their products and frequently update their products via functions included within the technology, but reliance on this or any one source for this information is not a sound practice. Often we focus solely on security data pertaining only to the technology our organization consumes, but it's also important to have a general level of understanding for the vulnerabilities present in other platforms or applications because one day, we may be asked to weigh in on the security liabilities of a technology not currently present within our environment.

NOTE

Not every post to a vulnerability disclosure list should cause you to panic and set off the corporate alarms. Eight vulnerabilities, on average, are discovered daily (as of August 2006). Trying to assess each newly announced vulnerability is a waste of time and resources, because only a fraction of new vulnerabilities will actually apply to most organizations.

Monitoring vulnerability data can be challenging due to the sea of information available and the disparate methods by which it is shared. Most organizations find it difficult to manage the breadth of new security information and use it effectively.

However, it can be done. In essence, monitoring is composed of two key steps: collating the new vulnerability information, and communicating the filtered information to the appropriate recipients. In-house or external sources can be responsible for gathering the VA data; internal members generally gather the information from locations such as vendor notices, vulnerability disclosure groups, security groups, and National CERTS (Computer Emergency Response Teams). You then can catalog applicable vulnerabilities according to the systems they affected; you should be able to leverage your current inventory data to draw this correlation. Once you know what systems are subject to each vulnerability, you can communicate this information to the asset owner or custodian. This enables faster and more effective resolution.

Here are some best practices to assist in vulnerability monitoring:

- Centralize the acquisition of vulnerability data/information.

- Disseminate vulnerability data to impacted parties.

- Utilize tools to assist in prioritizing and alerting the organization of vulnerability data.

- Have a process in place to ensure that urgent alerts are sent in a timely manner.

- In situations where patches have not yet been released but vulnerabilities are publicly known, consider the use of other defenses, such as intrusion prevention systems.

- Have security teams and lines of business discuss new vulnerabilities, virus activity, malicious activity, and other important security issues frequently.

Governance (What the Auditors Want to Know)

In light of recent corporate scandals and the security liabilities that are present in our highly connected, highly technology-based world, corporate governance based on IT controls and attestation to such controls is on the radar of every C-level executive these days. If information security wasn't important to organizations in the past, government legislation and industry regulations such as the Sarbanes-Oxley Act, the Gramm-Leach-Bliley Act, the Health Insurance Portability and Accountability Act, and the Payment Card Industry Data Security Standard have brought information security to the forefront.

In response, many organizations have had to reevaluate their approach to IT governance. This review has led to an understanding that information security is not just a technical issue that the CIO's office can address, but rather an issue that the organization's CEO must sponsor and champion throughout the heart of the business and across all lines of business.

When the auditors come knocking, and you know they will, they will be very interested in your vulnerability management program because this program is key to reducing an organization's level of IT risk and protecting the organization's assets. To prepare for the auditors you should ensure the following:

- Appropriate sponsorship and buy-in have been established for the vulnerability management program and associated processes.
- Members from the business, IT, and security groups represent and participate in the program.
- Key stakeholders have been identified and appointed.
- The scope of assets has been appropriately defined.
- Information security policies, standards, and guidelines exist, are documented, and are accessible.
- Risk-based determination and classification of risks exist.
- Roles and responsibilities have been defined, documented, and communicated.
- Effective communication and escalation processes have been documented and communicated.
- The capability to track remediation of vulnerabilities exists.
- A method of quickly identifying new vulnerabilities is available.
- Monitoring controls have been integrated to minimize the impact of vulnerabilities.
- Measurement of the effectiveness of the program has been established.
- Reports are routinely created and distributed to key stakeholders and interested parties.

Measuring the Performance of a Vulnerability Management Program

Measuring the performance of a vulnerability management program is a complicated affair, because there is no definitive process to follow. For example, first measuring the statistics of the vulnerabilities identified during the assessment stage and then measuring the number of vulnerabilities remediated is one form of measurement. Unfortunately, it's not the best form. Nor is measuring the time between when a vulnerability was released to the public and when it was remediated within your organization.

This is because as your vulnerability management program matures, the number of new vulnerabilities capable of impacting your organization should diminish because you have established process and compensating controls to mitigate vulnerabilities, as well as a more mature method of assessing vulnerability risk. Coupled with this, studies show that the number of vulnerabilities released in the coming years is only going to increase. As such, the number of vulnerabilities remediated within your environment is not a meaningful unit of measurement. With the increasing number of vulnerabilities released each year, you should naturally remedy more this year than last, and so on.

Measuring the maturity of a vulnerability management program is a more effective method of determining the current state of your program. Table 7.1 represents a scorecard that you can use to measure the maturity of your vulnerability management program.

Instructions

Score yourself by ticking off the tasks/processes your organization operates and performs. Your score for that section is then the level in which your organization managed to achieve all bullet points. As an example in the first row we have scored our organization at Level 1 despite having an item in Level 2 ticked and have a score of 1.

Table 7.1 Vulnerability Management Program Scorecard

Level 0 (Ad Hoc)	Level 1 (Reactive)	Level 2 (Proactive)	Level 3 (Continuous/ Validated)	Score
Identification and Assessment Maturity				
No process is in place to identify vulnerabilities.	Vulnerabilities are assessed when a vendor releases an announcement. Scanning may occur to determine the extent of the vulnerability.	Mailing lists are monitored for applicable vulnerabilities. Proactive network scanning for vulnerabilities is in place. Loose integration with asset management and infrastructure administration processes exists.	Participate in a National CISRT. Alert service and profiling software are utilized. Proactive network and host vulnerability detection capabilities for critical assets are in place. Medium to tight integration with asset management and infrastructure administration processes are in place.	
Management Maturity				
No process is in place to manage the assignment of responsibilities.	High-level policies define the risk model. Little or no documented processes (e.g., call lists) are in place.	Manual processes, review and assess responsibilities Some process documentation exists. Risk classification criteria are predefined.	Vulnerabilities are reviewed and assessed on a periodic basis based on predefined criteria that are tied to business criticality (risk/asset criticality). Response mechanisms are predefined and automated where appropriate (e.g., alert notifications, etc.).	

Continued

Table 7.1 continued Vulnerability Management Program Scorecard

Level 0 (Ad Hoc)	Level 1 (Reactive)	Level 2 (Proactive)	Level 3 (Continuous/ Validated)	Score
Application Maturity				
No process is in place for risk the mitigation defined.	Some procedures are defined for some business areas and platforms. Informal linkages to change management exist. Informal reporting on results and metrics is in place. Informal linkages with administration and change management exist.	Formal linkages with change management exist. Application/ deployment target windows are linked to risk classification. Formal reporting on results and metrics exists. Applicability for managed devices exists. Semi-formal linkages to administration and change management exist.	Medium to tight integration with software management processes is in place. Policies for both managed and unmanaged devices are in place. Predefined and automatic (where appropriate) deployment mechanisms are in place. Formal linkages to administration and change management are in place.	
Compliance Maturity				
No process is in place to check compliance.	Manual and informal reporting exist. Limited metrics are available.	Formal reporting exists. Technology is used to validate application of patches/fixes; usually through deployment software.	Independent validation on the mitigation of vulnerabilities is performed.	

Continued

Table 7.1 continued Vulnerability Management Program Scorecard

Level 0 (Ad Hoc)	Level 1 (Reactive)	Level 2 (Proactive)	Level 3 (Continuous/ Validated)	Score
Maintenance Maturity				
No process is in place for updating baselines, standards, and configurations.	Manual, informal, or inconsistent updating of baselines, standards, and configurations exists. Usually based on discovery after deployment.	Update of baselines, standards, and configurations after remediation of vulnerabilities has performed.	Update of baselines, standards, and configurations prior to or in parallel with remediation of vulnerability is performed.	
Governance Maturity				
No policy is in place to address vulnerability management. No executive insight into vulnerability management processes exists.	Executive management has approved vulnerability management policies and processes. Executive management insight into vulnerability management processes is in place.	Exceptions are detected and executives are required to formally sign off on associated risks. Responsibilities are clearly assigned and enforced. Enterprise wide consistency in results of the VM program exists.	Vulnerability management program is benchmarked against others. Tight linkages between objectives of vulnerability management and overall infrastructure administration (e.g., availability, etc.) exist.	

TOTAL

Score total from all six sections.

A score of 12 or more indicates a well-established and practiced vulnerability management program. Anything less than 12 reflects a vulnerability management program that is a little rough around the edges. In such cases, you must tweak your program to align it with what are considered industry best practices.

Common Problems with Vulnerability Management

The term *vulnerability management* has always been misunderstood, because it was never conceived to be a collection of security practices and procedures, all working together. However, after reading this chapter, you should have a better understanding of vulnerability management, its dependencies (e.g., patch management, an accurate asset database, etc.), and how they are interrelated. Vulnerability management poses several challenges and has numerous dependencies, so it should be of no surprise to hear that effective vulnerability management isn't an easy thing for organizations to attain.

Here are some of the problems organizations typically encounter:

- **Problem: Vulnerabilities are not being remediated.** The first and most abundant problem in many organizations is the discovery of vulnerabilities. Assessing assets for vulnerabilities across an enterprise can be a daunting task. Nothing is worse than going through this exercise to discover that the asset owners or the remediation team responsible for remedying the vulnerability hasn't patched the vulnerability or instituted a compensating control.
- **Solution:** Ensure that the entity responsible for remediation is held accountable for the vulnerability. This party must be informally as well as formally responsible for remediation.

- **Problem: Patching is perceived as the vulnerability management panacea.** Patching a vulnerability is not the same as vulnerability management!

- **Solution:** You cannot effectively mitigate many vulnerabilities simply via patching. In some instances, you need to modify policies, processes, and perhaps system configurations to ensure that vulnerabilities are expunged from your environment. Changing the policies and processes that introduced the vulnerability may be the appropriate solution to ensuring the longer-term removal of the vulnerability from your environment. This is a much better solution than the "Patch Tuesday" process of fire fighting.

- **Problem: Failure to prioritize vulnerability information and assets.** Organizations tend to focus on the small and quick remediation wins instead of remediating more critical company assets or focusing on more task-intensive vulnerability management efforts.

- **Solution:** It's important to remediate all unacceptable vulnerabilities within your environment. Instead of focusing only on the test machine at your desk, you should develop a remediation matrix, disseminate it to the appropriate parties, and highlight company assets that need to be remediated in order of importance.

NOTE

It's quite common to hear an end user or asset owner defending the presence of a vulnerability after being audited. "Oh, that's a test machine," or "We are replacing that next week" are typical comments you'll hear from users attempting to justify the existence of a vulnerability. Unfortunately, these are just excuses, because often such vulnerabilities will remain for months, if you allow them to.

Summary

In this chapter, we discussed the elements and aspects of an effective vulnerability management program. We talked about setting goals for the program and the need to get buy-in from senior management. We also highlighted the importance of communication and the inclusion of all parties (lines of business, IT, and security) to the success of a program

As you now know, vulnerability management is composed of six stages: identification, assessment, remediation, reporting, improving, and monitoring. We explained the intricacies of each stage and suggested best practices for each. We also briefly mentioned governance and its impact on a vulnerability management program, as well as the roles which regulations have played in elevating IT governance within corporate America. We gave pointers as to what to expect when the auditors come knocking.

In addition, we detailed how to measure a vulnerability management program and gave examples of how to do this. We also discussed the more effective method of measuring the maturity of a vulnerability management program, and a method for determining the current state of a program. We mentioned that the term *vulnerability management* has always been misunderstood, and that as a result, some common problems often surface. We also provided solutions to these problems.

Vulnerability management is a tough job, and no snake oil will help. Proper vulnerability management requires that you roll up your sleeves and get a little dirty, but once you do, you'll see that establishing or enhancing your organization's vulnerability management program and associated strategy will be well worth the effort.

Solutions Fast Track

The Vulnerability Management Plan

☑ Get approval and senior management buy-in or your organization's vulnerability management program.

☑ The C-Level suite typically does not understand or considers vulnerability management a serious risk management problem; its an IT problem.

☑ Communicate to all involved parties that the vulnerability management program is in alignment with the organization's risk management strategy.

☑ Define vulnerability classifications levels and timeframes in which each classification of vulnerability is expected to be remediated.

What is Vulnerability Management Comprised of?

☑ Vulnerability management is comprised of six stages: Identification, Assessment, Remediate, Report, Improve and Monitor.

☑ Identification

- Maintain an accurate asset inventory.

- Include all IP connected devices to your asset inventory

- Identify and assign asset owners.

- Ensure the classification of the asset is recorded in the asset inventory database.

☑ Assessment

- Prioritize the scanning effort (assess the most important assets first).

- Evaluate and develop assessment strategies in a lab environment first.

- Leverage configuration, remediation, and security tools to assess our environment.

- Create a standard operating procedure for conducting assessments.

☑ Remediate

- Automate the process of communicating vulnerability data to asset owners.

- Create remediation baselines so that remediation efforts are measurable.

- Get the business units to sign-off on remediation timeframes.

☑ Report

- Make sure reports identify what remains unfixed and who is accountable.

- Create reports based on expected audience.

- Focus reporting efforts on high risk vulnerabilities and how they map to critical corporate assets.

☑ Improve

- Leverage enhancements in the asset, configuration, and assessment management processes to improve your vulnerability management program

- Modify your security practices and procedures to improve the effectiveness of the program where applicable.

☑ Monitor

- Understand, at a high level, all critical security vulnerabilities being discovered.

- Don't panic though only a fraction of new vulnerabilities will actually apply to our organization.

- Monitoring includes two key elements: the collation of new vulnerability information and n   communicating applicable vulnerability data to the appropriate parties

- Utilize tools to assist in the prioritization and alerting of vulnerabilities

- Have a process in place to ensure that urgent alerts are sent in a timely manner.

Governance (What the Auditors want to know)

- ☑ To some extent industry and government regulations are driving vulnerability management within corporations.

- ☑ The public and more importantly the shareholders are demanding better accountability from public firms.

- ☑ Has the organization included the business, IT, and security groups in the creation of its vulnerability management program?

- ☑ Have roles & responsibilities have been defined, documented and communicated?

- ☑ Has measurement of the effectiveness of the program been established and currently evaluated?

- ☑ Are reports routinely created and distributed to the key stakeholders and interested parties?

Measurement

- ☑ Measuring the performance of the vulnerability management program is hard.

- ☑ Measuring just the statistics of the vulnerabilities identified and remediation efforts aren't enough.

- ☑ Measuring the maturity of a vulnerability management program is a more effective method.

Common Problems with Vulnerability Management

- ☑ "Vulnerability Management" has always been misunderstood.

- ☑ Problem One: Vulnerabilities not being remediated.

- ☑ Problem Two: Patching perceived as the vulnerability management panacea.

☑ Problem Three: Failure to prioritize vulnerability information and assets.

Frequently Asked Questions

The following Frequently Asked Questions, answered by the authors of this book, are designed to both measure your understanding of the concepts presented in this chapter and to assist you with real-life implementation of these concepts. To have your questions about this chapter answered by the author, browse to **www.syngress.com/solutions** and click on the **"Ask the Author"** form.

Q: Why do I have to plan, write, and communicate so much regarding vulnerability management when all I'm going to do is patch a system?

A: You are not just patching! You're assessing business risk based on vulnerability data and associated risks. As a result, you may choose to patch, you may choose not to patch, or you may elect to instrument a compensating control; this is the essence of vulnerability management. It's more than just patching. You are assisting your company in managing its business risk and providing C-level executives with detailed information regarding this.

Q: How can I get people involved and enthused about creating a through and robust vulnerability management program?

A: This requires top-down pressure. Management should be able to see the benefits of a vulnerability management program; auditors especially do. However, if your organization begins to suffer unexpected outages due to malware and, in part, the lack of a vulnerability management program, I'm sure management will come knocking on your door, insisting on the creation of such a program. (By no means do we encourage purposely inserting malware into your organization to spur the creation of such a program. Trust us when we say it's only a matter of time before this will happen on its own.)

Chapter 8

Vulnerability Management Tools

Solutions in this chapter:

- The Perfect Tool in a Perfect World
- Evaluating Vulnerability Management Tools
- Commercial Vulnerability Management Tools
- Open Source and Free Vulnerability Management Tools
- Managed Vulnerability Services

☑ Summary

☑ Solutions Fast Track

☑ Frequently Asked Questions

Introduction

Numerous tools are available to assist with vulnerability management. However, determining which tool(s) to leverage is not easy, because no one product can address all of the aspects of vulnerability management, as we discussed in Chapter 7. Therefore, when deciding which vulnerability management tool(s) to use, it's important that you understand each tool's capabilities, and how the available tools work with each other. In this chapter, we will discuss what to look for when evaluating vulnerability management tools, as well as discuss some of more popular commercial and open source tools available today.

The Perfect Tool in a Perfect World

To determine what to look for in a vulnerability management tool it helps to think about what the perfect tool would offer. The perfect vulnerability management tool would include capabilities for asset management, vulnerability assessment, configuration management, patch management, remediation, reporting, and monitoring, all working well together, and it would integrate well with third-party technologies.

Ideally, the tool's asset management, vulnerability management, and patch management capabilities would work particularly well together, for three reasons. First, asset management represents the foundation of a vulnerability management program. Without a complete and up-to-date asset inventory, your vulnerability management program will be only marginally effective. Therefore, it's critical that your tools leverage this repository for the list of assets represented within your environment.

Second, you're developing a vulnerability management program, so it would be nice if your vulnerability management tools and auxiliary tools could communicate with one another. A primary example is in your vulnerability assessment (VA) scanner leveraging the asset database to obtain the list of devices that are present within your environment. From that list, the VA scanner knows which assets to assess for security liabilities. VA tools are also helpful in developing system configuration baselines within your environment. You can use these baselines later to identify possible weaknesses and points of exposure within your infrastructure.

And third, patching and configuration management are key elements of the remediation process and, more important, of your vulnerability management plan. Understanding which systems are patched, along with their respective configurations, is one thing; but having this information populated within your asset database and being able to extract this data and use it to make informed security decisions is a capability which all security practitioners wish they had.

Notes from the Underground...

Useful Sites: INFOSEC
Mailing Lists, Tools, and Information

Here are some rather useful sites for security tools and security mailing lists:

- Tools and mailing lists: www.securityfocus.com
- Tools: packetstormsecurity.nl
- Mailing list: lists.apple.com/mailman/listinfo/security-announce
- Mailing list archives: seclists.org
- Tools and security advisories: www.frsirt.com/english/index.php
- Tools and security advisories: www.microsoft.com/technet/security/

Evaluating Vulnerability Management Tools

Vendors typically market their tools as the panacea for everything; vulnerability management vendors are no exception. Although some products address multiple areas of the vulnerability management life cycle, others attempt to bridge the gap between vulnerability management tools in an effort to provide synergy among products—for example, integrating patch management tools with vulnerability scanners. In the end, no one vendor or solution provides all of the components necessary to support a vulnerability management program.

Prior to deciding upon a tool, you must understand its capabilities as well as its shortcomings. To aid you in this you should consider the following points when evaluating vulnerability management technologies:

- **Asset management.** Does the technology provide an asset inventory database? If so, can you extend the database schema to support additional fields, such as asset classification? If not, can the technology integrate with other asset management repositories?

- **Coverage.** What's the breadth and platform coverage of the technology? Many technologies can perform operations against the Windows family of products, but you'll need technologies that can operate in a heterogeneous environment and can support a variety of platforms, applications, and infrastructure devices.

- **Aggregation of vulnerability data.** Does the product interoperate with other security technologies? Can the product aggregate data from security technologies such as Internet Security Systems' IIS Scanner, Microsoft's MBSA, Tenable Network Security's Nessus, McAfee's Foundstone, eEye's Retina, and Symantec's BindView bvControl? The ability to aggregate data from multiple and disparate sources is key.

- **Third-party vulnerability references.** Is the product Common Vulnerabilities and Exposures (CVE) compliant? Does it identify the source from which it received its information?

- **Prioritization.** Can the tool prioritize remediation efforts?

- **Remediation policy enforcement.** Does the product provide the capability to designate the selected remediation at varying enforcement levels, from mandatory (required) to forbidden (acceptable risk), via a centralized policy-driven interface?

- **Remediation group management.** Does the tool allow for the grouping of systems to manage remediation and control access to devices?

- **Remediation.** Can you use the product to address vulnerabilities induced by a system misconfiguration as well as vulnerabilities represented by not having the appropriate patch? For example:

  - Patch management, or deploying patches to the operating system or applications

  - Configuration management, or deploying changes to the operating system or application, such as disabling and removing accounts (i.e., accounts with no password, no password expiration, etc.), disabling and removing unnecessary services, and so on

  - The ability to harden services for NetBIOS, anonymous FTP, hosts.equiv, and so on

- **Patch management.** Does the product include or integrate with existing patch management tools?

- **Distributed patch repository.** Does the product provide the capability to load balance and distribute the bandwidth associated for patch distribution to repositories installed in various strategic locations?

- **Patch uninstallation support.** Can the tool report whether a patch was unsuccessful and whether it needs to be reapplied?

- **Workflow.** Does the product have a workflow system that allows you to assign and track issues? Can it auto-assign tickets based on rule sets defined (i.e., vulnerability, owner, asset classification, etc.)? Can it interface with common corporate workflow products such as BMC Software's Remedy and the Hewlett-Packard HP Service Desk?

- **Usability.** Can the tool participate in network services with minimal impact to business operations? Is the user interface intuitive?

- **Reporting.** Does the tool provide reports to determine remediation success rates? Can you use the tool for trending remediation efforts? Is the reporting detailed and customizable?

- **Appliances.** Is the tool software based or appliance based? Appliances often offer performance and reliability advantages. However, software solutions are more affordable and may be able to run on existing hardware, helping to reduce upfront capital expenditures.

- **Agents.** Does the application require agents? Is the application capable of leveraging existing agents on the system? If agents are necessary, can you deploy agents to groups of assets simultaneously, to facilitate ease of deployment? Agents generally provide more information on a particular system, but also increase the system's complexity. An ideal application would allow for the collection of system information with or without the use of agents.

- **Configuration standards.** Does the technology possess predefined security configuration templates that you can use to assess the system? Some products have defined operating system standards and are able to perform reporting based on defined templates to support some regulatory requirements (e.g., Sarbanes-Oxley, HIPAA, and the ISO/IEC 27000 series).

- **Vulnerability research.** Does the vendor have its own vulnerability research team? Does the vendor actively participate in the security community through the identification and release of security vulnerabilities? Does the vendor practice responsible disclosure? Does the vendor release checks for vulnerabilities it has discovered prior to the OEM remediating the vulnerability? How has the vendor responded to vulnerabilities in its own products?

- **Vulnerability updates.** How frequently does the vendor release updates? How are the updates distributed? Does the distribution mechanism leverage industry-recognized security communications protocols?

- **Interoperability.** Can the application integrate into existing patch management, configuration management, and/or monitoring tools and services?

Note that the items in the preceding list aren't applicable to all vulnerability technologies. We presented a germane list of points that apply to the collection of tools which support a vulnerability management program.

Commercial Vulnerability Management Tools

The vulnerability management space is changing frequently due to mergers, acquisitions, and new partnerships. In the remainder of this section, we will discuss some of the vendors that offer solutions in this space.

eEye Digital Security

www.eEye.com

eEye Digital Security is a leader in vulnerability research. It also develops a suite a tools that can assist you in vulnerability management. The suite consists of the Retina Network Security Scanner (a vulnerability assessment tool), Blink Professional (a host-based security technology), and the REM Security Management Console. The management console provides the centralized management interface for the company's other products. It also handles vulnerability management workflow, asset classification, and threat-level reporting, and it can integrate with CA's UniCenter, IBM's Tivoli, and HP's OpenView.

Symantec (BindView)

www.bindview.com

BindView's Compliance Manager is a software-based solution which allows organizations to evaluate their assets against corporate standards or industry best practices, without the need for agents in most cases. Assets are evaluated against standards and practices based on a pass/fail notion; either an asset is compliant or it's not. Data is then aggregated and assembled to produce reports that the remediation team can leverage to support their efforts, or the internal audit group can use for compliance issues. You also can use the reports generated to support other initiatives.

As mentioned, you can evaluate assets against internal standards or to industry best practices. The industry standards included are CIS Level 1 and Level 2 Benchmarks for Windows, Red Hat Linux, BindView's Security Essentials for Sun Solaris, and NetWare. In addition to these standards, the Compliance Manager also provides Report Views for the following regulations and frameworks: ISO 17799, Sarbanes-Oxley based on COBIT, FISMA based on NIST SP 800-53, HIPAA, Basel II, and GLBA.

The Compliance Manager does not include its own workflow capability, but it does provide an interface that allows users to open incidents in Remedy and HP Service Desk. In addition, leveraging its bvControl technology, BindView is capable of delivering patch and configuration management to Windows hosts.

Attachmate (NetIQ)

www.netiq.com

NetIQ's Compliance suite, a combination of NetIQ's Security Manager and Vulnerability Manager tools, brings together vulnerability scanning, patch management, configuration remediation, and reporting. The NetIQ Vulnerability Manager enables users to define and maintain configuration policy templates, vulnerability bulletins, and automated checks via AutoSync technology. It also has the capability to evaluate systems against those policies. Predefined templates are available for Sarbanes-Oxley, HIPAA, and ISO/IEC 27000. These allow you to report and score your information systems against these standards.

The Compliance suite also supports a classification system that allows you to adjust risk scores based upon the asset's classification. The NetIQ suite also looks for common signs of system compromise, such as modified Registry keys and known malicious files, and it has an OEM relationship with Shavlik to provide integrated patch management.

StillSecure

www.stillsecure.com

StillSecure is the manufacturer of VAM, an integrated suite of security products that perform vulnerability management, endpoint compliance monitoring, and intrusion prevention and detection. It also includes a built-in workflow solution (Extensible Vulnerability Repair Workflow) which automatically performs assignment of repairs, scheduling, life cycle tracking, and repair verification, all while maintaining detailed device histories.

VAM interoperates with other third-party scanners too, taking input from Nessus, the ISS Internet Scanner, Harris STAT, and others. Enterprises may want to be wary regarding VAM, because its reporting module is not as well refined as the other vendors' and it relies on third-party information and integration for asset management, patch management, and vulnerability resolution.

McAfee

www.mcafee.com

McAfee's Foundstone Enterprise is an agentless solution that offers asset discovery, inventory, and vulnerability prioritization with threat intelligence, correlation, remediation tracking, and reporting. It integrates with McAfee's IntruSheild network-based intrusion prevention system (IPS), McAfee's Preventsys Compliance Auditor, and other vulnerability and trouble-ticket management systems. One of its more appealing features is its SSH credentialed scans for Red Hat Enterprise, Solaris, AIX, Microsoft Windows, and to the surprise of many, Cisco IOS!

Compliance templates for Sarbanes-Oxley, FISMA, HIPAA, BS7799/ISO17799, and the Payment Card Industry (PCI) standard are included, expediting the preparation of audits. Foundstone Enterprise can also auto-assign tickets, streamlining and simplifying the remediation process.

Open Source and Free Vulnerability Management Tools

The open source community has created some great security tools over the years. However, none of them represents a complete vulnerability management solution. In some cases, though, the open source tools integrate well together, forming a formable foe to the commercial offerings.

In the following sections, we cover open source tools that you can use to support your vulnerability management program.

Asset Management, Workflow, and Knowledgebase

One tool we recommend in this space is Information Resource Manager (IRM), available at http://irm.stackworks.net. IRM is a powerful Web-based asset tracking and trouble-ticket system built for information technology (IT) departments and help desks. All elements are interwoven into a seamless Web application, with a MySQL engine at the back end doing the heavy lifting.

Host Discovery

For host discovery, Nmap (www.insecure.org) is a free, open source utility for network exploration or security auditing. It was designed to rapidly scan large networks, although it works fine against single hosts. Nmap uses raw Internet Protocol (IP) packets in novel ways to determine what hosts are available on the network, what services (application name and version) those hosts are offering, what operating systems (and versions) they are running, what type of packet filters/firewalls are in use, along with dozens of other characteristics. Nmap runs on most types of computers and both command-line and graphical versions are available.

Vulnerability Scanning and Configuration Scanning

Nessus, from Tenable Network Security (www.tennable.com), is a tool for vulnerability scanning and configuration scanning. The Nessus Project was started by Renaud Deraison in 1998 to provide the Internet community with a free, powerful, up-to-date, and easy-to-use remote security scanner. Nessus is the best free network vulnerability scanner available, and the best to run on UNIX at any price. It is constantly updated (more than 11,000 plug-ins are available for as a free feed), but registration and EULA acceptance are required. Key features include remote and local (authenticated) security checks, client/server architecture with a GTK graphical interface, and an embedded scripting language for writing your own plug-ins or understanding the existing ones.

Nessus 3 is now closed source, but it is still free unless you want the very newest plug-ins. If you decide to rely on only Nessus for vulnerability scanning, consider also choosing a product that can manage and schedule scans, such as Tenable Security's Security Center product (www.tenablesecurity.com).

Configuration and Patch Scanning

Microsoft's Baseline Security Analyzer (MBSA) is an easy-to-use tool designed for the IT professional that helps small and medium-size businesses determine their security state in accordance with Microsoft security recommendations, as well as offers specific remediation guidance. Built on the Windows Update Agent and Microsoft Update infrastructure, MBSA ensures consistency with other Microsoft management products including Microsoft Update (MU), Windows Server Update Services (WSUS), Systems Management Server (SMS), and Microsoft Operations Manager (MOM). MBSA on average scans more than 3 million computers each week! For more information, visit www.microsoft.com.

Vulnerability Notification

Advchk (Advisory Check), available at http://advchk.unixgu.ru, reads security advisories so that you don't have to. Advchk gathers security advisories using RSS feeds, compares them to a list of known services, and alerts you if you are vulnerable. Because adding hosts and services by hand would be a boring task, Advchk leverages NMAP for automatic service and version discovery.

Also available in this space is SIGVI (http://sigvi.sourceforge.net). This product is a recent release but could be a promising solution if maintained and developed further. SIGVI downloads vulnerabilities from defined sources, stores them to a database, and then compares them to the products currently installed on the assets (as previously defined in the main application).

The application is flexible in the way that it lets you define your own sources. By default, the application supports the NVD (National Vulnerability Database at http://nvd.nist.gov) format. Periodically, the application will contact the sources, download the vulnerabilities, and store them into the SIGVI database. Those vulnerabilities are then available through the pages of the SIGVI main window.

Security Information Management

Ossim (www.ossim.org) stands for Open Source Security Information Management. Innately a SIM, OSSIM does incorporate several aspects of vulnerability management and over time should become a more comprehensive and complete vulnerability management tool. OSSIM's goal is to provide a comprehensive compilation of tools which, when working together, grant a network/security administrator a detailed view of the network and devices.

Besides getting the best out of open source tools, some of which are described in the following list, OSSIM provides a strong correlation engine, detailed reporting, and incident management tools. Here is a list of open source tools that integrate with OSSIM:

- **Arpwatch.** Used for Media Access Control (MAC) address anomaly detection.

- **P0f.** Used for passive operating system detection and operating system change analysis.

- **Pads.** Used for service anomaly detection.

- **Nessus.** Used for vulnerability assessment and cross-correlation (IDS versus Security Scanner).

- **Snort.** An IDS, used for cross-correlation with Nessus.

- **Spade.** A statistical packet anomaly detection engine, used to gain knowledge about attacks without a signature.

- **Tcptrack.** Used to gather session data information that can provide useful information for attack correlation.

- **Ntop.** A network usage tool that builds an impressive network database from which you can derive aberrant and anomalous behavior.

- **Nagios.** Monitors host and service availability information.

- **Osiris.** A great host-based intrusion detection system (HIDS).

Managed Vulnerability Services

Many organizations have elected to outsource the challenging task of vulnerability management; if not in total, certainly in parts. Outsourcing a vulnerability management program can help you to reduce head count, administrative overhead, and equipment and personnel expenses. However, before you get too excited about the advantages of outsourcing vulnerability management, you need to keep in mind that an effective outsourced solution is going to be based in part on how well you've defined your requirements.

Tired and weary veterans of outsourcing know that clear and concise service-level agreements (SLAs), which have been drafted in conjunction with legal counsel, represent the foundation of all outsourcing relationships and aid in remedying issues that arise during the term of a contract.

NOTE

One mistake people often make is to believe that business risk is transferred when you outsource a portion of your security program, such as vulnerability management. However, risk is not transferable. Organizations remain responsible, even when their operations are completely outsourced, although they may shift the financial liability to the third party. With that said, it's critical to assess a provider's financial stability when considering outsourcing.

When leveraging a third party to support all or part of your vulnerability management program you should consider the following:

- **Escalation procedures.** Ensure that escalation procedures exist and communication processes are defined. Also ensure that ownership is well documented and agreed upon in writing by both parties.

- **Data access.** Ensure that you have access to the data that the outsourcer is collecting. Many times an outsourcer will collect data from your assets, but won't provide you with access to the data. You could use this data to better ascertain risk within your environment, and it could help you to make appropriate risk-based decisions. If the outsourcer doesn't allow you access to your data, you should think twice before signing the contract. Also, it is important that you understand how the outsourcer shares your data within its own organization. Is your data privy to everyone who works for the outsourcer?

- **The toolset.** Before selecting a vendor, you should confirm which products the vendor uses, and why. There may be a conflict between the vendor's tools and yours, or the vendor may simply be using inferior technology to support your operations.

■ **Metrics.** How will the provider be evaluated/measured? It is important that you ensure that these metrics are clearly defined. Depending on the level of service the outsourcer is providing, the metrics used to evaluate the outsourcer may be different; for example, if the provider is providing path management, how long does the provider have before it must patch all of the assets it manages? You should define, understand, and clearly agree upon these metrics up front.

Summary

In Chapter 7, we discussed the methodology behind vulnerability management. In this chapter, we discussed what an ideal vulnerability tool features, although we know and understand why such a tool doesn't exist. However, as we discussed, some vendors are getting close to delivering complete solutions in this comparatively new discipline in information security.

We briefly discussed some of the players, but gave no suggestions regarding the pros and cons of the tools because there is no one tool that fits all the requirements of an organization. Although the open source community has a wealth of great tools available, there isn't one tool that supports all of the facets of vulnerability management; rather, there are bits and pieces scattered among many authors.

To close out the chapter, we discussed some of the pros and cons of leveraging an outsourcer to manage parts of a vulnerability management program. It's conceivable, and many organizations do it, but it's imperative to put in place some serious guidelines and detailed service-level agreements beforehand to ensure that no one becomes disappointed with the delivery of the service.

Solutions Fast Track

The Perfect Tool in a Perfect World

☑ The perfect vulnerability management tool would include asset management, vulnerability assessment, configuration management, patch management, remediation, reporting, and monitoring capabilities.

☑ All of these components interoperate, pushing and pulling data as each task is performed.

Evaluating Vulnerability Management Tools

☑ No one vendor has a solution or set of technologies that completely addresses all aspects of the vulnerability management life cycle.

☑ Several key questions can assist you in evaluating vulnerability management tools and, hopefully, in identifying gaps in terms of capabilities.

Commercial Vulnerability Management Tools

☑ The vulnerability management market is changing frequently due to mergers, acquisitions, and alliances. Numerous vendors provide tools in this space, so you must identify your needs prior to evaluating technologies.

Open Source and Free Vulnerability Management Tools

☑ The open source community has created some great security tools.

☑ No one tool provides a complete vulnerability management solution.

☑ It may not require much effort to create interoperability between open source vulnerability management tools.

Managed Vulnerability Services

☑ Set some serious guidelines and detailed service-level agreements to ensure that no one becomes disappointed with the delivery of a service.

☑ Before selecting a vendor, confirm which products the vendor is using and how the information is distributed to interested parties.

☑ Ensure that you have access to the raw data.

www.syngress.com

Frequently Asked Questions

The following Frequently Asked Questions, answered by the authors of this book, are designed to both measure your understanding of the concepts presented in this chapter and to assist you with real-life implementation of these concepts. To have your questions about this chapter answered by the author, browse to **www.syngress.com/solutions** and click on the **"Ask the Author"** form.

Q: How do I decide which tool to use?

A: Demo the technology first. Most vendors provide trial-ware offerings of their products. Even if it's an appliance-based solution, most vendors are usually willing to provide you with a loaner unit. Managed vulnerability providers also allow for interactive demonstrations.

Q: Should I seriously consider an open source solution?

A: That depends on your aversion to technology. If you're looking for creative technologies and novel intellectual property, and you are seeking to fill a gap within your vulnerability management program, you should definitely consider open source. If your organization is taking the creation of a vulnerability management program seriously (i.e., you have a budget), you should look into a combination of commercial tools and open source tools.

Chapter 9

Vulnerability and Configuration Management

Solutions in this chapter:

- Patch Management
- Building a Patch Test Lab
- Patch Distribution and Deployment
- Configuration Management
- Change Control

☑ Summary

☑ Solutions Fast Track

☑ Frequently Asked Questions

189

Introduction

Dealing effectively with vulnerabilities in today's networks includes not only managing and dealing with the vulnerability process itself, but also integrating the previous approach toward vulnerability assessment (leveraging scanners to discovery vulnerabilities) into the correlative frameworks and processes of patch management, configuration management, and change control. This chapter focuses on these frameworks and processes. Understanding what these processes are, their similarities and differences, and how they integrate with the vulnerability life cycle is essential to pulling an effective vulnerability management program together.

Patch Management

Why patch a system? This question can seem rather remedial in nature, but it is certainly a valid question. Far too often our answer is, "Because the vendor said to." You should never patch a system unless it is absolutely necessary; otherwise, causing system instability is well within the realm of possibility. Patching a system is as much an art as it is a science. There are numerous reasons why you may want to patch a system, but patches are generally applied to do the following:

- Enable new functionality
- Mitigate discovered vulnerabilities or security risks
- Fix stability issues

Patches can be software or hardware related, and the results of one patch can often affect the operation of both the primary and secondary functions of another patch. One common example that is often overlooked is the upgrade of a system's BIOS. Functions or features enabled (or re-enabled) in the system BIOS can have widespread consequences from the operating system perspective. Let's look at the release notes for a common BIOS upgrade available from Dell, remembering that each BIOS upgrade is a "roll-up" of previous fixes and changes. So if you are going from A07 BIOS revision to A09, all of the fixes/changes introduced in A08 will also be present.

```
BIOS Release Notes

Systems: OptiPlex GX110
Version: A09
Release Date: 01-22-2003


The following changes have been made to BIOS rev A08 to create A09:


1. Fix LPT code for HP All-in-one printers



BIOS Release Notes

Systems: OptiPlex GX110
Version: A08
Release Date: 08-30-2001


The following changes have been made to BIOS rev A07 to create A08:


1. ESCD is cleared when asset tag PASS:xx/xx changes.

2. Added ability to turn the USB controller on and off in setup.

3. Updated selectable boot capability. When a device is removed
its place in the boot list is saved in case it is ever readded.

4. Updated some CPU microcodes.

5. Added BBS calling interface to SMBIOS.

6. During NVRAM updates the reset and power buttons are now disabled.

7. Added support for 48-bit LBA disk drives.

8. System now beeps when CTRL-ALT-F10, or F12 is pressed

9. Fixed a few potential Plug & Play configuration errors.
```

```
10. Added a fix to allow certain cards (PERC/3) to work properly.
```

```
11. IRQ 12 is now reserved.
```

From the release notes listed here, several of these changes could potentially impact our system from the operating system perspective—most notably, number 2: "Added ability to turn the USB controller on and off in setup." This particular addition to the BIOS can also play an important role in the mitigation process if a patch for a related vulnerability is not available. Figure 9.1 shows the typical life cycle of a patch. Patches are issued, tested, deployed, and superseded, and eventually reach an end-of-life. When an operating system reaches end-of-life, patches typically stop being issued by an OEM, although it is often possible to obtain them for a substantial fee.

Figure 9.1 The Life Cycle of a Patch

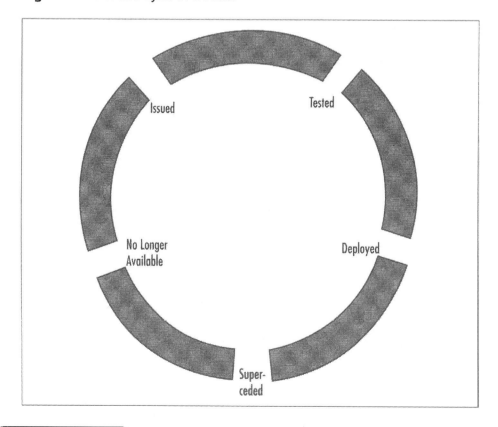

Perhaps one of the most crucial components of a vulnerability management framework lies in the establishment of a patch management program. Figure 9.2 shows a rudimentary patch management process. This much-simplified, scaled-down process consists of steps involving system classification, system inventory, and the Patch Management Tracking System (PMTS), which all interoperate with the change control and testing and deployment mechanisms.

For smaller organizations and companies just starting to implement a comprehensive vulnerability management program, this simplified approach can often yield fairly satisfactory results with a low margin of error, and it directly compliments the more in-depth approach we'll cover later in this chapter.

Figure 9.2 A Rudimentary Patch Management Program

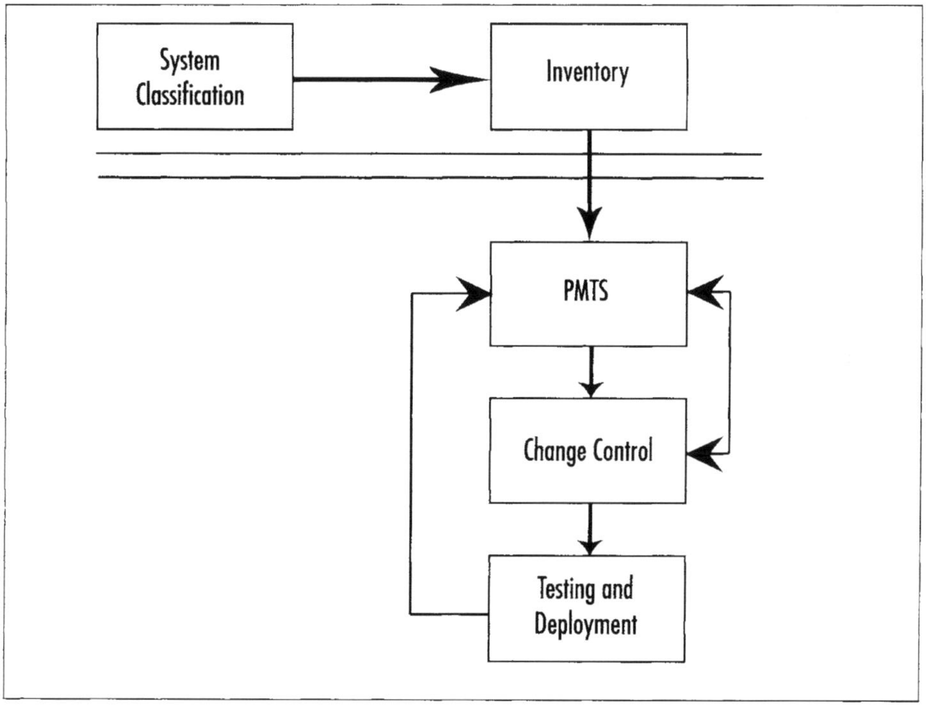

A more common patch management process (shown in Figure 9.3) typically has many moving parts to it. As you can see, there are many components to an effective patch management framework. This is the preferred framework for enterprise use, and in this chapter we'll cover each component in detail.

A patch management framework consists of the following:

- System inventories
- System classification
- System baselines
- Notification
- Mitigation
- Policy
- Prioritization
- Research and testing
- Distribution and deployment
- Logging and reporting

Figure 9.3 A More Common Patch Management Process

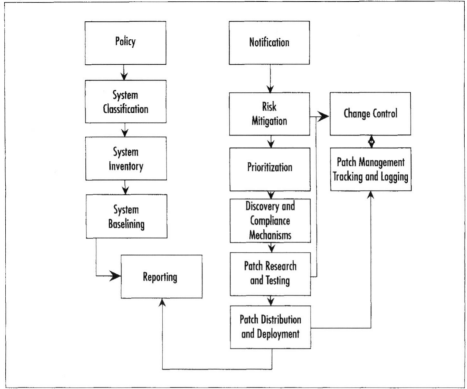

System Inventories

A *system inventory* is a process used to garner as much available information about a system as possible. Remember Y2K? This was probably the last time that many organizations conducted a full system inventory. Your vulnerability discovery process will no doubt assist in garnering a plethora of information about your systems, but additional information is essential to successfully integrating this into your patch management framework. You often can collect a wealth of information, but it's entirely possible in some cases that you can collect *too much* information. As is the general rule with log information, you should never collect more information than you can possibly hope to use or interpret. That having been said, the following elements are typically collected in a system inventory:

- **The system name and physical location.** This is a "no-brainer." The primary reason you need this information is that different patch standards could exist due to language packs and other local settings that may not be evident at first glance.

- **The operating systems and applications, including versions.**

- **Existing patch levels.** In order to be effective in the following steps, it is imperative that you understand what patch level (if any) the system state is currently in. Some vendors require some patches to be applied in a certain order; deviating from that order can result in an inoperable system.

- **System owner and contact information.** You often can obtain this information by enumerating the user accounts on the system, the system's NetBIOS name, or the user profiles stored on the system.

- **Services running and open ports.**

- **Proximity in relation to other systems.** The primary reason you need this information is so that you can derive a more accurate picture as to relative risks to the environment. If the system is contained or isolated by network segmentation, the risk factor and weight can be lower. In Chapter 8, we covered several tools that can assist in this regard. Another tool that is free (but unfortunately is no longer being maintained) is Cheops, available at www.marko.net/cheops.

- **Open shares.** Open shares create an avenue for worm propagation.

- **BIOS revision.** As stated previously, your system BIOS revision can have a significant impact on your overall risk.

- **Processor type.** In the case of patches that have stringent hardware requirements, this is a must-have. There are also patches that are processor dependent—for example, RISC versus x86.

- **Network information.** This includes Internet Protocol (IP) and Media Access Control (MAC) addresses, single or dual homed, manufacturer name, and adjustable properties.

As we've discussed here, a full system inventory should consist not only of existing patches, but also of all installed applications, dependencies, and correlations to other programs. The GDI+ vulnerability in Microsoft products and most MSDE vulnerabilities are prime examples of why you need this data.

For your first baseline you shouldn't worry so much about getting everything, as this will expand and the amount of detail and accuracy will improve over time. You should break down these inventories into independent categories within the individual system role inventory for easier management. Common examples of this include "Productivity Application" (such as Microsoft Office or Open Office), "BIOS/Firmware," "Operating System," "Network Application" (such as DNS and NTP), "Web Application," "Database," and so on.

System Classification

System classification is defined as the classification of systems based upon their particular function in the enterprise. As you can see in Figure 9.4, you can divide systems into three major categories: devices, servers, and desktops. You can get as granular with these classifications as you want, but for a first pass at classification it is suggested that you keep it simple and add one classification at a time. The key to setting an effective classification for a system is to find the common denominator with them. Within your classifications, you should also assign roles that these systems play within their given classification. In this example, we have assigned the roles of "Web," "Database," and "Application" within the Server classification. Given our environment we could easily classify "Infrastructure" as another classification for domain controllers, domain name system (DNS), print servers, and so on.

Figure 9.4 Classification of Systems

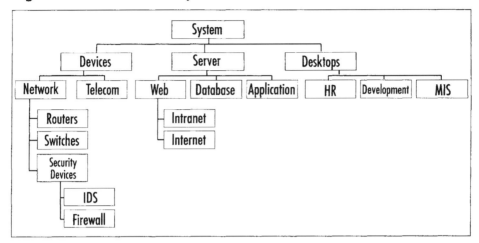

You may be asking, "What is the importance of classifying systems and assigning roles?" The answer to this question is fairly simple. You assign classifications and roles to systems for some of the following reasons:

- **It makes it easier to assign risk weight.** Not all vulnerabilities will have the same weight (or priority) assigned to them. Some influences on vulnerability weighting include your overall risk classification scheme, the timeline for testing and deployment, and your particular business model. For instance, if your company is an application service provider, those systems supporting your application service provider's services would more likely have a higher weight and priority assigned to them than systems which are used only internally.

- **Different risks are associated with different system types.** A Microsoft Word vulnerability may not impact your SQL servers, for instance, but if the patch happens to be a core operating systems patch, it may come up flagged as "missing." Knowing what risk is acceptable for what given length of time will assist you immensely in your patch research, testing, and deployment cycles.

- **It assists in identifying and assigning priority based in part upon system roles.** System roles are a key part of the classification process and you should not overlook them. You have to define the system's role in order to fully understand its operational impact on your organization, as well as the potential impact on the systems around it. A GPO locking vulnerability would be applicable to the classification mentioned previously as "Infrastructure" and to the role of Domain Controller.

System Baselines

What is *patch management baselining*? In a nutshell, patch management baselining is the common fundamental frame of tested and deployed patches for a given device which meet established levels of acceptable security risk. In other words, this is the minimum acceptable patch level of any given system or device. Baselining enacts a forward-moving starting point for patch testing, deployment, and maintenance. If you have never performed a patch baseline you can start either from scratch with a bare operating system, or "as is" with an existing system. You should bear in mind that an existing system will prove to be more time consuming and complex in the way of system inventory and risk classification. A bare-bones system will allow you more flexibility in documenting the system fully, and allow you to test the functional impact of patches as you move forward.

Why establish baselines? In order to have an effective patch management strategy for your enterprise, it is important that you have a way to measure progress and implement changes that *minimally* impact the operation of systems across the enterprise. Every patch in existence alters the system or device in some fashion, even though the results may not be readily apparent to the naked eye. A baseline helps with a "roll back" as well as a "move forward." Just because a patch was released, it doesn't necessarily mean that it is needed and *must* be deployed. Mitigation should *always* precede patching as a first line of defense, but patching is a necessary "evil" for a healthy security posture.

Creating a Baseline

Now that we've defined what a baseline is and laid out some key areas contained within the process, let's put this all together in a quick, step-by-step formation of a simple baseline on a base operating system installation, briefly explaining each step:

1. **Assign system roles.** You should assign system roles to each system in your environment so that you can make an "apples to apples" comparison of specific baselines. This comparison can help you identify where deficiencies lie in regard to existing patch management policy and where patches can be deployed in a more expeditious manner the next time the same conditions exist. The system roles probably will not change, but exposure and priority may. A role is generally assigned to a system based on its particular function in the enterprise, and its relationship to the systems around it. A simple network diagram will often tell you the number and type of roles that already exist in your environment.

2. **Inventory individual systems.** Inventory and document all of the packages and applications installed on a system or device. You should store these results in a spreadsheet or database for easier correlation and comparison to the same system roles later. From this you can derive your inventory matrix of approved applications. Inventory the systems for current patch levels compared to what is currently available from the vendor. Plenty of patch management tools and vulnerability assessment (VA) scanners are available to help you collect this information; we covered many of them in Chapter 8.

3. **Evaluate vulnerability/patch applicability.** Decide whether the patch or vulnerability is applicable to the system at this point in time, and consider the consequences of someone (or something) being able to change the state of the system that would affect applicability. One example of this would be the vulnerability listed in Microsoft Security Bulletin MS02-028, "Heap Overrun in HTR Chunked Encoding Could Enable Web Server Compromise (Q321599)." If you do not have *.htr* mapped on your Web server, you will not be immediately affected, and you could consider the patch to be "not applicable." However, if someone were to enable *.htr* mapping on that particular Web server, the system would be placed in a vulnerable state.

4. **Evaluate level of exposure.** Based on factors such as system placement and available access to untrusted or semitrusted systems and
users, you can get a good idea of a system's exposure level to a given
vulnerability for which a patch has been released:

   a. **Internal.** Internally accessible systems generally have a lower risk
   value in relation to border or external systems due to internal
   users being granted a certain degree of trust to participate on the
   network in the first place.

   b. **External.** External systems are border area systems accessible to
   any extent to anyone outside your network. Web, e-mail and
   DNS servers and firewalls are all examples of external systems.

   c. **Bridged.** These are systems or devices that can connect to any
   external resources. If your users have Internet access via browser,
   instant messaging, FTP, and so on, this is a prime example of
   bridged access. Remote/virtual private network (VPN) users and
   proxy servers are other examples. Bridged is typically the highest
   risk of the three exposure classifications outlined here.

5. **Timing.**

   a. **Exploit or virus available that uses vulnerability/required
   patch.** If a virus, or exploit code, has been released to the general public using an existing vulnerability, this will often change
   patch applicability and affect your baseline.

   b. **Average time to complete deployment of patch.** If the
   system is going to remain vulnerable for a period outside what is
   considered acceptable for the exposure level, this will obviously
   affect your future baseline. You should flag this patch and document it as a follow-up item, as well as add it to the baseline once
   you can test it properly. An example of this would be a patch that
   you can apply, but that you cannot enable until you reboot the
   system at a later date.

6. **Risk weight/priority.** When you have evaluated the preceding factors, you can assign a weight/priority to each patch to add to your baseline. Some organizations prefer to use a numeric rating system (e.g., 1–5), and others prefer to keep with Microsoft's ratings of "Low," "Moderate," "Important," and "Critical."

Baseline Example

Having a better understanding of the components and interdependencies of a patch management framework, you can now look back at Figure 9.2 with a greater appreciation and understanding. Say, for instance, that the first patch you look at for addition to your base operating system configuration happens to be an Internet Explorer vulnerability for which Microsoft released a patch labeled "Critical." What should you do? Based on what we've covered thus far, you should leverage the following steps to understand the overall risk the vulnerability presents:

1. After researching the impact, you determine that for this vulnerability to work, it requires user intervention and administrative rights on the applicable system. Looking at Figure 9.2 you determine that the systems that have Internet Explorer installed and are used most frequently with elevated rights are the MIS systems and possibly some developer systems. Although other systems have Internet Explorer installed by default, your policy and practices prohibit the use of Internet Explorer on the other systems (Web, DB, Application, Infrastructure, etc.). You assign a risk weight of "2".

2. Comparing this to your recent system inventory and scan reports, you determine that all desktops do not already have this patch applied. A few MIS folks updated some of the systems via automatic updates, but most of the systems do not have this patch. You do not assign a weight to this item.

3. All systems are internally placed, but have external Internet access via Internet Explorer. No other Web browser is used on these systems, so the vulnerability is applicable. You assign a risk weight of "3".

4. You look at your exposure classifications, and see that all desktops can be classified as "bridged". This raises the risk factor. You assign a risk weight of "3".

5. Exploit code is currently available. However, antivirus and content management can help mitigate the overall risk. Patch installation requires reboot, which is not an issue with desktop systems. You assign a risk weight of "4".

6. The total risk weight assigned based on the preceding factors is 12 out of 20. Your patch management policy states that any patch with an applicable risk weight or priority score of 14 or better should be added to the patch baseline. This one falls a bit short.

7. Lather, rinse, and repeat for each patch that is not in your baseline.

8. When you think you've reached the end of the available list of patches (and this will take a lot of research initially), you now have your baseline.

The Common Vulnerability Scoring System

The Common Vulnerability Scoring System (CVSS; www.first.org/cvss) is a joint initiative started by CERT/CC, Cisco, DHS/MITRE, eBay, Internet Security Systems, Microsoft, Qualys, and Symantec to assign universal numeric risk ratings on reported vulnerabilities. It uses a fairly flexible approach toward classification and numeric risk weight assignment, and it works well within the patch management framework discussed here. Figure 9.5 shows an example. Here you can see three vulnerabilities and their relative scores of severity, as calculated by the CVSS scoring methods. CVSS scoring is based on a number of metrics explained fully at www.first.org/cvss/cvss-guide.html.

Creating a baseline is not a complicated process, but it does require attention to detail, process methodology, accountability, planning, and hindsight. It is important that you continually evaluate additions to your baseline to keep your systems on an even keel. It's not as important *what* tools you use to assist you in establishing your baseline, but it *is* important that you understand the process methodology, and the variables that drive the processes.

Figure 9.5 Vulnerability Scoring Worksheet

Common Vulnerability Scoring System (CVSS) Version 0.2

	Microsoft Outlook Express Scripting Vulnerability	Microsoft LSASS Vulnerability	BGP potential DOS
Vulnerability			
CVE number	CAN-2004-0380	CAN-2004-0533	CAN-2004-0589
URL			
Access Vector	REMOTE	REMOTE	REMOTE
Access Complexity	HIGH	LOW	HIGH
Authentication	NOT-REQUIRED	NOT-REQUIRED	NOT-REQUIRED
Confidentiality Impact	COMPLETE	COMPLETE	NONE
Integrity Impact	COMPLETE	COMPLETE	NONE
Availability Impact	COMPLETE	COMPLETE	COMPLETE
Impact Bias	NORMAL	NORMAL	AVAILABILITY
BASE SCORE	5.9	10.0	4.0
Exploitability	FUNCTIONAL	FUNCTIONAL	UNPROVEN
Remediation Level	OFFICIAL-FIX	OFFICIAL-FIX	UNAVAILABLE
Report Confidence	CONFIRMED	CONFIRMED	CONFIRMED
TEMPORAL SCORE	6.6	8.3	3.4
Collateral Damage Potential	NONE	NONE	NONE
Target Distribution	HIGH	HIGH	HIGH
ENVIRONMENTAL SCORE			

Building a Patch Test Lab

Establish a Patch Test Lab with "Sacrificial Systems"

Ideally, your Patch Test Lab will have one copy of every mission-critical system in a similar isolated networked environment. Obviously, this could get quite expensive from a hardware perspective, and it is often not within the realm of possibility, with today's technology and security budgets being as lean as they are. The average security budget in the mid-market sector, for example, is roughly 2% to 5% of the overall technology budget. In order to meet your goals, therefore, you must often improvise and use the solutions that are available, being creative at times. As a result, one of the best strategies for your test lab can be the use of simulation. The two key concepts we'll cover here briefly include:

- Using virtualization
- Using environmental simulation programs

Another way that you can accomplish this is to take a sampling of actual live systems on your network to use for testing. Some organizations are large enough to have systems or users that can be interrupted on an occasional basis, and although this isn't the best way to do things in a world of tight budget constraints for both cash and time, it is sometimes the only choice.

Let's jump back to the better way to do things and talk about how, if you had the time and budget, you could really do things right.

Virtualization

We've all heard of VMware, and even Microsoft has jumped on the virtualization bandwagon with Microsoft Virtual PC. Disk space and memory are relatively cheap these days, so setting up a lab with virtual systems may be just what the doctor ordered for fast, easy, and cheap testing of patch management scenarios.

Figure 9.6 shows a screenshot of the VMware Server Console. The VMware Server is available for download at www.vmware.com/download/server. It is completely free and it allows you to take a snapshot of a system so that you can roll back to any previous image at any time. You can create a virtual network of interconnected devices, test the results of your patching, and then roll back to either your baseline image or any deviation. Backing up theses images is as easy as including the VMware image directories in your backup plan.

In the example shown in Figure 9.6, you can see Checkpoint's Secure Platform version R60, a Windows XP Professional system, a BEA Weblogic 8.1 SP4 server, and an IBM DB2 server running SUSE. All of these images and a number of others (except Windows XP) are available for download free of charge on VMware's Virtual Appliance page, located at www.vmware.com/vmtn/appliances. Figure 9.7 illustrates VMWorkstation 5.0's Snapshot Manager, where you can manage your rollbacks.

Figure 9.6 VMware Server Console

Figure 9.7 VMware Snapshot Manager

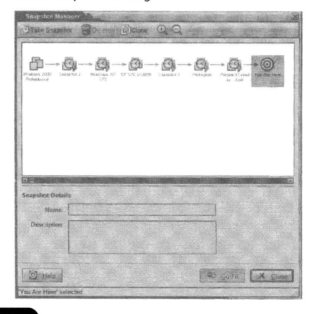

Environmental Simulation

Environmental simulation programs such as Karalon's Traffic IQ Pro and RedSeal's Security Risk Manager (SRM) can also be extremely helpful in your lab environment for inspecting traffic conditions that may be induced by system changes in real time, and you can use them to replay certain exploits in order to test that vulnerabilities are fully remediated. One of the really cool things about these products is that you don't necessarily need to have the actual routing and networking devices in the environment, just the configuration files. When used with the virtualization technique just described, you can simulate nearly any condition that could present itself in a production environment. Figures 9.8 and 9.9 show RedSeal's SRM solution.

Figure 9.8 RedSeal's Threat Graph

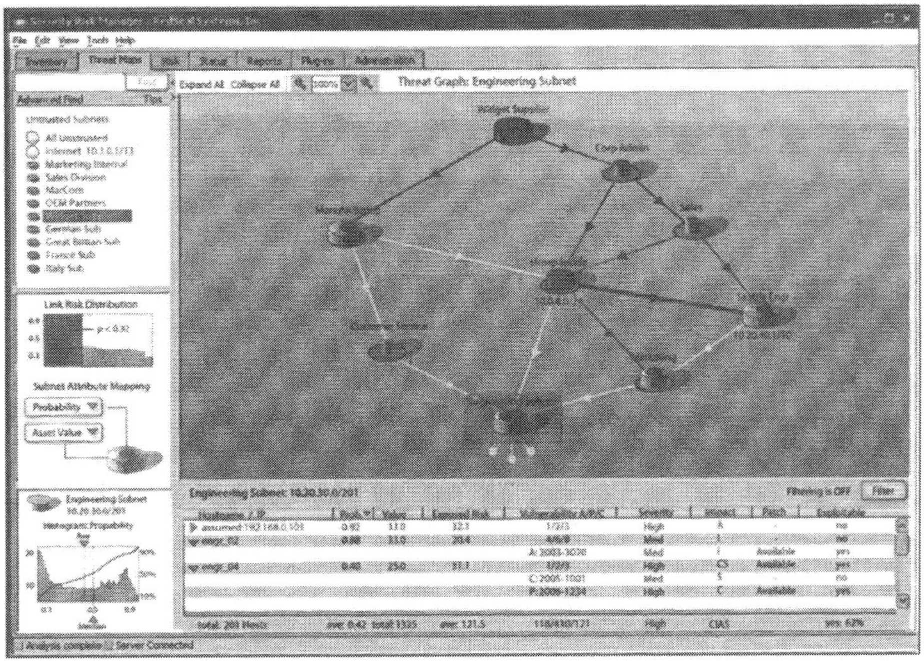

Figure 9.9 RedSeal's Risk Trend Virtualization

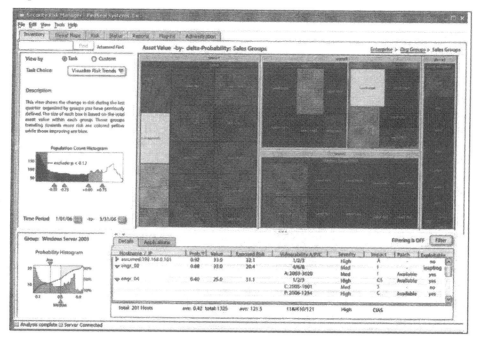

Your fundamental concern and priority with your patch deployment lab should be to determine how a given patch will affect the system's operation, or the operation of the environment into which it is placed. Some root-cause issues that will help you to make these vital determinations include:

- **Reboot.** Does the system(s) require a reboot or a service to be restarted in order to work effectively after the patch has been applied? This will no doubt affect the operation of the system or device from the service perspective, as well as in relation to the environment into which it is placed. Can your other servers handle the increased load while you round-robin the patch?

- **Rollup patch.** If the patch is a "rollup," it will most likely supersede many previous patches, not only affecting the patch baseline that you previously established, but also perhaps requiring additional reboots and frequent system snapshots.

- **How deep the patch goes into the system.** A patch can have far-reaching consequences to system operation, affecting not only network performance but also operations to other functions that you would not typically associate with its current classification or role. If your system will be "recycled" for use in the future to include operations outside of its current scope, you should plan for this in advance. An Internet Explorer or MSXML patch, for example, could affect not only the application itself, but also the operating system.

- **Integration issues with third-party applications.** You should test critical services and applications first, in order of priority to the system's classification and role. For example, a Dynamic Host Configuration Protocol (DHCP) server's capability to perform lease reservations and BOOTP operations would be of paramount concern for that role.

So, what other scenarios do you need to consider when testing a patch or configuration change? How about failures? In some cases, a patch can fail due to a variety of reasons. Some scenarios to test to see how your patches react are:

- Loss of network connectivity during package delivery
- System shutting down, rebooting, or losing power during the installation
- Normal and higher-than-normal system use during the patch install
- Other scenarios that can cause an interruption of the install or delivery process

The whole point of creating an in-depth plan and testing this plan is to minimize surprises. You need to account for every possible scenario, not just application incompatibilities.

Patch Distribution and Deployment

Patch distribution and deployment are much more complicated than simply pushing a patch to a system or having someone click a button and update a system. You need to consider numerous factors, only some of which include the following:

- The location of the system from a protocol perspective
- The bandwidth needed and the tools (if any) used
- Personnel (plan on something going not quite right)

You can deploy patches in a number of ways, each with their own benefits and drawbacks. They are:

- **Push technology.** Tools such as Microsoft SMS use what is called *push technology*, in which a centralized console must have a copy of the patch, sometimes called a *package*, and then pushes that patch to each system specified. The biggest drawback of this method is reliability of delivery. You have no real way to ensure that a system is online and will remain online long enough to receive the package. It also requires more administration overhead, especially in cases where you have to create your own custom package.

- **Pull technology.** Tools such as the built-in Microsoft Windows Update and even Red Hat's RHN are considered *pull technology* because each client will, on its own, contact the update server and pull the patches down and then install them. Note that you can set up your own patch repositories internally; instead of having all your systems access the Internet, you can have them access an internal system instead. The drawback to this technology is that it typically offers less control to administrators and in some cases can have a higher impact on network utilization.

- **Sneakernet.** Although some of you may chuckle when you read this, the unfortunate reality of some organizations is that some systems are not as easily accessible via the network as others are. This means that important upgrades and patches need to be delivered and installed manually, usually via CD or USB device. The drawbacks to this method are very obvious, as this is the most time-consuming way to patch systems.

Logging and Reporting

So, after you have deployed all of your patches, how do you know for sure that they have installed correctly and that your systems are no longer vulnerable? Most patch deployment tools offer some sort of logging capability—some centralized and some stored on the individual systems. In addition, it is highly recommended (and this will become evident in the last chapter of this book) that you rerun the vulnerability scans that identified that the systems needed patching in the first place. This will ensure, especially if you are using a quality scanning product that actually tests against the vulnerability, that the patch was not only successfully installed, but also properly fixes the issue.

Configuration Management

One area we have not talked about very much in this chapter is configuration management. The principles behind configuration management are very similar to those of patch management. The rule of document, test, deploy, and test again are as true here as they are with patch management.

There are two main reasons for having to worry about patch management. The first is enterprisewide system configuration change and the second is vulnerability mitigation. Over the past few years, the concept of secure desktop and secure server configuration has become increasingly popular because it is a viable option to prevent certain attack vectors from being successful. The initial problem with this practice is that it has always been a struggle for information technology (IT) departments to roll out and then change system configurations once systems are in production. A multitude of configuration management vendors have stepped up to the plate to solve this issue, and as suspected, this aligns closely with patch management.

So, we have a choice here. We can retype this entire chapter, replacing the words *patch management* with *configuration management*, or you the reader can simply understand that the concepts presented here apply to any change to your systems, be they patch installations or configuration changes.

For some ideas on secure configuration options for your organization, look at the NIST Security Configuration Checklists (http://checklists.nist. gov/repository/1014.html) and adapt them to your organization.

Change Control

No matter what you are doing on your network, be it a simple patch installation or a configuration change, you have to do it in a controlled and logical manner. All of the concepts discussed in this chapter should fit into your organization's existing change control procedures.

If computing asset change is not planned properly, it will fail, and ultimately your security initiatives will fail along with it. You need to plan, test, track, and retest all changes to all systems. This will ensure that any bad changes will be caught before they affect the overall user base, and possibly more important, it will ensure that you completely understand and plan for any security impact these changes may have.

When creating your change and patch management process you need to ensure that you cover the following steps:

1. Create a test group that is a sampling of all assets on your network.
2. Document the proposed change in detail.
3. Document a "roll-back" plan to undo the change.
4. Obtain sign-off from asset owners on the planned change.
5. Implement the change on your test group.
6. Monitor for adverse effects.
7. Roll out the change enterprisewide if the test group is successful.
8. Undo the change if the test group is not successful.

Although this appears to be a lengthy list of steps that could be time consuming and not conducive to quickly addressing vulnerabilities, with the right tools and the proper organizational buy-in, this process can move fairly quickly and even account for emergency changes. The key is proper documentation and testing; this will save you a lot of work when things go badly.

Tools & Traps…

Types of Documents That Require Tracking

This sidebar presents samples of documents you can use to perform and track the progress of your security assessment. Specific naming of documents is organizationally dependent, so this list may not include all the names you may encounter. All documents should be logged on a simple document-tracking sheet.

Policy Documents:

- Acceptable-Use/Internet Usage Policy
- Business Strategy
- Corporate Mission
- Employee Code of Conduct
- Information Security Policy
- Information Systems Security Policy
- Internet Usage Policy
- IT Strategy
- Mission Statement
- Organization Chart
- Organizational Description
- Organizational Security Policy/Procedures
- Personnel Security Policy
- Physical Security Policy
- Security Policy
- Security Strategy
- Strategy Document

Continued

Guideline/Requirements Documents:

- Administrative Security Requirements (Marking, Labeling, Storage, Transport of Documentation and Removable Media)
- Business Continuity/DRP
- Communications Security (COMSEC) and COMSEC Key Management Procedures
- Concept of Operations (CONOPs)
- HR Procedures (Hiring, Transfer, Retirement, Termination)
- List and Description of HW, SW, FW, OS, DB, GOTS, COTS, DOI/NBC Unique Applications
- Maintenance Standards/Change Control
- Mission Needs Statement (MNS)
- Network Connection Rules (External)/ External Connection MOU/MOA
- Operational Requirements Document (ORD)
- Security Concept of Operations (SECCONOPS)
- Security Department/Committee Mandates
- Security Programming/Testing Standards
- Technical Standards/Guidelines

System Security Plan Documents:

- Contingency Plan/Continuity of Operations Plan (COOP)
- Configuration Management Plan
- Network Diagrams/Architecture with Narrative
- Network Diagram (High and Low Level) *Required*
- Personnel Security Plan
- Physical Security Plan
- Prior Assessment (Threat/Risk/Security)
- Prior Audits (Internal or External)
- System Security Authorization Agreement (SSAA)
- Security Test Plans

Continued

User Documents:

- Account Management and Data Transfer Procedures in Hiring, Transfer, Retirement, Termination
- Audit Procedures
- Data Backup Procedures
- Desktop Support Security Procedures
- Desktop Support End-User Security Awareness
- Identification and Authentication Procedures
- Incident Response Plan
- Maintenance Plan/Procedures
- Password Management Procedures
- Personnel Security Procedures
- Physical Security Procedures
- Rules of Behavior
- Security Administrator Procedures
- Security Administrator's Manual
- Security Education Awareness Training Plan
- Security Features User's Guide
- Server/OS Administration Procedures
- Standard Operating Procedures (SOPs)
- Systems Admin Professional Development
- Systems Admin Security Procedures
- User's Guide
- Vendor Documentation
- Virus/Malicious Code Protection

Summary

This chapter covered the process of remediating vulnerabilities. In reality, an entire book could be written on this subject, as this is probably the most diffi- cult and time-consuming part of the vulnerability management process. That being said, this chapter gave you the tools you need to properly build a test environment, to test patches and configuration changes, to document those changes, and to ultimately increase the overall security of your organization.

Solutions Fast Track

Patch Management

☑ Why Patch to enable new system functionality?

- To remediate vulnerabilities.

- To solve issues with system stability.

Keys To Patch & Configuration Management

☑ Document the change.

☑ Test the change in a lab or other test environment.

☑ Document an emergency system restore procedure.

☑ Test the emergency restore procedure.

☑ Roll out changes.

☑ Monitor for success or failures.

Change Management Process

☑ Create a test group that is a sampling of all assets on your network

☑ Document the proposed change in detail

☑ Document a "roll back" plan to undo the change

☑ Obtain sign off from asset owners on the planned changes

☑ Implement the change on your test group

☑ Monitor for adverse effects

☑ Roll out changes enterprise wide if test group is successful

☑ Undo changes if not successful

Frequently Asked Questions

The following Frequently Asked Questions, answered by the authors of this book, are designed to both measure your understanding of the concepts presented in this chapter and to assist you with real-life implementation of these concepts. To have your questions about this chapter answered by the author, browse to **www.syngress.com/solutions** and click on the **"Ask the Author"** form.

Q: Can system hardening alone secure my systems so that I do not need to patch?

A: Absolutely not. While system hardening and secure configuration standards are an excellent idea and can limit the attack surface of a system it will not protect you from every vulnerability.

Q: My Host Based Intrusion Prevention vendor says that with their solution I no longer need to patch. Is this true?

A: I hope you can get your money back. No end point protection product can protect your completely and these products should never be considered a replacement for patch management.

Q: Should I trust a non-vendor third party patch?

A: That depends on who produces that patch and your level of trust for that individual or organization. Third party patches have their place as a temporary solution if no other mitigation is available.

Q: I have users that are not only remote but also mobile on a constant basis. Is there a strategy for keeping those systems up to date?

A: Absolutely, vendors like Configuresoft, that use a Central Managed Database (CMDB) model are able to handle updating, albeit not as quickly as stand alone desktops, on remote and unreliable connections.

Q: We need to increase our internal network security. Should we buy a vulnerability scanner and scan our entire Class B internal network?

A: No, you need to classify your assets, create security zones for scanning, then test each range based on the needs of the specified security zone.

Q: What should we do if a new vulnerability and exploit is released publicly in the wild?

A: Don't panic, first you need to update your vulnerability scanners to reflect the vulnerability (if your vendor has not updated their tool yet, *then* you can panic!). Scan your security zones starting with the most critical ones first, and based on the results assign the remediation efforts for each zone to responsible parties as soon as they are completed.

Q: Does the SANS/FBI Top 20 favor Unix or Windows?

A: The SANS/FBI Top 20 is actually a list of the top 10 Windows vulnerabilities and a list of the top 10 Unix vulnerabilities.

Q: How do I handle a finding that I cannot determine to be a false positive or false negative?

A: If the onsite data gathering is performed correctly by following the 10 baseline activities, you should not be faced with this issue. The evaluation team's expertise of knowing what tool to use, when to use it, and how to use it, in accordance with a comprehensive methodology, will play a big role in eliminating this problem.

At times, though, a TCP port could be interrogated and the service or application on the listening port cannot be determined. We say "listening" because a traffic analyzer is utilized to verify a full TCP handshake to the port. The listening port must be reported to the customer so that source of the listening port on the server can be researched in more detail. Once the source has been identified, the testing perspective and business justification of the identified application and how it should be accessed will be accounted for in the customer's decision process.

## Chapter 10

Regulatory Compliance

Solutions in this chapter:

- Regulating Assessments and Pen Tests
- Drafting an Information Security Program

☑ Summary

☑ Solutions Fast Track

☑ Frequently Asked Questions

Introduction

Vulnerability assessments (VAs) and penetration tests (pen tests) have long been major components of information security programs. In fact, security managers have historically defined when and how they would conduct these exercises, as well as the scope of such exercises. Nevertheless, a missed assessment or pen test traditionally wasn't a big deal. Considering the resource constraints of most information security departments, missing an assessment period, or even two, was quasi-acceptable.

But that is no longer the case. Today businesses and industries are being besieged by compliance statutes. As security professionals and business leaders, we are no longer left to our own accord regarding how we create and implement our information security programs. In this chapter, we'll discuss the impact that regulations have had on vulnerability assessment and pen testing, as well as how to draft an information security program to meet an ever-changing business environment. See Appendix A for more information on the legal ramifications of regulatory compliance.

Regulating Assessments and Pen Tests

Unless we're operating a family diner, have an insignificant number of patrons, don't offer a healthcare plan to our employees, and run our entire business on cash, our organization is probably subject to at least one government/industry regulation. In fact, most organizations today are feeling the compliance burden and are subject to not one, but many compliance statutes. For instance, hospitals and healthcare providers are being besieged by the Health Insurance Portability and Accountability Act of 1996 (HIPAA), and many companies are still grappling with the Sarbanes-Oxley Act (SOX). Merchants and credit card processors now face the Payment Card Industry (PCI) standard, and government agencies must endure the Federal Information Security Management Act (FISMA). Financial institutions, probably the most regulated, are subject to the Gramm-Leach-Bliley Act (GLBA), Basel II, and a slew of other compliance regulations.

To complicate this, very few organizations are subject to only one regulatory statute. Take, for example, a Fortune 500 company that has an online storefront and outsources its healthcare program, but subsidizes its employees' healthcare costs. This company must comply with at least SOX, PCI, and HIPAA. In this section, we'll provide a high-level overview of each regulation and discuss their impact on vulnerability assessment and penetration testing.

The Payment Card Industry (PCI) Standard

Credit card theft has been with us ever since there have been credit cards. In the past, though, before the advent of the Internet and electronic commerce, a thief's accessibility to credit card data was relatively limited. Sure, a thief could compromise our credit card number and maybe the credit card number of 10, 20, or perhaps 100 other people, but it was relatively unlikely, with the exception of organized crime, for a criminal to have access to hundreds of thousands or even tens of thousands of credit card numbers. The advent of the Internet, coupled with the adoption of electronic commerce and online storefronts, has changed this. Now, upon exploiting a repository that supports an online storefront, a thief can easily gain access to hundreds of thousands, if not millions, of customer records and credit card numbers.

In an effort to address the liabilities associated with credit card theft, credit card companies, beginning with Visa in 2001 with its Cardholder Information Security Program (CISP), began enacting data protection standards governing the processing, transmission, and storage of credit card data. Other credit card companies soon followed suit and developed and enacted their own credit card legislation.

As a merchant or service provider, complying with the credit card data protection standards initially could be quite cumbersome and exhaustive, because no credit card vendor acknowledged and honored the other's credit card program. After three years of credit card mayhem, Visa and MasterCard collaborated and sponsored the PCI data protection standard. PCI doesn't usurp the data protection standards of the respective credit card companies, but Visa, MasterCard, Discover, American Express, Diners Club, and the Japan Credit Bureau (JCB) all endorse it.

Having garnered credit card unification and support, and with a rise in credit card theft, by the end of 2004 credit card companies began mandating that all merchants and service providers comply with either PCI or the data protection standard for the credit cards they accept or process. Attesting to PCI requires that organizations submit a report on compliance (ROC) and a remediation plan to VISA. The ROC is intended to identify an organization's level of compliance to the PCI standard and the remediation plan is intended to detail what an organization is doing to become compliant.

Part of securing the processing, transmission, and storage of credit card data is identifying vulnerabilities within the supporting infrastructure: servers, switches, routers, and applications used to support the credit card process. In an attempt to ensure that vulnerabilities do not exist or are identified and remediated within the credit card process, PCI requires vulnerability assessments and a penetration test of the merchant or service provider's cardholder environment. Table 10.1 lists PCI's VA and pen testing requirements.

Table 10.1 PCI VA Requirements*

Requirement #	Requirement Description
11	Regularly test security systems and processes.
11.2	Run internal and external network vulnerability scans at least quarterly and after any significant change in the network (e.g., new system component installations, changes in network topology, firewall rule modifications, product upgrades). *Note that external vulnerability scans must be performed by a scan vendor qualified by the PCI.*
11.3	Perform penetration testing on network infrastructure and applications at least once a year, and after any significant infrastructure or application upgrade or modification occurs (e.g., operating system upgraded, subnetwork added to environment, Web server added to environment).

*http://usa.visa.com/download/business/accepting_visa/ops_risk_management/cisp_PCI_Data_Security_Standard.pdf.

As noted in Table 10.1, external vulnerability scans must be performed by an approved PCI vendor. Table 10.2 reflects a partial list of approved PCI VA vendors. For a complete list, go to https://sdp.mastercardintl.com/vendors/vendor_list.shtml. For further information regarding PCI, visit http://usa.visa.com/business/accepting_visa/ops_risk_management/cisp.html.

Table 10.2 Approved PCI VA Vendors

Vendor Name	Product Name	Locations Served
403 Labs, LLC	PCI Compliance Testing	Global
Accume Partners	SDP Compliance Assessment	Global
Accuvant	Accuvant Compliance Scan	North America
Akibia, Inc.	Credit Card Security Compliance Services	Global
AlertSite	AlertSite Security Vulnerability Scan	Global
Alexander Open Systems, Inc.	Alexander Open Systems, Inc.	North America
Ambersail Ltd.	Ambersail Assured	UK and Europe
AmbironTrustWave	TrustKeeper	Global
Ascure nv	Ascure SDP Assessment Services	Global
Avanteg Bilgi ve lletisim Hizmetleri Ticaret A.S.	Avanteg Preventive Solutions–SDP Compliance Testing	Global

TIP

PCI focuses heavily on protecting a credit card number throughout its life cycle. It does not address protecting the customer's personal data associated with that credit card number—for example, street address, customer name, and so on. As we evaluate credit card exposure within our environment, we should also assess the customer data we possess and create a strategy that mitigates the security liabilities associated with the unauthorized disclosure of both.

The Health Insurance Portability and Accountability Act of 1996 (HIPAA)

When visiting a physician's office these days we're frequently presented with a document detailing our rights as a patient. Not only are we presented with our rights, but we're also given our physician's process for ensuring the security, confidentiality, and integrity of our health data. Securing patient health data hasn't always been a major concern; it wasn't prior to the last decade. A lot has changed since then, and this has become a focal point, thanks in large part to the Health Insurance Portability and Accountability Act of 1996 (HIPAA).

Congress passed HIPAA in August 1996. The intent of the legislation was to make healthcare delivery more efficient by:

- Simplifying the administrative process
- Defining the underwriting process for medical coverage
- Standardizing the electronic transmission of billing and claims information

By standardizing the transmission of billing and claims data, the potential for theft and abuse of patient health information (PHI) increased. To lessen this threat Congress expanded HIPAA and included safeguards to protect the confidentiality and security of patient data. These safeguards dictate that only authorized individuals have access to patient information and only to the information necessary to support a given task. HIPAA was also expanded to regulate not only PHI such as printouts, but also electronic PHI (ePHI) such as voice mails and e-mails.

HIPAA went into effect April 14, 2001, but organizations were given until April 2003 to become compliant. After April 13, 2003, organizations could be penalized for noncompliance.

Hospitals, as we might expect, are subject to HIPAA, but they aren't the only ones. Following is a list of entities that must be HIPAA compliant as of today (see NIST Special Publication 800-66):

- **Covered healthcare providers** Any provider of medical or other health services, or supplies, who transmits any health information in electronic form in connection with a transaction for which the Department of Health and Human Services (HHS) has adopted a standard.

- **Health plans** Any individual or group plan that provides, or pays the cost of, medical care, including certain specifically listed government programs (e.g., a health insurance issuer and the Medicare and Medicaid programs).

- **Healthcare clearinghouses** A public or private entity that processes another entity's healthcare transactions from a standard format to a nonstandard format, or vice versa.

- **Medicare prescription drug card sponsors** A nongovernmental entity that offers an endorsed discount drug program under the Medicare Modernization Act. This fourth category of "covered entity" will remain in effect until the drug card program ends in 2006.

Logically we would expect healthcare providers, clearinghouses, and drug card sponsors to be subject to HIPAA. Many health plans have been caught off guard by this legislation, though. Recall that a health plan is any individual or group plan that provides or pays for the cost of medical care. Because of this definition many companies are subject to HIPAA, for they provide employee assistance programs and subsidize their employees' healthcare costs.

Entities subject to HIPAA must appoint a security official. This official is responsible for conducting and filing a HIPAA risk assessment, usually with the entity's fiduciary. The main purpose/intent of the assessment is to ensure that PHI and ePHI are protected with appropriate controls and measures; the ePHI that a covered entity creates, receives, maintains, or transmits must be protected against reasonably anticipated threats, hazards, and impermissible uses and/or disclosures. Table 10.3 (from NIST Special Publication 800-66) outlines HIPAA's vulnerability assessment requirements. For a detailed listing of the HIPAA security requirements, visit www.hhs.gov/ocr/hipaa/.

Table 10.3 HIPAA VA Requirements

Standard	Section	Implementation Specifications
Security awareness and training	Protection from malicious software	Determine the health plan's level of vulnerability to the threat of malicious software.
Security awareness and training	Protection from malicious software	Review adequacy of current safeguards for guarding against, detecting, and reporting malicious software.
Security awareness and training	Protection from malicious software	Develop a policy and procedure for protection from malicious software.
Security awareness and training	Log-in monitoring	Determine the health plan's level of vulnerability to the threat of unauthorized access to ePHI or the health plan's information system by internal or external individuals inappropriately using a workforce member's log-in information.

NOTE

HIPAA, unlike other compliance statutes, doesn't require us to submit our risk assessment to an external party; not to HHS or any other independent agency. Although HHS has received more than 19,000 HIPAA-related complaints, it has yet to levy a fine. HHS has the authority to impose fines for civil violations ranging from $100 to $25,000, and officials can refer possible criminal violations to the Department of Justice (www.kaisernetwork.org/daily_reports/rep_index.cfm?DR_ID=37687).

The Sarbanes-Oxley Act of 2002 (SOX)

The early part of the twenty-first century was marred by corporate financial scandals and collapses. At Enron, WorldCom, Adelphia Communications, and more, many corporate executives were manipulating investors and stakeholders alike by inflating the profits of their respective companies via unethical accounting practices. As a result, many of these once admired and idolized companies imploded; filing bankruptcy, laying off thousands of employees, and staving off the myriad retaliatory lawsuits brought by shareholders. In response to this and in an effort to restore the integrity of financial reporting, the Sarbanes-Oxley Act of 2002 (SOX) was enacted.

NOTE

In 15 years, Enron grew from nowhere to become America's seventh largest company. But the firm's success turned out to be an elaborate scam. Enron lied about its profits and stands accused of a range of shady dealings, including concealing debts so that they didn't show up in the company's accounts (for more, visit http://news.bbc.co.uk/1/hi/business/1780075.stm). After more than four years of criminal inquiry, Enron's former CEO, CFO, and other corporate executives were found guilty and some have been imprisoned for their corporate wrongdoings. Prior to facing sentencing Ken Lay, Enron's former CEO, died on July 5, 2006 after suffering a massive heart attack in his Aspen, Colorado vacation home. The irony is that by dying, Lay achieved something he could not do when he was alive. He cleared his name and wiped a conviction that it took the US Government more than four years to win. This is for when a defendant who pleads not guilty dies before being sentenced, the conviction is wiped out on the grounds that the defendant did not have the opportunity to appeal (for more, visit http://www.theage.com.au/news/business/in-death-as-in-life-lay-cheats-his-detractors/2006/07/07/1152240489467.html).

The Sarbanes-Oxley Act has fundamentally changed the business, regulatory, and information technology (IT) environments (the entire document can be viewed at http://www.isaca.org/Content/ContentGroups/Research1/Deliverables/IT_Control_Objectives_for_Sarbanes-Oxley_7july04.pdf). By holding corporate executives, chief executives, and financial officers explicitly responsible for establishing, evaluating, and monitoring the effectiveness of internal control over financial reporting, SOX strengthens internal checks and balances, corporate accountability, and ultimately, corporate financial reporting.

Unlike with HIPAA and PCI, many feel that the compliance requirements articulated within SOX are somewhat vague and disconcerting; especially section 404. Within section 404, organizations must attest to their financial and general IT controls. Financial controls measure and verify our accounting practices and general IT controls assess the accessibility and safeguards we have governing our technology, our financial systems, and our supporting infrastructure.

As a part of measuring, testing, and attesting to our general IT controls, we must identify the risks related to our IT systems and design and implement safeguards or compensating controls to mitigate these risks. Part of identifying and assessing this risk is conducting vulnerability assessments and pen tests against our IT systems. Though SOX doesn't specifically define a frequency for these activities, all publicly traded companies, for the most part, must annually undergo a SOX audit, and such an organization needs to annually conduct at least one vulnerability assessment and pen test. In seeking due diligence, many internal audit departments are asking that these exercises be conducted more frequently and by a recognized third party. Note that the recognized third party cannot be the same independent auditor that's used to substantiate the company's financial reporting process.

Compliance Recap

As noted in the previous section, regulatory statutes are beginning to exert force upon and shape our VA and pen test processes; ultimately impacting our information security programs. Figure 10.1 represents a partial list of the regulatory landscape.

Table 10.4 lists the primary industry each form of legislation impacts and provides a brief summary of each statute.

Figure 10.1 Partial Regulatory Landscape

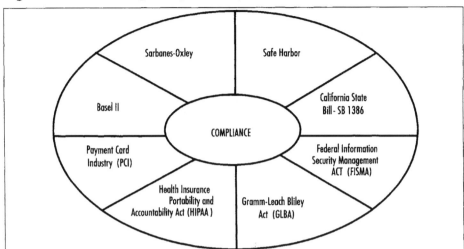

Table 10.4 Compliance Summary

Regulation/Standard	Sector Affected	Summary	Effective Date
PCI	Cross-sector	Data protection standard governing the processing, storage, and transmission of cardholder data.	2004
HIPAA	Healthcare	Regulation governing the privacy, security, availability, and confidentiality of patient health data.	2003
GLBA	Financial	Privacy requirements for customers' financial data. Mandates the publication of privacy standards used by financial institutions and restricts the use and transfer of data between organizations.	2004

Continued

Table 10.4 continued Compliance Summary

Regulation/ Standard	Sector Affected	Summary	Effective Date
FISMA	Government	Act requiring government agencies to secure the information and systems supporting their operations and assets.	2002
California State Bill– SB 1386	Cross-sector	Requires individuals and organizations to properly notify California residents if their personal identifiable information (PII) is disclosed as part of a security breach or any other exposure.	2004
Safe Harbor	Cross-sector	U.S. complement to the European Union's (EU's) Directive on Data Protection, which prohibits the transfer of personal data to entities that do not meet the EU's "adequacy" standard for privacy protection.	2000
SOX	Cross-sector	Created to restore investor confidence in corporate financial reporting through good corporate governance, ethical business practices, and sound financial and IT auditing and controls.	2003
Basel II Accord	Financial	Regulation to introduce a more risk-sensitive capital framework in international financial institutions.	2006

Drafting an Information Security Program

Coupled with the fact that we live in a very litigious society, as security practitioners and business leaders we also now live in a highly regulated business environment. Because of this, drafting policies and standards and delivering an information security program that meets all of the compliance statutes, as well as an organization's needs, can be quite daunting.

Smaller or siloed business may be able to structure an information security program around the major regulatory statute they're subject to, but this simply doesn't scale for large enterprises because, as illustrated earlier, most organizations are subject to many statutes. Complicating this, many organizations partner with others that operate outside their primary industry and have other regulatory compliance obligations. Therefore, you often see security addendums attached to contracts to protect the compliance requirements of each partner. Figure 10.2 is an excerpt from of a standard security addendum.

Figure 10.2 Security Addendum Excerpt

1.   **Governance**. VENDOR will maintain Information Security Policies and Procedures that meet the standards of its respective industry and privacy regulations applicable it.

2.   **Audits**

2.1 Security Audits

a.   VENDOR and its contractors (to the extent that such contractors have access to the COMPANY's information) must have a comprehensive risk management program for its systems that contain the COMPANY's data. This should include a process for identifying newly released information about security patches for any such systems.

b.   If VENDOR has not already had a security audit performed by a mutually agreed upon third party, VENDOR will have such audit conducted within a timeframe agreeable to both parties. This initial audit will determine the state of security and readiness within VENDOR's environment. Prior to VENDOR accessing, gathering, storing, or processing COMPANY data, VENDOR will resolve any issues identified through the initial security audit as mutually agreed upon by the parties.

c.   If VENDOR has had a security audit performed by an industry recognized third party as mutually agreed upon by the parties, then the requirements of Section 2.b above will be waived and the following obligations will apply:

i.   Prior to VENDOR accessing, gathering, storing, or processing COMPANY data, VENDOR will provide COMPANY with the scope and summary of the most recent security audit performed by that third party. The scope of this audit must include the proposed COMPANY-related environment.

So what are we to do? Do we draft policies around HIPAA, SOX, or perhaps PCI? Prior to making this decision, we must remember that the most effective information security programs are tailored around an organization's people, process, and technology. Figure 10.3 shows the relationship among these three elements.

Figure 10.3 Relationship Among People, Process, and Technology

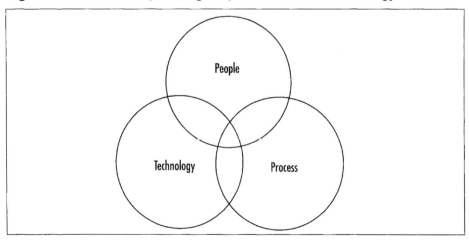

Information security isn't all about technology. If we were to align people, process, and technology in order of importance, our output would look similar to Figure 10.4, with people representing the foundation of our information security program, followed by process and technology. A lot of the time, we can get by with inferior technology if we have well-defined and functioning processes being executed by individuals with an elevated security IQ.

Figure 10.4 Order of Importance of People, Process, and Technology

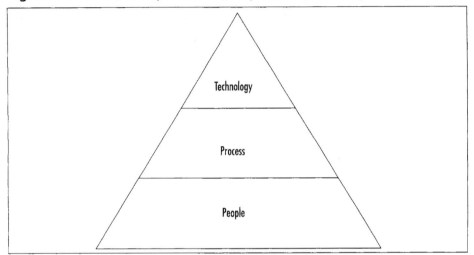

Because of today's regulatory environment, drafting and executing an information security program is somewhat of a challenge. In the past, many of us have adopted the International Organization for Standardization (ISO) standard, ISO 17799, and our internal audit departments have leveraged the Committee of Sponsoring Organizations (COSO) or Control Objectives for Information and related Technology (COBIT) to evaluate our information security programs. ISO is a good and well-established framework, but it lacks defining elements. ISO articulates that statements such as auditing should be enabled, and many of the regulations we're subjected to dictate the level of auditing and the frequency with which it should be reviewed. Independent of whether we're using ISO or another security framework, we should develop and tailor our programs with risk mitigation in mind. Figure 10.5 is a Risk-Management-Based Policy Framework.

NOTE

COBIT is a set of best practices (a framework) for IT management created in 1992 by the Information Systems Audit and Control Association (ISACA) and the IT Governance Institute (ITGI). COBIT provides managers, auditors, and IT users with a set of generally accepted measures, indicators, processes, and best practices to assist them in maximizing the benefits derived through the use of IT and developing appropriate IT governance and control in a company.

Figure 10.5 Risk-Management-Based Policy Framework

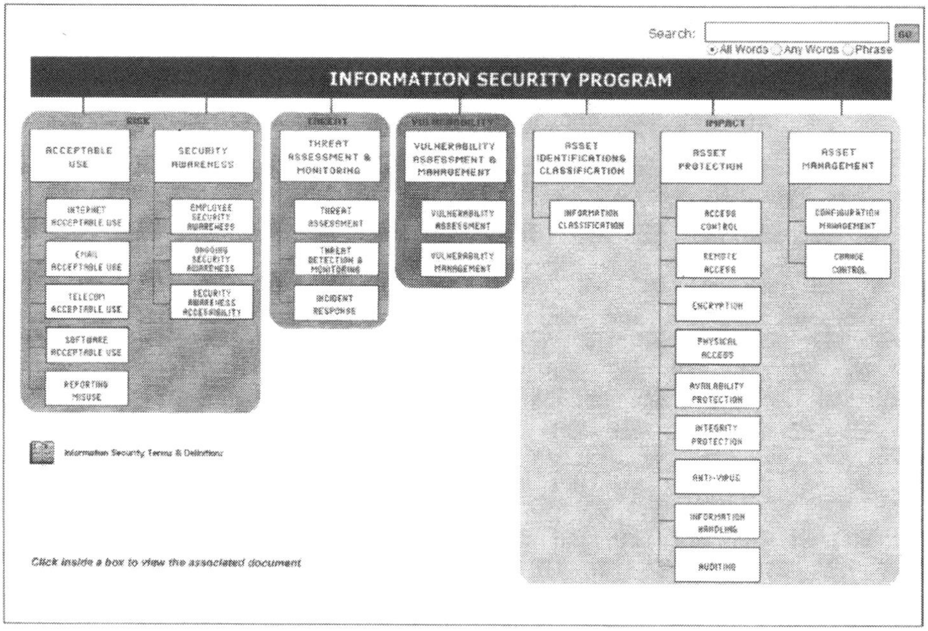

Leveraging a framework such as that shown in Figure 10.5 or organizing our existing framework in the same fashion will allow us to:

- Organize our information security programs into digestible modules that our employee groups can easily understand

- Adapt to changing threats, environments, and regulations

- Focus on the people and process elements of information security

Upon organizing our program in this fashion, we can then develop a compliance matrix associated with the various regulations we're subject to. Figure 10.6 is an example of such a matrix. To accomplish this we don't necessarily have to modularize our information security program into high level policy statements with supporting standards, as illustrated in Figure 10.5, but as chief information security officers or security/compliance leaders we are typically responsible for the program's policies and standards and by modularizing our program we can:

- Communicate changes to the program in an easy and concise manner. We simply have to communicate the policy or standard that has changed and not the entire program.

- Easily make changes to the program to support new threats or other security / business concerns

- Potentially make modifications to the program without requiring executive signoff. While senior management needs to signoff on the program, executive sponsorship usually isn't required when modifying standards or supporting procedures.

Over the past several years, technologies such as Symantec's Bindview Policy Manager have come to market. Policy Manager maps created policy to best-practice frameworks, such as ISO 17799, and multiple regulations, like HIPPA, and supplies proof of compliance to policy through integration with Symantec and third-party infrastructure assessment software (for more, visit www.symantec.com/Products/enterprise?c=prodinfo&refId=1261&cid=1004). For CISOs and Compliance Officers the beauty of Policy Manger and similar technologies is that it:

- negates the need for compliance matrixes like Figure 10.6 for we no longer have to physically map regulatory controls to our company's policy statements

- aids us in drafting information security programs in alignment with the regulatory environment we are subject to

- allows organizations to automatically, via technology, attest to their level of compliance

Figure 10.6 Compliance Matrix*

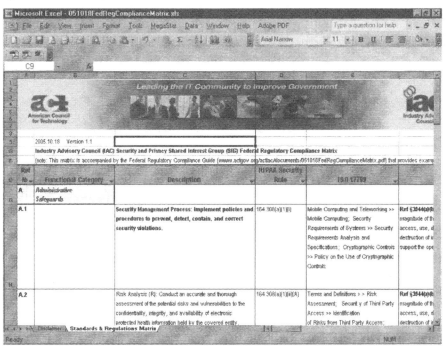

*(www.actgov.org/actiac/documents/051018FedRegComplianceMatrix.pdf)

Drafting an information security program in this day and age is somewhat of a chore, but if we take a holistic view of the challenge and tailor it toward risk mitigation, drafting policies and standards to meet today's evolving and regulated environment, while minimizing the security liabilities faced by our organizations, is certainly attainable.

Summary

Protecting corporate assets has long been on the minds of security professionals and business leaders. Protecting the data which resides on those assets is now even more important, given the regulatory environment in which we operate.

PCI, HIPAA, and SOX reflect the first wave of compliance statutes that our organizations are subject to. The next wave may include state, and possibly federal, notification and disclosure statutes governing our organization's responsibility to publicly disclose security breaches to our constituents.

The regulatory landscape is fairly new, so we should expect the expected—more regulations—and the unexpected—changes to existing regulations. Drafting an information security program that is modular, flexible, and focused on risk mitigation and common-sense security will go a long way toward tackling the ever-evolving compliance landscape.

Solutions Fast Track

Regulating Assessments and Pen Tests

☑ Merchants and service providers must adhere to the Payment Card Industry (PCI) data protection standard when processing, transmitting, or storing credit card data.

☑ HIPAA, the Health Insurance Portability and Accountability Act of 1996, now governs the confidentiality, integrity, and availability of patient health information.

☑ As of 2004, the Sarbanes-Oxley Act (SOX) presides over the financial reporting of most publicly traded companies. SOX attempts to ensure that there are general safeguards around the financial and general IT controls associated with financial reporting.

Drafting an Information Security Program

- ☑ Understand your business and your industry.
- ☑ Understand the compliance landscape.
- ☑ Develop a compliance matrix associated with the regulations your organization is subject to.
- ☑ Create an information security program tailored to your organization and the regulations it's subject to.

Frequently Asked Questions

The following Frequently Asked Questions, answered by the authors of this book, are designed to both measure your understanding of the concepts presented in this chapter and to assist you with real-life implementation of these concepts. To have your questions about this chapter answered by the author, browse to **www.syngress.com/solutions** and click on the **"Ask the Author"** form.

Q: I've gone through the PCI standard and it appears that the credit card companies want us to encrypt everything everywhere—for example, credit card numbers in repositories and even administrative connections to infrastructure devices. How can I achieve this, given my legacy environment?

A: The credit card companies realize that this is a challenge for many organizations. Because of this, they are relaxing PCI's encryption requirements. For specifics, contact your PCI auditor.

Q: One auditor is measuring me using COBIT and another via COSO. Which solution should we use?

A: Auditors should assess your environment and your processes based upon due diligence. Are you diligent in the safeguards and processes you've implemented? Storing usernames and passwords in protected Excel spreadsheets would be an example of negligence and not due diligence. A control framework should be instituted within your environment. At the end of the day, it may behoove you to adopt a recognized framework to ensure that you, your auditors, and your partners are all on the same information security page.

Q: Do we really need to spend the time and money to become HIPAA compliant if no one will know whether we indeed are?

A: Though HIPAA fines haven't been levied, that's not to say they never will be. With that said, neither we nor our companies want to become the case study for HIPAA noncompliance.

Q: Is there some sort of compliance broker that I can enlist and have one interface and reporting mechanism for all regulations?

A: Unfortunately, compliance clearinghouses such as this currently don't exist. The best approach is to have a single set of internal and external auditors to assist with your compliance efforts. As such, the auditor should be able to leverage data garnered from previous audits to support additional audit requests.

Q: Should we expect an environment that is more regulated or less regulated in the coming years?

A: More, of course, but we should also expect changes to existing legislation, too. Many of these are fairly new and regulators like organizations are still trying to figure everything out.

Q: What new compliance statutes should we expect in the foreseeable future?

A: A federal notification and disclosure statute is certainly foreseeable, as well as new statutes focusing on protecting personal identifiable information (PII).

Q: Many of the statutes have overlapping control statements. Can I leverage output from a previous audit—say, PCI—to support SOX compliance?

A: To some extent, absolutely. Your auditor will determine to what extent, though. They can't totally rely on another auditors' work, but they can leverage some of it.

Chapter 11

Tying It All Together

Introduction

Congratulations on reaching the final chapter of the book! We hope you have been able to use the examples we've presented throughout in your daily battles, securing and monitoring your systems. One of the things that we have been annoyed with in the past is books written by multiple authors who do not fit together well. This book was written by three different authors, all of whom are very talented in their respective fields and all of whom have many years of experience dealing with vulnerabilities and, more important, with securing corporate networks. We took great pains to ensure that we collaborated fully when writing this book, and we hope you feel that our work has paid off in the form of a book that flows well and provides consistent advice and concepts.

If we failed to accomplish this in the preceding chapters, this chapter should tie everything together nicely and give you a concise guide to vulnerability management. Concepts, examples, and product screen shots aside, we want readers to literally tear this chapter from the book and keep it handy on their desks as a comprehensive methodology checklist for vulnerability management.

A Vulnerability Management Methodology

Unless you are friend or family member of one of the authors, you bought this book because you need a guide to vulnerability management. If you have ever had the pleasure of writing a book, or even online content, you are aware that it can drive even the best of authors into a 12-step program to recovery. So, in honor of such programs, we offer the following eight essential steps for vulnerability management. Perform the following steps for a year and you won't get a token or a certificate, but you will find yourself having successfully created a vulnerability management program that becomes easier to administer day by day:

- Step one: know your assets.
- Step two: categorize your assets.

- Step three: create a baseline scan of all of your assets.

- Step four: perform a penetration test on certain assets.

- Step five: remediate vulnerabilities and risk.

- Step six: create a vulnerability assessment (VA) schedule.

- Step seven: create a patch and change management process.

- Step eight: monitor for new risks to assets.

- Wash, rinse, and repeat.

We discuss each step in the sections that follow. Within those sections, we provide the following information:

- What you need to do

- Why you need to do it

- How to do it

- What tools exist to help you do it

Step One: Know Your Assets

What You Need to Do

You should document every asset on your network that "speaks" the Transmission Control Protocol/Internet Protocol (TCP/IP) language—at both a logical and a physical level. As simple as this may sound, you should read it over and over again in order to truly understand that when we say *every asset* we *mean* every asset. This can include obvious things, such as workstations and servers, but it can also mean equipment such as printers, copy machines, routers, switches, Internet Protocol (IP) phones, and network attached storage, and even items such as game consoles, toasters, and fridges (yes, some kitchen appliances actually speak TCP/IP; go to www.lge.com).

Even if your VA tool does not support the scanning of more obscure devices, you still need to know they exist.

> **NOTE**
>
> Are you running IPv6? Even if you are not officially running it, you might want to perform network scans for both IPv4 and IPv6 devices, because it's not uncommon for organizations to find unsupported networks in their environments. Be sure to check that your chosen tools support IPv6 as well. What about other protocols, you ask? Although you cannot scan them, you should always be aware of what is in your environment.

Why You Need to Do It

Although on the surface, this appears to be a simple inventory task, it is actually a very important security step. We know of organizations that have identified devices that should not exist on their networks. This is also an important part of the compliance puzzle; the last thing an information technology (IT) administrator wants is an auditor finding systems that are not only unknown, but also do not comply with specific regulatory issues. In addition, multiple presentations have been given at various conferences, showing how you can use various devices such as game consoles to allow unauthorized access to corporate networks. So consider this step as something that should become a constant task which you schedule along with your vulnerability scans.

How to Do It

You can use a number of tools to document assets on your network. There are a few different ways to accomplish this task, as well:

- **ICMP discovery.** This is the simplest method of identifying systems on a network. An Internet Control Message Protocol (ICMP) packet is also known as a *ping packet*. Although it is the most reliable way to identify hosts, many IT professionals are taught to disable a system's (or switch's) capability to respond to ICMP as a form of mitigation from unauthorized scans. Of course, while you have protected your network against unauthorized ICMP scans, you have also effectively hidden your systems from legitimate scans as well.

- **TCP port discovery scan.** This is a good way to identify hosts when ICMP might be disabled. Simply put, this method will attempt to connect to every IP address in the scan range on a specific port. If that port is open and is listening for connections, the host will be considered alive. If none of the selected ports is alive and listening, the host will be considered dead.

- **UDP discovery scan.** This type of scan works a little differently. Whereas a TCP port scan looks for a response on an open port, a User Datagram Protocol (UDP) scan will actually look for closed ports. When a UDP scan hits a port that is closed, a specific error will be returned which proves that there is, in fact, a live system at that IP address.

When identifying assets you should document some key things. Table 11.1 summarizes what you should document, and why.

Table 11.1 Things to Document When Identifying Assets

What to Document	Why to Document It
IP address of the asset	Even if your organization is using dynamically assigned IP addresses (DHCP), you cannot scan a system unless you know the IP address. In addition, keeping track of the IP address that a system is assigned leaves a good audit trail in the event that an incident needs to be investigated.
MAC address of the asset	As we discussed before, this is the physical address of the system. This is a static 12-character value—for example, *00-0E-35-E9-98-A6*—that will allow you to map physical systems to the IP address assigned.

Continued

Table 11.1 continued Things to Document When Identifying Assets

What to Document	Why to Document It
DNS/NetBIOS name of the asset	This is the name of the system; typically the domain name system (DNS) name and the NetBIOS name will be the same. This is one more way to map the system to the IP address and the Media Access Control (MAC) address.
Operating system of the asset	Although obvious, this is important to the patch management process. If you don't know what your systems are running, it is difficult if not impossible to know what vulnerabilities to monitor for, and to plan the patching stages.
Listening services on the asset	One of the oldest concepts in information security is the one of least privilege. Systems should not have services listening on them that are not being used. Documenting what is listening on each system and what is needed on each system is a critical step.
Physical location of the asset	This is the physical location and department of the asset. This is an obvious thing to document, because from time to time, IT resources may have to physically access the system.
Owner of the asset	There are two data points for this category. You should know both who the typical user of the system is, as well as whom in the organization is ultimately responsible for that asset on both an IT and a management level.
Classification of the asset	This is the classification of the asset and the data contained on that asset. As we discussed, this is an important step in the entire vulnerability management process.

What Tools Exist to Help You Do It

One of the unfortunate realities that has constantly plagued IT and security administrators is the fact that no one tool does everything perfectly. This has forced many administrators to use multiple tools and to piece together the data the tools provide.

For commercial tools, we talked about many that can collect this data. Although it would be easy to simply recommend a tool, it is far better for an organization to test each product and judge for itself which one meets its minimum criteria. In Chapter 3, we talked about what a good VA tool should do for you. By using this chapter as a guide, you should be able to select the tool that is best for your organization.

If you were using the free and open source tool, Nmap, to perform these tasks, you would do the following, logged in as *root* on a *nix system or as *Administrator* on a Windows system:

```
#NMAP -sV -O -p1-65535 <ip address range> -oN <scanname.txt>
```

This would perform a scan of the specified IP range and log the host, the operating system of that host, and the services, including the version number listening on that host. The *–p* option tells Nmap to scan all TCP ports, meaning that your scans may take a long time. More information on Nmap and the various options you can use to make this first step easy to perform is available in the online documentation, and is included in the Nmap help file, which you can download from www.insecure.org. We also covered the various Nmap options in Chapter 4.

As for commercial tools, in this book we used the two leading products in our examples: Tenable Network Security's Nessus and eEye Digital Security's Retina. Here is a more complete list of commercial products that, in our opinion as practitioners, are worth taking a look at to see whether they fit into your organization:

- Retina (eEye Digital Security, www.eeye.com)
- Nessus (Tenable Network Security, www.tenablesecurity.com)
- QualysGuard (Qualys, www.qualys.com)
- Network Security Inspector (Sunbelt, www.sunbelt.com)

- IP360 (nCircle, www.ncircle.com)

- ISS Scanner (Internet Security Systems, www.iss.net)

- Foundstone (McAfee, www.mcafee.com)

- BindView bvControl (Symantec, www.bindview.com)

Step Two: Categorize Your Assets

What You Need to Do

As we discussed in Chapter 4, ISO17799 states:

> The organization should be in a position to understand what information assets it holds, and to manage their security appropriately.

Asset classification is the art of assigning a value to an asset in order to organize it according to its sensitivity to loss or disclosure. The major steps required for asset classification and controls are:

- Identification of assets

- Accountability of assets

- Classification of assets

Although it is great to simply repeat the high-level information provided by the various standards, this doesn't really specify exactly what you need to do to classify your assets. Basically, you need to organize every asset in a way that best suits your organization. The example we used in Chapter 4 was based on the following criteria:

- Physical location

- Organizational location

- Asset classification

Physical location is quite obvious because this is the actual place the asset is located. You can use a city or even an office name, which is a good idea if you have multiple locations in one city.

> **NOTE**
>
> An issue that many organizations have struggled with is remote workers. If you have employees who work offsite or from home you should be sure to add them to a group or create a separate group for them. Imagine the impact to your organization and your career if the home workstation of a developer who telecommutes is compromised and is used to attack the corporate network because you failed to account for it in your vulnerability management program.

Organizational location is valuable because it helps determine who the asset owner or owners may be in your organization. For smaller organizations this isn't a big deal, but larger corporations can have multiple departments or even multiple suborganizations, each with their own IT functions.

Finally, asset classification is the stage in which you determine the value of the asset and assign it a classification, such as *unclassified*, *internal only*, or *confidential*. Base this classification on the impact the asset or the data on that asset would have to your organization if it was lost or stolen.

Why You Need to Do It

Although asset classification, and probably asset identification, is typically considered to be very boring and time consuming, it is important, especially for large organizations where it can be difficult to perform a full network assessment in a timely manner. As corporations grow, their networks grow, meaning that it takes a longer time to scan these networks. Many organizations battle this by deploying distributed scanners, all reporting to a central reporting server, but deploying enough scanners can quickly become cost prohibitive, and the reports they generate can become a new bottleneck. So, the solution is to scan parts of your network in stages, starting with the more-critical assets and finishing with the less-critical ones. In addition, critical assets or critical locations are typically scanned more often as well.

It's also good to perform this step in case an attacker compromises your network. Without knowing every detail of your network, along with their value to the organization, you cannot possibly determine what the lapse in security cost the organization.

How to Do It

To perform this step you must have completed the preceding step, because the data from the first step is essential. For an organization that has never undergone this sort of task, this will be difficult and time consuming to accomplish.

During this stage, you must sort every system that was detected in step one, into categories based on location and importance. It can be helpful to sort each group in the following way:

- Geographic location 1/Confidential
- Geographic location 2/Confidential
- Geographic location 3/Confidential
- Geographic location 1/Internal Only
- Geographic location 2/Internal Only
- Geographic location 3/Internal Only
- Geographic location 1/Unclassified
- Geographic location 2/Unclassified
- Geographic location 3/Unclassified

Obviously your organization may have more or fewer geographic locations, and in some cases more or fewer asset classifications.

What Tools Exist to Help You Do It

This is an area on which vendors have not focused in terms of providing great solutions. Data classification tools are available, but none of them supports the rest of the process, and VA tools do not completely support the asset classification process.

Some tools try to fill this gap, but in our opinion (and please email us if you think otherwise), none of them completely helps with this step. In all honesty, we have found that what works best is to create a spreadsheet with your favorite spreadsheet application and then import that data into your VA tool, or manually create your groups if your tool doesn't support importing.

Step Three: Create a Baseline Scan of Assets

What You Need to Do

After you have documented and classified your assets, you can move on to the more fun and interesting step of actually performing a baseline vulnerability assessment. In Chapter 5, we addressed the issue of credentialed scans versus noncredentialed scans. Table 11.2 provides a summary.

Table 11.2 Credentialed Scans versus Noncredentialed Scans

Option	What It Does	Benefits	Problems
Scan without credentials	The scanner will attempt to audit the target systems without authenticating to those systems with any user rights.	This gives you the "hacker's" view of a system, as the typical attacker would not have credentials.	Scanning in this manner will not identify the patch level of the system, or vulnerabilities that a user with credentials could leverage.
Scan with credentials	The scanner will use administrator-level credentials to connect to the target system and audit Registry entries, files, and other configuration options.	This gives a more complete scan of the system and allows the scanner the capability to check for vulnerabilities in things such as client-side software, as well as configuration issues that equate to vulnerabilities.	Some feel that this does not give a true hacker's view of a system. Although this is a true statement, getting the true hacker's view of a system and actually securing a system are two different things.

Based on the benefits and drawbacks listed in Table 11.2, it is clear that if your goal is to improve security through vulnerability management, you will want to run your scans with credentials because that will give you the most coverage. There is also the question of internal versus external scans. For this step you will want to concentrate on running your scans internally. If you are responsible for a large organization, these scans may take some time to complete. It is important that you scan all assets in this step, because you are creating a baseline of your current security posture.

Why You Need to Do It

This step is pretty obvious, because it is the most important step of a vulnerability management program: detecting vulnerabilities. This step is your first initial scan which will create a baseline of your current security posture and give you a point of reference to track improvements.

How to Do It

In this step, you will leverage the work you put into the preceding two steps. Smaller organizations (those with networks that have fewer than 500 hosts) will not need to go to as much trouble as larger organizations, so if you are lucky enough to have fewer than 500 hosts to manage, you can skip scanning by asset group and simply follow the directions we provide here for every asset on your network.

If you are scanning a larger network, you unfortunately will not have the luxury of simply entering your network addresses and scanning, because the time required to perform large scans, regardless of what tool you use, is dramatically high when running an in-depth scan such as that which we need to do to create an initial baseline scan.

As noted earlier, this is where the asset groups you created in step two can be very helpful. As we discussed in Chapter 5, you will want to start with the most-critical assets and work your way down to the less-critical ones. When you conduct your scans be sure to check your tool's settings to ensure that you are:

- Enabling a full port scan for both TCP and UDP ports.
- Enabling operating system detection.
- Enabling all vulnerability checks.

If any of the VA tool vendors were to read the preceding list, they would immediately object because the options we suggested will cause your scans to take a considerable amount of time to complete. In this case, this is a good thing because you want your baseline to be as complete as possible, which means you have to scan for everything. To get around the time issues such scans create you should consider running your scanners in a distributed model, which means having multiple scanning engines scanning different asset groups and reporting the results to a central console or reporting server.

Enabling a full port scan on both TCP and UDP ports will allow you to identify every potential service running on the system—both legitimate and illegitimate. Remember, a lot of Trojans and other malware use high ports to communicate, so this is also a great way to detect any systems that are compromised.

Operating system detection will help you fill out the list of assets and what is running on them. As we have said multiple times, this is an important step when it comes to monitoring for both new vulnerabilities and patches.

Enabling all vulnerability checks, while adding to the scan time, is the only way you will get a complete list of all vulnerabilities, configurations, and policy issues with your systems. On the positive side, you won't have to always scan for all ports and all vulnerabilities, as you will see in upcoming steps.

What Tools Exist to Help You Do It

In this book, we used the two leading products in our examples: Tenable Network Security's Nessus and eEye Digital Security's Retina. Here is a more complete list of commercial products that, in our opinion, are worth investigating to see whether they fit into your organization:

- Retina (eEye Digital Security, www.eeye.com)
- Nessus (Tenable Network Security, www.tenablesecurity.com)
- QualysGuard (Qualys, www.qualys.com)
- Network Security Inspector (Sunbelt, www.sunbelt.com)
- IP360 (nCircle, www.ncircle.com)
- ISS Scanner (Internet Security Systems, www.iss.net)
- Foundstone (McAfee, www.mcafee.com)
- BindView bvControl (Symantec, www.bindview.com)

Remember to judge these tools based on the criteria presented in Chapter 3, as well as additional criteria that are specific for your organization.

Step Four: Perform a Penetration Test on Certain Assets

What You Need to Do

Those of you who have experienced vulnerability assessment and management before are probably asking "Why haven't they covered penetration testing?" Although pen testing is arguably a waste of time and money for most organizations (see sidebar, "Wasted Security Budget?"), it does still have its place in the vulnerability management life cycle.

NOTE

We are sure the comment in this chapter about pen testing being somewhat of a waste of time and money will raise some eyebrows, so hopefully we can explain here exactly what we meant by that comment. Most organizations will hire a third-party firm to perform a pen test before doing any of their own work to build an infrastructure. This almost guarantees that the pen test team will successfully compromise your hosts. Does it not make more sense to build an infrastructure first, and then to test it via a pen test?

The argument that a pen test is needed to show that the infrastructure, or better yet, the budget for the infrastructure, is needed is no longer valid. Today, every executive understands the need for an effective information security program.

Now that you have a plan in place, it is time to perform a pen test. Because you can do this only if you have a plan in place, you need to make sure that you have already set aside time and, more important, money for steps five through eight before performing this step. Otherwise, consider this stage completely optional and, in times of budget cuts, the first budget item to be cut.

That being said, there is great value in performing a pen test on assets that are accessible externally to your organization.

Why You Need to Do It

Although the value of a pen test is up for debate, when such tests are conducted at the right time and on the right assets, they can be very helpful. This is truly the only way you can get a real attacker's view of your network, as we explained in previous chapters of this book.

How to Do It

You have a number of options when performing a pen test. You can do it yourself or you can contract the work out to a third party. When performing this step yourself you will have the advantage of having a more accurate view of your network versus if an outside third party conducted the test.

You will want to concentrate on only the assets that are accessible from the outside world. If yours is one of the unlucky organizations that have multiple assets exposed to the world, you will want to approach the pen test in the same manner that you approach the baseline vulnerability assessment. Start with the highest-risk assets and work down to the lower-risk ones.

Remember, depending on your network configuration, each asset will have, or should have, been scanned during step three, but from the inside of your corporate network. So this is also a good time to compare the results of the pen test with those of the vulnerability scan from the internal interface. In addition, note that most pen tests include some level of application security testing that a typical vulnerability scanner cannot perform. So to perform your pen test you will want to be sure to cover the following steps:

- Profile external systems
- Profile external applications
- Identify potential architectural weaknesses
- Identify potential exploitable vulnerabilities
- Exploit weaknesses and vulnerabilities
- Report

In your profile of external systems you will document everything that is publicly available about your externally facing network. This includes open ports, DNS records, and domain name records.

You also should document externally facing applications, including what the application is running, what types of user input it accepts, and what type of data is saved on the application servers. Externally, it should be possible to get an idea of the general architecture and layout of your applications.

Once you have created the initial profile it should be easy to identify both potential architectural weaknesses that can expose systems to unnecessary risk, as well as potential vulnerabilities that could be exploited. After you've validated each weakness, you should create a report that shows what was found and what was exploited. It is important to also document potential issues because the failure of your pen testing team to exploit something does not equal system security, and these weaknesses should still be manually addressed.

What Tools Exist to Help You Do It

What tools you use for your pen test will depend on whether you are doing the work yourself or are outsourcing the project to a third party. In terms of free open source tools, you have a lot of choices. The following two tools are among the more popular today:

- Framework (Metasploit, www.metasploit.org)
- Nmap (Insecure.org, www.insecure.org)

On the application side of the house, we recommend using the resources and tools available at the Open Web Application Security Project (OWASP), located at www.owasp.org.

Multiple options also are available in the commercial tools arena. Probably the best and most advanced pen testing tool is Core Impact; the following list includes another one you may want to check out:

- Core Impact (Core Security Technologies, www.coresecurity.com)
- Immunity CANVAS (Immunity Inc., www.immunitysec.com)

In the application security arena these commercial tools are useful:

- AppDetective (Application Security Inc., www.appsecinc.com)
- AppScan (Watchfire Corp., www.watchfire.com)

Step Five: Remediate Vulnerabilities and Risk

What You Need to Do

Each of the four preceding steps should have generated a lot of reports, each with their own level of detail. Once you have progressed to this step, you should have a list of every asset on your network and what vulnerabilities and risks those assets face.

This is the step where you actually go out and fix the vulnerabilities present in your systems. When you get to this step, remember our definition of a vulnerability from Chapter 1:

> A vulnerability is a software or hardware bug or misconfiguration that a malicious individual can exploit.

We remind you of this because many people fail to realize that issues such as configuration management also apply when dealing with vulnerabilities, because a misconfigured system that is completely patched can still be vulnerable to a number of issues that can lead to system compromise.

Why You Need to Do It

The reason to remediate at this stage should be obvious. You have a long list of vulnerable systems from your baseline scans, so now you must bring these systems up to a secure state before moving forward with your vulnerability management plans.

This step isn't meant to replace step seven, but it is meant to set the framework and make step seven a lot easier to accomplish.

How to Do It

The larger your organization is, the harder this step will be to complete. We suggest that you approach this in much the same way that we have recommended you approach large-scale vulnerability assessments. Start with higher-risk assets and finish with lower-risk ones.

There are two different types of issues that you will have to remediate. The first, of course, is vulnerabilities, and the second is configuration issues. To add a level of confusion to your remediation plans, some vulnerabilities may not have patches and may need to be addressed via configuration changes.

Unfortunately, it isn't a safe bet to simply apply patches and configuration changes, so the first step of remediation is to take a sample of your systems and make those your test case. These are the systems that you will use to test patches and configuration changes, so be sure to get a true sampling of your network. When choosing systems think about what custom applications and third-party software may react adversely to patch or configuration changes. These are the systems you want in your test group.

Once you have tested each configuration change and patch on your test systems, you will be ready to roll out your changes to the entire network. Again, you will want to start with the higher-risk systems and move to the lower-risk ones when applying the changes and patches.

NOTE

One concept that can be difficult to grasp for new security practitioners is that of accepting risk. There will be systems on your network which, for whatever reason, you will not be able to patch or reconfigure. Although this goes against building a secure infrastructure, it is a reality in most corporate environments. Typically in such cases, the asset owner will sign a document that lists the security risks and the reasons for not making the necessary changes to the system. As a security professional, you will become very familiar with the phrase *cover your ass*. Although this document will do that, you also should try to place such systems on their own network that have mitigating controls to prevent attacks.

One of the mistakes that many IT and security administrators make is that once they have rolled out their configuration changes, they fail to validate that the changes took place and that the systems are actually secure. That's why it's important to repeat step three after you have patched. You might be surprised to see that some systems, for various reasons, were not actually patched or reconfigured. With that in mind, these are the steps we recommend you follow during this stage:

1. Create an accurate sampling of your assets.

2. Test all patches and configuration issues on your sampling.

3. Document results and document accepted risk for sign-off.

4. Roll out patches and configuration changes.

5. Repeat step three to validate roll-out.

What Tools Exist to Help You Do It

This is not an area where you will find a lot of open source tools that can help you, so you will be forced to look at a commercial solution. One such solution that we recommend is ECM, from Configuresoft, but do not take our word for what tools to use, because your organization may have different requirements. Do, however, review Chapter 8 and, as we recommend when picking any tool, create a list of your requirements and evaluate each tool and how it meets your requirements. Here are some tools to look at:

- ECM (Configuresoft, www.configuresoft.com)

- PatchLink Update (PatchLink Corp., www.patchlink.com)

- Microsoft Systems Update Services (Microsoft, www.microsoft.com)

- bvControl (Symantec, www.symantec.com)

- UpdateEXPERT (St. Bernard Software, www.stbernard.com)

Step Six: Create a Vulnerability Assessment Schedule

What You Need to Do

By now, you should have a pretty good idea of how long it will take to not only scan your entire network, but also remediate any issues found. So, now is the time to create a schedule to continue your vulnerability assessments.

Why You Need to Do It

As we said in previous chapters, and even in this one, a vulnerability manage-ment program is a perpetual activity which, although time consuming, does get easier over time. This is the step which, if you approach it logically, can make the entire process easy to deal with.

How to Do It

By now, you should have noticed a theme of starting with critical assets and working down to less-critical ones. This step is no different, and although your schedule will depend entirely on how paranoid your organization is, there are some basic guidelines to follow concerning when to perform assess-ments. Like we said in Chapter 5, there are three specific triggers that should cause you to initiate a scan of your network:

1. A new threat becomes evident and you want to verify that your sys-tems are not vulnerable or identify systems that are vulnerable.

2. A vendor releases a patch or a number of patches and you want to verify that your systems are patched and are not vulnerable, or some other event causes wide-scale changes to your environment.

3. You want a point-in-time assessment of your current security posture and a list of vulnerabilities affecting your organization.

How can you schedule around these three triggers so that your vulnera-bility management plans are more proactive than reactive? Luckily, many ven-dors that are serious about supporting their enterprise customers publish specific patch dates. If your vendor doesn't follow a specific schedule, you can create your own which, although hard to pin down, will at least let you plan scan and patch events more clearly. Table 11.3 provides a sample schedule we recommend for implementing vulnerability assessments.

Table 11.3 A Sample Schedule for Implementing Vulnerability Assessments

Scan Trigger	What to Scan	When to Scan	What to Scan For
Point-in-time assessment	Confidential Asset Groups	The last Monday of every month	All vulnerabilities and configuration issues.
Point-in-time assessment	Internal Only Asset Groups	The last Friday of every month	All vulnerabilities and configuration issues.
Point-in-time assessment	Unclassified Asset Groups	The second-to-last Monday of every quarter (three-month schedule)	All vulnerabilities and configuration issues.
Vendor releases a patch, or some other event causes wide-scale changes	Confidential Asset Groups	Immediately after the trigger event, and again after remediation is completed	Scan for the vendor-released patches or issues that the patch addresses. If a wide-scale change is the trigger, scan for all vulnerabilities related to the change.
Vendor releases a patch, or some other event causes wide-scale changes	Internal Only Asset Groups	Immediately after Confidential Asset Group scans are complete, and again after remediation is completed	Scan for the vendor-released patches or issues that the patch addresses. If a wide-scale change is the trigger, scan for all vulnerabilities related to the change.

Continued

Table 11.3 continued A Sample Schedule for Implementing Vulnerability Assessments

Scan Trigger	What to Scan	When to Scan	What to Scan For
Vendor releases a patch, or some other event causes wide-scale changes	Unclassified Asset Groups	Immediately after Internal Only Asset Group scans are complete, and again after remediation is completed	Scan for the vendor-released patches or issues that the patch addresses. If a wide-scale change is the trigger, scan for all vulnerabilities related to the change.
A new threat becomes evident	Confidential Asset Groups	Immediately after the trigger event, and again after remediation is completed	Scan for operating systems, applications, or configurations that are related to the new threat.
A new threat becomes evident	Internal Only Asset Groups	Immediately after Confidential Asset Group scans are complete, and again after remediation is completed	Scan for operating systems, applications, or configurations that are related to the new threat.
A new threat becomes evident	Unclassified Asset Groups	Immediately after Internal Only Asset Group scans are complete, and again after remediation is completed	Scan for operating systems, applications, or configurations that are related to the new threat.

As you can see, only one of the three trigger events is something you can actually plan for: you can partially plan for the patch release trigger if your vendor has a set schedule or if you are able to create your own schedule. By breaking the scans into groups, you decrease the amount of work required at each stage, and therefore, decrease the length of time from vulnerability to patch.

Step Seven: Create a Patch and Change Management Process

What You Need to Do

We listed this as a separate step, but in reality, you should do this the same time you create your VA schedule (step six), because each of these steps relies on the other. Any organization that allows change to its computing assets without some sort of logical testing and planning is doomed to experience long system downtime and will never achieve a successful vulnerability management program.

To prevent this from happening you need to create a process that covers all potential problems that patching or reconfiguration can cause. In our experience, this process will never be perfect, and it should be open to evolving with an organization and account for potential shortcomings. Change, when managed properly, can be a good thing, but even the process for handling change needs to be adaptable.

Why You Need to Do It

As we mentioned earlier, if computing asset changes are not planned for properly, the changes will fail, and ultimately, your security initiatives will fail along with them. You need to plan, test, track, and then retest all system changes. This will ensure that any bad changes will be caught before they affect the overall user base, and it will ensure that the organization understands and plans for any impact to its security that these changes will create.

How to Do It

When creating your change and patch management process, you need to ensure that you follow these steps:

1. Create a test group that is a sampling of all assets on your network.

2. Document the proposed change in detail.

3. Document a "roll-back" plan to undo the change.

4. Obtain sign-off from asset owners on the planned change.

5. Implement the change on your test group.

6. Monitor for adverse effects.

7. Roll out the change enterprisewide if the test group is successful.

8. Undo the change if the test group is not successful.

9. Initiate step 6.

Although this appears to be a lengthy list of steps that could be time consuming and not conducive to quickly addressing vulnerabilities, with the right tools and the proper organizational buy-in, this process can move fairly quickly and even account for emergency changes. The key is proper documentation and testing; this will save you a lot of work when things go badly.

What Tools Exist to Help You Do It

Unfortunately, some of the best, and even the worst, change management tools we have had the pleasure to work with over the years have been custom-built systems. That being said, there are a lot of commercial products that can help you, and some of them even integrate with some of the more popular VA tools. Here's a list of tools we like:

■ Tivoli (IBM, www.ibm.com)

■ netViz Change Management (netViz, www.netviz.com)

■ BMC Remedy (BMC Software, www.bmc.com)

Step Eight: Monitor for New Risks to Assets

What You Need to Do

This is the final step of our eight-step program to vulnerability management, and it's probably the one that can be the most frustrating for IT security engineers. Once you have completed the preceding seven steps you may feel like you are almost done, but unfortunately, now the hard work begins. After all of the work you put into creating a baseline and a plan for changes, you now have to sit back and wait for events that you have no control over but will create hard work for your team.

This is the reality of the security practitioner: just when your systems are secure, you have to remain vigilant and wait for the coming storm.

Why You Need to Do It

Although it would be easy to bury your head in the sand and pretend that after performing steps one through seven, you are done with this process and your organization is secure, as any attacker would gladly prove to you this is not the best strategy, because eventually something outside of your control will impact the security of your network.

So, the only thing you can do is constantly monitor for new events that have an impact on your security and deal with them in a timely manner. Think about the first chapter in this book, where we discussed windows of vulnerability. This is the key point to vulnerability management: reducing the length of time those windows are open.

How to Do It

Now that we have made you a little more paranoid than you already are, we will try to help you deal with that paranoid feeling that everyone is out to get you and your organization's network, because the reality *is* that everyone is out to get you and your organization's network.

Before you can monitor for new threats, you need to know what the threats could be. The following is a list of things you need to keep your IT security staff aware of on a constant basis. We are sure you will notice that all of these were trigger events for a vulnerability assessment:

- Vendor-released patches
- Configuration weaknesses
- 0 day vulnerability releases
- Large-scale attacks

> **NOTE**
>
> We addressed this issue at a high level in Chapter 1, where we talked about a speech given at the Black Hat Briefings in Europe, pertaining to vendors silently fixing vulnerabilities in their patches. Most vendors practice this and at least one vendor has admitted to rating the risk of the issues it is patching to reflect the true risk of the actual vulnerability it is patching. Although this makes sense, it makes it difficult for organizations to understand the true risk of a patch, and even more disturbing, it prevents vendors from offering signature-based (and reactive) protections from truly protecting against all potential issues.

Each issue in the preceding list can have an impact on your organization's security, so you need to come up with an easy way to say "in the know" when it comes to emerging issues. Unfortunately, this requires a lot of work.

What Tools Exist to Help You Do It

One of the ways you can track vendor-released patches is to subscribe to vendor patch release mailing lists. Table 11.4 provides a list of popular vendors and where you can find information on their release processes. You also should create a list of vendors you use in your environment (do not forget application vendors).

Table 11.4 Vendor Patch Release Mailing Lists

Vendor	Patch Release Information
Microsoft	www.microsoft.com/technet/security/default.mspx
Apple	www.apple.com/support/security/
Citrix	www.citrix.com/site/jumpPage.asp?pageID=22214
Sun Microsystems	http://sunsolve.sun.com/pub-cgi/show.pl?target=patchpage
Oracle	www.oracle.com/technology/deploy/security/alerts.htm
Red Hat Linux	www.redhat.com/security/updates/
Hewlett-Packard	www1.itrc.hp.com/service/index.do
Mozilla	www.mozilla.org/security/#Security_Alerts

Continued

Table 11.4 continued Vendor Patch Release Mailing Lists

Vendor	Patch Release Information
IBM	www-306.ibm.com/software/sw-bycategory/
Cisco	www.cisco.com/iam/unified/ipcc1/Cisco_Product_Security_Overview.htm
Juniper	www.juniper.net/support/security/security_notices.html
Nortel Networks	www130.nortelnetworks.com/go/main.jsp

Configuration weaknesses, security advisories, 0 day releases, and even large-scale attacks are typically reported via various mailing lists. A great resource for getting a complete list of every information security mailing list comes from our friends at Neohapsis, http://archives.neohapsis.com.

Table 11.5 provides a short list of good mailing list resources that you can use to monitor for various security issues.

Table 11.5 Mailing List Resources

List Name	URL
VulnWatch	www.vulnwatch.org
VulnDiscuss	www.vulnwatch.org
BugTraq	www.securityfocus.com/archive/1/description
Full-Disclosure (warning: unmoderated)	https://lists.grok.org.uk/mailman/listinfo/full-disclosure
North America Network Operators Group (NANOG)	www.nanog.org/mailinglist.html
Patch Management	www.patchmanagement.org/
Incidents Mailing List	www.securityfocus.com/archive/75/description

The typical network is a diverse environment, so manually monitoring all of these resources can be time consuming. As such, some organizations go so far as to hire security analysts whose job is to do nothing but monitor for new threats. Luckily, some vendors have stepped up to the plate and created solutions that are designed to help you battle the massive amounts of information this work generates, and concentrate only on the issues that matter to your organization. As with any software tool, we highly recommend that you test each solution based on your own criteria before committing to a specific one. There are a lot of players in this market, some with a lot of experience and others who are quite new to it, so be cautious with your decisions:

- Symantec DeepSight (www.symantec.com/Products/enterprise?c=prodcat&refId=1017)

- Computer Associates eTrust (www3.ca.com/services/subpractice.aspx?ID=5012)

- FrSIRT Alerting Service (www.frsirt.com/english/services/)

- Telus Assurent (www.assurent.com/)

- CyberTrust (www.cybertrust.com/solutions/managed_security_services/)

- Secunia (http://corporate.secunia.com/products/9/vulnerability_management_products_enterprise)

Summary

Here we are, at the end of our eight-step vulnerability management process and, of course, the end of the book. Hopefully, you have learned a thing or two that will help you design and implement a vulnerability management plan which will enable you to do your job and, most important, secure your networks.

We have covered a lot of concepts, each of them important but none of them a security solution on its own. Combine each step outlined in this book and summarized in this chapter, and you truly will be able to take your organization from vulnerability to patch in a quick but accurate manner.

We have presented various security tools here, and although our professional bias has led us to use specific tools in our examples, we want to point out yet again that you should select your tools based on your specific requirements. A tool that has worked great for one of us may not work as well in your environment or do exactly what you want it to, so evaluate carefully before spending those precious security budget dollars.

As you probably already have realized, the life of a security practitioner is one of constant education, so we have done our best to share with you the various resources on the Internet that we have used in our careers, to stay ahead of the curve and deal with security issues.

In this day and age, we are all faced with various compliance issues and standards against which we are regulated. This book explained some of the regulatory and compliance issues that may be affecting your organization, and how you can deal with them.

Finally, this book, and more specifically, this chapter, demonstrated the close link between vulnerability assessment, patch management, configuration management, and threat awareness in a way that should help you understand that each of these is a required step when dealing with vulnerabilities, and that each truly works to secure your network.

Of course, the one topic this book did not cover, because it requires a separate book in itself, is network defense technologies for detecting and defending against attacks. It is important to understand that although this book has given you a framework that will keep your computing assets from being compromised easily, we did not touch on the difficult subject of monitoring for and responding to actual attacks. We'll leave that as an idea for another quality Syngress book.

Legal Principles for Information Security Evaluations

by Bryan Cunningham

Solutions in this chapter:

- Uncle Sam Wants You: How Your Company's Information Security Can Affect U.S. National Security (and Vice Versa)

- Legal Standards Relevant to Information Security

- Selected Laws and Regulations

- Do It Right or Bet the Company: Tools to Mitigate Legal Liability

- What to Cover in IEM Contracts[2]

- The First Thing We Do...? Why You Want Your Lawyers Involved From Start to Finish

- ☑ Solutions Fast Track
- ☑ Frequently Asked Questions

WARNING: THIS APPENDIX IS NOT LEGAL ADVICE

This appendix provides an overview of a number of legal issues faced by information security evaluation professionals and their customers. Hopefully, it will alert readers to the issues on which they should consult qualified legal counsel experienced in information security law. This appendix, however, does not, and cannot, provide any legal advice or counsel to its readers. Readers should not, under any circumstances, purport to rely on anything in this appendix as legal advice. Likewise, following any of the suggestions in this appendix does not create an "advice-of-counsel" defense to regulatory or law enforcement action or to civil legal claims. Readers involved in information security are strongly urged to retain qualified, experienced legal counsel.

Introduction

You have watched the scene hundreds of times. The buttoned-down, by-the-book police lieutenant and the tough-as-nails, throw-out-the-rules-to-save-lives detective debate in front of the police chief. A child is kidnapped and the clock is ticking; a murder is about to be committed and the judge will not issue a warrant. The world-weary police chief has to make a split-second decision. Is there a way to live within the law but save the child? How does the police chief balance the duty to protect the people of the city with fealty to the rulebook? Is there a creative way to do both? On television, this scene usually happens in an aging, shabby, police headquarters office furnished with Styrofoam cups of stale coffee, full ashtrays, fading green walls, and rickety metal desks. Now, imagine this same drama being performed on an entirely different stage.

Uncle Sam Wants You: How Your Company's Information Security Can Affect U.S. National Security (and Vice Versa)

It is September 2011. As the tenth anniversary of al-Qa'ida's devastating attacks on our nation approaches, the president is faced with increasingly clear intelligence that what's left of the infamous terrorist group has fulfilled its long-standing ambition to be able to launch a devastating attack on the U.S. through cyberspace. Perhaps they will disable our air traffic control or financial exchange network. Perhaps they will penetrate Supervisory Control and Data Acquisition (SCADA) systems to attack dams or other energy facilities. Perhaps they will shut down power to hundreds of hospitals where surgery is underway. Or maybe they will directly target our heavily information systems-dependent military forces. The targets and magnitude are far from clear.

As September 11, 2011 dawns though, it becomes obvious that cyber-attacks are underway, even though the perpetrators are undetermined. What becomes increasingly clear is that the attacks are striking us directly, not from overseas; from dozens, perhaps hundreds, of university and corporate servers right here in the U.S. The scene that follows plays out in the stately, wood-paneled, electronically sophisticated confines of the Situation Room in the West Wing of the White House. Our protagonists here are The Secretary of Defense, the Director of National Intelligence, the National and Homeland Security Advisors to the president, and the Attorney General. And, of course, in this scene, the decision maker carrying the weight of the world is not a big city police chief, but the President of the United States.

In all likelihood, the president will receive conflicting advice from his senior advisors. Some will insist that U.S. law prohibits the government from disabling the servers within the U.S. from which the attacks are coming, or even trying to learn who is behind the attacks. These advisors urge caution, despite intelligence indicating that the attacks are actually coming from terrorists overseas, using the servers in the U.S. as "zombies" to carry out their plot. These advisors will further argue that the president has no option but to use the cumbersome and time-consuming criminal law process to combat these attacks. The attorney general's law enforcement officers must collect information, go to a federal judge, and get a warrant or, in this case, dozens or hundreds of warrants, to try to determine who is behind the attacks (unless emergency access without a warrant is authorized by law). Even in such emergencies, organizing and directing law enforcement control over hundreds or thousands of zombies is an overwhelming effort.

Other officials will advise the president that by the time any progress will be made going the law enforcement route, devastating damage to the critical infrastructure may already have occurred, and the overseas perpetrators disappeared, covering their tracks. These advisors will argue strenuously that the president has ample constitutional and legal authority to use any element of U.S. power (military, intelligence, or law enforcement) to defeat the attacks and defend the nation. They will argue that using the normal law enforcement route would not only be futile, but would amount to an abdication of the president's primary constitutional responsibility to protect our nation and its people from attack. Finally, they will respectfully remind the president of the sage advice of Vietnam War era U.S. Supreme Court Justice Arthur Goldberg that "While the constitution protects against invasions of individual rights, it is not a suicide pact."[3]

As a purely legal and constitutional matter, the president's more hawkish advisors will likely be correct.[4] However, that in no way will lessen the terrible moral, ethical, and political burden that will fall on the president: whether or not, in the absence of perfect information, to order counterattacks on information infrastructures inside the U.S.

While reasonable experts still disagree on the probability that such a scenario will arise in the next decade (and there are differences of opinion even among the authors of this chapter), most agree that the scenario is technically possible.[5] The U.S. National Strategy to Secure Cyberspace describes the following necessary conditions (which exist today) for "relative measures of damage to occur [to the United States] on a national level, affecting the networks and systems on which the Nation depends:

- Potential adversaries have the intent.

- Tools that support malicious activities are broadly available.

- Vulnerabilities of the Nation's systems are many and well known.[6]

Thus, even in an unclassified publication, the U.S. government has confirmed that our adversaries, whether terrorists, rogue states, or more traditional nation-state enemies, possess a classic combination for the existence of threat: intent + capability + opportunity. If September 11, 2001 taught us anything as a nation, it is that when these three are present, we had better be prepared.

More concretely, senior Federal Bureau of Investigation (FBI) officials and others have testified before Congress that terrorist groups have demonstrated a clear interest in hackers and hacking skills; the FBI predicts that, "terrorist groups will either develop or hire hackers."[7] Material found in former al-Qa'ida strongholds in Afghanistan showed al-Qa'ida's interest in developing cyber-terror skills.[8] Former U.S. government "cyberczar" Richard Clarke pointed out that a University of Idaho student, arrested by FBI agents on allegations of terror links, was seeking a PhD in cyber security. Clarke warns that, "similarly to the fact that some of the Sept. 11 hijackers had training in flight training, some of the people that we're seeing now related to [al-Qa'ida] had training in computer security."[9] Several experts, including cyber experts at Sandia National Laboratories and the U.S. Naval Postgraduate school, have bluntly asserted that adversaries could disrupt significant portions of the U.S. power grid, for time periods ranging from minutes, to days, and even longer.[10]

Cyber attacks have already been used to disrupt online elections in Canada, and attacks by terrorist groups have been launched to "crash" government computers during elections in Indonesia, Sri Lanka, and Mexico.[11] Finally, apart from terrorist groups and rogue states, a number of nations potentially adversarial to the U.S. now openly include cyber warfare as part of their existing military doctrine, including China and Russia.[12]

This scene, then, is plausible,[13] except that we will be lucky if it takes until 2011 to play out.

Many international legal experts assert that, under internationally recognized laws of armed conflict, attacks by foreign nations or international terrorists using bits and bytes through cyberspace can be acts of war just as can the use of guns or bombs or fuel-laden airliners.[14] If a nation determines that a cyber attack is an act of war against it, that determination, in turn, triggers a number of rights on the part of those attacked to take defensive or responsive action against their attackers.[15] Recognizing the threat of a cyber attack and the potential need for more than a law enforcement response, President Bush in 2003 announced a new U.S. policy with regard to such attacks:

> "When a nation, terrorist group, or other adversary attacks the United States through cyberspace, the United States response need not be limited to criminal prosecution. The United States reserves the right to respond in an appropriate manner. The United States will be prepared for such contingencies."[16]

In a cyber attack (unlike in a conventional military attack), it may be difficult for decision makers to know against whom to take action to stop the attack and/or respond. Unlike a terrorist bombing, though, or even the heinous September 11, 2001 attacks, a cyber attack may continue for a long enough period of time that rapid defensive action may dramatically reduce the damage done to the critical infrastructure and economy, even where the perpetrator is still unknown.

Thus, a cyber attack in progress using "zombied" servers inside the U.S. will present decision makers with a uniquely vexing dilemma. If they do nothing in the initial minutes and hours after the attack is underway, they may allow far greater damage than if they take decisive action to stop the attack and disable the attacking machines. Taking such action, however, risks damage or destruction to the zombied servers themselves, perhaps without identifying the guilty parties. Further, doing so can destroy information that may be needed later to identify and apprehend the perpetrator(s).

Making the situation even more dangerous and complex is the fact that, "distinguishing between malicious activity originating from criminals, nation state actors, and terrorists in real time is difficult."[17] In many cases, affirmative attribution will be nearly impossible with today's technology. Thus, decision makers facing the agonizing choice of taking action to disable or destroy zombied servers inside the U.S. or risking greater damage to our nation if they wait, may not know in time to make a sound decision on whether a true attack is underway or whether what looks like the initial stages of an attack is instead other malicious activity.

What does this mean to information security evaluation professionals and their customers? First and foremost, it means that *you do not want the "zombied" servers used in a cyber attack to be yours.* When the U.S. (or another nation)[18] decides to mount an official response against the hijacked servers being used to launch an attack, it will be a very bad day for the entity whose servers are being used. Additionally, though prudent information security consultants will remain current on all potential threat vectors for purposes of protecting your customers' networks, the identity of any particular threat will be largely irrelevant, even if the origin could be determined. Custodians of sensitive information of any kind have myriad reasons to develop and maintain a reasonable information security posture: business operational needs; preventing economic loss and industrial espionage; mitigating potential litigation, regulatory, and prosecution risks; and maintaining a reputation for responsible security vis-à-vis others in the same business.

The risk of involuntarily becoming part of a cyber attack, or defending against such an attack, adds another important incentive to do what most businesses and educational institutions already recognize as the right thing to do. Unlike other motivations for information security, however, avoiding involvement in a cyber attack is important even if an organization does not maintain any "sensitive" information. Unlike "traditional" hackers, criminals, and others who might exploit information security vulnerabilities, terrorists do not ignore companies simply because they are unable to find sensitive information. Instead, terrorists care about what damage can be done using your servers as proxies. And governments (ours or others) also will not care what information you have or do not have, if it is determined that your servers are involved in an attack and must be neutralized (or worse).

Second, understanding the way governments see information security provides a context for understanding how policy statements contribute to the development of a legal "duty" for individuals and organizations to secure their portions of cyberspace (discussed in greater detail below). In a nutshell, the actual knowledge or constructive knowledge (i.e., information in the public domain) of public policy mandating private "owners" of cyberspace to secure their components, may create a legal "duty" to do so, which could be the subject of future litigation. Likewise, emerging federal policy on potential cyber attacks could well contribute to the movement, already gathering steam, to further regulate private information security at the federal level.

Legal Standards Relevant to Information Security

Laws are made by politicians and politicians are driven by public and media reaction to specific incidents. Laws, therefore, are made piecemeal, at least until a critical mass is reached, which then leads lawmakers to conclude that an emerging patchwork of related, but often inconsistent, laws and regulations require an omnibus law to create consistency and greater predictability. In the absence of such a unifying federal law, particular industries or sectors are targeted for regulation as perceived problems in those industries become public. Laws and regulations covering targeted industries are gradually expanded through civil litigation and regulatory action that is limited only by the patience of judges and the imagination of plaintiffs' lawyers, prosecutors, and regulators.

This is the current situation in the law of information security. As discussed in "Selected Federal Laws" below, federal law regulates information security for, among other things, personally identifiable health care information, financial information of individuals, and, to an increasing degree, financial information in the hands of publicly traded companies. Though there is no "omnibus" federal statute governing all information security, the standards of care being created for these specific economic sectors are being "exported" to other business areas through civil litigation, including by regulators and state attorneys general.[19]

For information security practitioners, this is a good news/bad news story. Often, attempts at "comprehensive" regulation turn out to be a jumbled mess, particularly when multiple economic sectors with differing operational environments and needs are being regulated. Such regulation can be particularly ineffective (or worse) when promulgated before the private sector, which has developed solid, time-tested best practices, implements a workable solution. On the other hand, a patchwork of different federal, state, and international laws and regulations (as is the current state of information security law), can be confusing and puts a premium on careful, case-specific legal analysis and advice from qualified and experienced counsel

Selected Federal Laws

To illustrate the array of laws that impact information security, the following provides a general survey of statutes, regulations, and other laws that may govern information security consultants and their customers. This list is not exhaustive, but may help identify issues in working with customers and in understanding which "best practices" have actually been adopted in law.

Gramm-Leach-Bliley Act

One of the earliest U.S. government forays into mandating information security standards was the Gramm-Leach-Bliley Act (GLBA).[20] Section 501(b) requires each covered financial institution to establish "appropriate safeguards" to: (1) ensure the security and confidentiality of customer records and information; (2) protect against anticipated threats or hazards to the security or integrity of those records; and (3) protect against unauthorized access to, or use of, such records or information which could result in substantial harm or inconvenience to any customer.[21] GLBA required standards to be set by regulation for safeguarding customer information.[22] This task was accomplished with the promulgation of the Interagency Guidelines Establishing Standards for Safeguarding Customer Information (the "Guidelines").[23]

The Guidelines apply to Customer Information maintained by covered "financial institutions," both of which terms are broadly defined under applicable law and regulations. The Guidelines require a written security program specifically tailored to the size and complexity of each individual covered financial institution, and to the nature and scope of its activities.[24]

Under the Guidelines, covered institutions must conduct risk assessments to customer information and implement policies, procedures, training, and testing appropriate to manage reasonably foreseeable internal and external threats.[25] Institutions must also ensure that their board of directors (or a committee thereof) oversees the institution's information security measures.[26] Further, institutions must exercise due diligence in selecting and overseeing, on an ongoing basis, "service providers" (entities that maintain, process, or otherwise are permitted access to customer information through providing services to a covered institution).[27] Institutions also must ensure, by written agreement, that service providers maintain appropriate security measures.[28]

Health Insurance Portability and Accountability Act

The Health Insurance Portability and Accountability Act of 1996 (HIPAA) became law in August 1996. Section 1173(d) of HIPAA required the secretary of Health and Human Services (HHS) to adopt security standards for protection of all Electronic Protected Health Information (EPHI).[29] Development of these security standards was left to the HHS secretary, who promulgated the HIPAA Security Final Rule (the "Security Rule") in February 2003.[30] All covered entities, with the exception of small health plans, must now comply with the Security Rule.[31]

Because HIPAA has, in some ways, the most elaborate and detailed guidance available in the realm of federal law and regulation with regard to information security, we focus more on the HIPAA Security Rule than any other single federal legal provision. In addition, many of the general principles articulated in the Security Rule are common to other legal regimes dealing with information security. As a general framework, the HIPAA Security Rule: (a) mandates specific outcomes; and (b) specifies process and procedural requirements, rather than specifically mandated technical standards. The mandated outcomes for covered entities are:

- Ensuring the confidentiality, integrity, and availability of EPHI created, received, maintained, or transmitted by a covered entity[32]

- Protecting against reasonably anticipated threats or hazards to the security or integrity of such information[33]

- Protecting against reasonably anticipated uses or disclosures of EPHI not permitted by the HIPAA Privacy Rule[34] and

- Ensuring compliance with the Security Rule by its employees.[35]

Beyond these general, mandated outcomes, the Security Rule contains process and procedural requirements broken into several general categories[36]:

- **Administrative Safeguards**[37] Key required processes in this area include: conducting a comprehensive analysis of reasonably anticipated risks; matrixing identified risks against a covered entity's unique mix of information requiring safeguarding; employee training, awareness, testing and sanctions; individual accountability for information security; access authorization, management, and monitoring controls; contingency and disaster recovery planning; and ongoing technical and non-technical evaluation of Security Rule compliance.

- **Physical Safeguards**[38] Physical security safeguard measures include: mandated facilities access controls; workstation use and workstation security requirements; device and media controls; restricting access to sensitive information; and maintaining offsite computer backups.

- **Technical Safeguards**[39] Without specifying technological mechanisms, the HIPAA Security Rule mandates automated technical processes intended to protect information and control and record access to such information. Mandated processes include authentication controls for persons accessing EPHI, encryption/decryption requirements, audit controls, and mechanisms for ensuring data integrity.

The Security Rule contains other requirements beyond these general categories, including: ensuring, by written agreement, that entities with whom a covered entity exchanges EPHI, maintain reasonable and appropriate security measures, and holding those entities to the agreed-upon standards; developing written procedures and policies to implement the Security Rule's requirements, disseminating such procedures, and reviewing and updating them periodically in response to changing threats, vulnerabilities, and operational circumstances.

Sarbanes-Oxley

The Sarbanes-Oxley Act of 2002 (SOX) creates legal liability for senior executives of publicly traded companies, potentially including stiff prison sentences and fines of up to $5,000,000 per violation, for willfully certifying financial statements that do not meet the requirements of the statute.[40] Section 404 of SOX requires senior management, pursuant to rules promulgated by the Securities and Exchange Commission (SEC), to attest to: "(1) the responsibility of management for establishing and maintaining an adequate internal control structure and procedures for financial reporting; and (2) ...the effectiveness of the internal control structure and procedures of the issuer for financial reporting." [41] Section 302, also requires that pursuant to SEC regulations, officers signing company financial reports certify that they are "responsible for establishing and maintaining internal controls," and "have evaluated the effectiveness" of those controls and reported their conclusions as to the same.[42]

Federal Information Security and Management Act

The Federal Information Security and Management Act of 2002, as amended, (FISMA) does not directly create liability for private sector information security professionals or their customers.[43] Information security professionals should be aware of this law, however, because the law:

- Legally mandates the process by which information security requirements for federal government departments and agencies must be developed and implemented

- Directs the federal government to look to the private sector for applicable "best practices" and to provide assistance to the private sector (if requested) with regard to information security

- Contributes to the developing "standard of care" for information security by mandating a number of specific procedures and policies

FERPA and the TEACH Act

The Family Educational Right to Privacy Act (FERPA) prohibits educational agencies and programs, at risk of losing federal funds, from having a policy or practice of "permitting the release of" specified educational records.[44] FERPA does not state whether or not the prohibition places affirmative requirements on educational institutions to protect against unauthorized access to these records through the use of information security measures. It is certainly possible that a court could conclude in the future that an educational institution, which fails to take reasonable information security measures to prevent unauthorized access to protected information, is liable under FERPA for "permitting the release" of such information. The 2002 Technology, Education and Copyright Harmonization Act (the "TEACH Act") explicitly requires educational institutions to take "technologically feasible" measures to prevent unauthorized sharing of copyrighted information beyond the students specifically requiring the information for their studies, and, thus, may create newly enforceable legal duties on educational institutions with regard to information security.[45]

Electronic Communications Privacy Act and Computer Fraud and Abuse Act

These two federal statutes, while not mandating information security procedures, create serious criminal penalties for any persons who gain unauthorized access to electronic records. Unlike laws such as HIPAA and GLB, these two statues broadly apply, regardless of the type of electronic records that are involved. The Electronic Communications Privacy Act (ECPA) makes it a federal felony to, without authorization, use or intercept the contents of electronic communications.[46] Likewise, the Computer Fraud and Abuse Act of 1984 (CFAA) makes the unauthorized access to a very wide range of computer systems (including financial institutions, the federal government, and any protected computer system used in interstate commerce) a federal felony.[47] As a result, information security professionals must take great care—and rely on qualified and experienced legal professionals—to ensure that the authorizations they receive from their customers are broad and specific enough to mitigate potential criminal liability under ECPA and CFAA.[48]

State Laws

In addition to federal statutes and regulations implicating information security, there are numerous state laws that, depending on an entity's location and the places in which it does business, can also create legal requirements related to the work of information security professionals.

Unauthorized Access

In Colorado (and in other states), it is a crime to access, use, or exceed authorized access to, or use of, a computer, computer network, or any part of a computer system.[49] It is a crime to take action against a computer system to cause damage, to commit a theft, or for other nefarious purposes. However, it is particularly important for information security professionals to be aware that it is also a crime to knowingly access a computer system without authorization or to exceed authorized access. This is one reason it is critical for information security professionals, with the advice of qualified and experienced counsel, to negotiate a comprehensive, carefully worded, Letter of Authorization (LOA) with each and every customer (discussed in detail below).

Deceptive Trade Practices

Deceptive trade practices are unlawful and may potentially subject anyone committing them to civil penalties and damages.[50] In Colorado (as in many other states), "deceptive trade practices" include:

- "Knowingly mak[ing] a false representation as to the characteristics… [or] benefits of goods, …services, or property"[51]

- "Fail[ing] to disclose material information concerning goods, services, or property which information was known at the time of an advertisement or sale if such failure to disclose such information was intended to induce the consumer to enter into a transaction"[52]

Deceptive trade practices laws have been used by regulators to impose (through lawsuits) information security requirements on entities in industries not otherwise subject to statutory or regulatory standards.

These are only two of the many types of state laws potentially applicable to information security professionals and their customers. In addition, common law negligence doctrines in every state can create civil legal liability for information security professionals and their customers (discussed below in "Do it Right or Bet the Company: Tools to Mitigate Legal Liability").

Understanding the myriad state laws that apply to information security, and to any particular entity, and how such laws overlap and interact with federal laws, is complex and constantly evolving. Information security professionals and their customers should consult qualified and experienced legal counsel to navigate this challenging legal environment.

Enforcement Actions

What constitutes the "reasonable standard of care" in information security, as in all areas of the law, will continue to evolve, and not only through new statutes and regulations. Prosecutors and regulators will not be content to wait for such formal, legal developments. In lawsuits, and enforcement actions against entities not directly covered by any specific federal or state law or regulation, prosecutors and regulators have demonstrated the clear intent to extend "reasonable" information security measures even to those entities not clearly covered by specific existing laws. This is being done through legal actions leading to settlements, often including consent decrees (agreements entered into to end litigation or regulatory action) wherein a company agrees to "voluntarily" allow regulators to monitor (e.g., for 20 years) the company's information security program.[53]

Since these agreements are publicly available, they are adding to the "standard of care" to which entities will be held, in addition to providing added impetus for similar enforcement actions in the future. Thus, customers of information security professionals should take scant comfort in the fact that there are not yet specific laws explicitly targeted at their economic sectors or industries.

Three Fatal Fallacies

Conventional wisdom is a powerful and dangerous thing, as is a little knowledge. Unfortunately, many entities realizing they have legal and other requirements for information security have come to believe some specific fallacies that sometimes govern their information security decisions. More disturbingly, a significant number of information security providers, who should know better, also are falling victim to these fallacies. Herewith, then, let the debunking begin.

The "Single Law" Fallacy

Many information security professionals, both within commercial and educational entities, and among the burgeoning world of consultants, subscribe to the "single law" fallacy. That is, they identify a statute or set of regulations that clearly apply to a particular institution and assume that, by complying with that single standard, they have ended all legal risk. This assumption may be true, but in many cases is not. Making such an assumption could be a very expensive error, absent the advice of qualified and experienced legal counsel.

Take, for example, a mid-sized college or university. Information security professionals may conclude that, since FERPA clearly applies to educational records, following guidance tailored to colleges and universities based on what they conclude are the appropriate Department of Education standards, is sufficient to mitigate any potential legal liability. Worse yet, they may decide to gamble that, given current ambiguity about whether FERPA requires affirmative action to prevent unauthorized access to such records, they need not take any affirmative steps to try and prevent such access. This could be an expensive gamble, particularly if the educational institution does not ask itself the following questions:

- Does the school grant financial aid or extend other forms of credit? If so, it could be subject to GLBA.

- Does it operate hospitals, provide psychiatric counseling services, or run a student health service? If so, it could be subject to HIPAA.

- Does the school's Web site contain any representations about the security of the site and/or university-held information? If so, it could be subject to lawsuits under one or more (depending on whether it has campuses in multiple states) state deceptive trade practices laws.

The Private Entity Fallacy

Focusing on SOX and the resulting preoccupation with publicly traded companies, some institutions take solace in being private and in the fact that, so the argument goes, they are not subject to SOX and/or that they can somehow "fly under the radar" of federal regulators and civil litigants. Again, a dangerous bet. First, the likelihood of comprehensive federal information security regulation reaching well beyond publicly traded companies grows daily. Second, anyone who believes that lawyers for future plaintiffs (students, faculty, victims of attack or identity theft) will be deterred by the literal terms of SOX is misguided. The argument (potentially a winning one) will be that the appropriate "standard of care" for information security was publicly available and well known. The fact that one particular statute may not apply, by its plain terms, does not relieve entities of awareness of the standard of care and duty not to be negligent. Third, and most importantly, a myopic focus on SOX (or any other single law or regulation) to the exclusion of the numerous other potential sources of liability, will not relieve entities of the responsibility to learn about, and follow, the dictates of all other sources of law, including, but not limited to, HIPAA, GLBA, state statutes, and common law theories and, depending on where an entity does business, international and foreign law, such as the complex and burdensome European Union Privacy Directive.[54]

The "Pen Test Only" Fallacy

Every information security professional has dealt with the "pen test only" customer, probably more than once. This customer is either certain that their information security posture is so good that they just need an outside party to try and "break in" (do a penetration test) to prove how good they are, or feels an internal bureaucratic need to prove to others in the company how insecure their systems are. Generally, the customer has a limited budget or simply does not want to spend much money and wants a "quick hit" by the information security professional to prove a bureaucratic point. One variation on this theme is the customer who wants the penetration test as a first step, before deciding how far down the Information Security Assessment/Evaluation road to walk.

There is no way to say this too strongly: **starting with a penetration test is a disaster**, particularly if there is no way to protect the results from disclosure (see "Attorney-client Privilege" below). At least as important are the horrendous legal consequences that can flow from starting with a penetration test without establishing a more comprehensive, longer-term relationship with qualified and experienced lawyers and, through them, information security technical consultants. Not only will the customer almost certainly "fail" the penetration test, particularly if done as the first step without proper assessment, evaluation, and mid-stream remediation, but this failure will *be documented in a report not subject to any type of attorney-client privilege or other protection from disclosure.*

In short, testing done at the worst possible time in the process in terms of exposing vulnerabilities will be wide open to discovery and disclosure by your customers' future adversaries. From the standpoint of the information security technical professional, this also could lead to your being required later to testify, publicly and under oath, as to the minutest of details of your work for the customer, your methodology and "trade secrets," and your work product.[55]

Do It Right or Bet the Company: Tools to Mitigate Legal Liability

In recent years, numerous articles have been written on how to protect your network from a technical perspective,[56] but, at least throughout mid-2005, the headlines swelled with examples of companies that have lost critical information due to inadequate security. Choice Point, DSW Shoes, several universities, financial institutions including Bank of America and Wachovia, MasterCard and other credit providers, and even the FBI have been named in recent news articles for having lost critical information. As one example, ChoicePoint was sued in 2005 in actions brought in states ranging from California to New York and in its home state of Georgia. Allegations in the lawsuits included that ChoicePoint failed to "secure and maintain confidential the personal, financial and other information entrusted to ChoicePoint by consumers"[57]; failed to maintain adequate procedures to avoid disclosing some private credit and financial information to unauthorized third parties; and acted "willfully, recklessly, and/or in conscious disregard" of its customers rights to privacy.[58] Legal theories used in future information security-related lawsuits will be limited only by the imagination of the attorneys filing the suits.

It is hardly a distant possibility that every major player in information security will be sued sooner or later, whether a particular suit is frivolous or not. It is a fact of business life. So, how can information security consultants help their customers reduce their litigation "target profile?"

We Did our Best; What's the Problem?

Many companies feel that their internal information technology and security staffs are putting forth their best efforts to maintain and secure their networks. They may even be getting periodic penetration tests and trying to make sense out of the hundreds of single-spaced pages of "vulnerabilities" identified in the resulting reports. So why isn't that good enough? The answer is that "doing one's best" to secure and maintain a network system will not be enough unless it is grounded in complying with external legal standards (discussed above).

Penetration tests alone are likely not enough to demonstrate reasonable efforts at meeting the standard of care for information security. In ChoicePoint's case, at least based on what has been made public as of mid-2005, penetration tests would not have helped. ChoicePoint appears to have fallen victim to individuals who fraudulently posed as businessmen and conned people into giving them what may have been otherwise secure information.

Ameliorating any one particular potential point of failure will almost never be enough. Companies today must understand the potential sources of liability that apply to all commercial entities, as well as those specific to their industry. Only through understanding the legal environment and adopting and implementing policies to assure a high level of compliance with prevailing legal requirements can a company minimize the risk of liability. Of course, this system approach cannot be not static. It requires ongoing review and implementation to assure compliance in an ever-changing legal environment.

The Basis for Liability

A company's legal liability can arise as a result of: (a) standards and penalties imposed by federal, state, or local governments; (b) breach of contractual agreements; or (c) other non-contractual civil wrongs (torts) ranging from fraud, invasion of privacy, and conversion to deceptive trade practices and negligence. Avoiding liability for criminal misconduct also involves an understanding of the statutes and regulations applicable to your business and adhering to those requirements. Federal and state statutes may impose both criminal penalties as well as form the basis for private lawsuits.

Negligence and the "Standard of Care"

The combination of facts and events that can give rise to civil claims when information security is breached and the specific impact on business operations, are too numerous to discuss in detail. Understanding the basis for liability and conducting business in a manner designed to avoid liability is the best defense. In many cases, the claim of liability is based in a charge that the company and its officers and directors acted "negligently." In law, "negligence" arises when a party owes a legal duty to another, that duty is breached, and the breach causes damages to the injured party. Generally speaking, acting "reasonably" under the circumstances will prevent information security consultants or their customers from being found "negligent."[59] The rub is that what is "reasonable" both: (1) depends on the particular circumstances of individual situations; and (2) is constantly evolving as new laws and regulations are promulgated and new vulnerabilities, attack vectors, and available counter-measures become known.

Certainly, when a company maintains personal or confidential customer information, or has agreed to maintain as confidential the trade secret information of another business, its minimum duty is to use reasonable care in securing its computer systems to avoid theft or inadvertent disclosure of the information entrusted to it. Reasonable care may range from an extremely high standard when trust and confidence are reposed in a company to secure sensitive information, to a standard of care no more than that generally employed by others in the industry.

A reasonable "standard of care" is what the law defines as the minimum efforts a company must take not to have acted negligently (or, put another way, to have acted reasonably). A strong foundation to avoid liability for most civil claims begins with conducting the company's affairs up to the known standard of care that will avoid liability for negligence.

The appropriate, reasonable standard of care in any given industry and situation can arise from several sources, including statutes, regulations, common law duties, organizational policies, and contractual obligations. Courts look to the foreseeability of particular types of harm to help determine an industry standard of care. In other words, a business must exercise reasonable care to prevent an economic loss that should have been anticipated. As a result of ongoing public disclosure of new types of harm from breaches in information security, it is increasingly "foreseeable" that critical information may be lost through unauthorized access, and the policies and practices used to protect that information will take center stage in any negligence action.

What Can Be Done?

Fully understanding the risks, as assessed by qualified and experienced counsel, is an essential first step. Taking action that either avoids liability or minimizes the consequences when things go wrong is the next stride. The following are some suggestions that will help in the journey.

Understand your Legal Environment

Mitigating legal liability begins with understanding the laws applicable to a company's business. (A variety of potentially applicable legal requirements are outlined in the "Legal Standards Relevant to Information Security" section above.) Ignorance of the law is no excuse, and failure to keep pace with statutory requirements is a first source of liability. Working with professionals, whether inside or outside of the company, to track changes in legislation and tailor your information security policies is the first line of defense. Careful compliance with laws not only helps reduce the potential for criminal liability or administrative fines, but also evidences a standard of care that may mitigate civil liability.

Comprehensive and Ongoing Security Assessments, Evaluations, and Implementation

Working with qualified and experienced legal counsel and technical consultants, a company must identify and prioritize the information it controls that may require protection, and catalogue the specific legal requirements applicable to such information and to the type of business the company is in. Next, policies must be developed to assure that the information is properly maintained and administered and that the company's personnel conduct themselves in accordance with those policies. Policy evaluations must include the applicable legal requirements, as well as reasonable procedures for testing and maintaining the security of information systems.

Critically, the cycle of using outside, neutral, third-party assessments/evaluations, implementation and improvement, and further assessment, must be ongoing. A static assessment/evaluation sitting on your shelf is worse than none at all. Almost equally bad is actually implementing the results of assessments/evaluations, but never reassessing or modifying them or insufficiently training employees on them, or evaluating those employees on their understanding and implementation of such results.

Use Contracts to Define Rights and Protect Information

Most businesses understand the process of entering into contracts and following the terms of those contracts to avoid claims of breach. What is not so easily identified is how contractual obligations impact the potential of civil liability based on how information is secured and managed within a particular business? Many areas within a company's business require contracts to be developed and tailored to avoid liability and preserve the integrity of the business. One example is the Uniform Trade Secrets Act (UTSA), adopted in nearly all states and intended to protect confidential information of value to a company's business. Under the UTSA, confidential information may include formulas, patterns, compilations, programs, devices, methods, techniques, or processes that derive independent economic value from not being generally known to the public and for which the company has made reasonable efforts to maintain confidentiality. Almost every company has trade secrets—from its customer lists to its business methodologies afford a competitive advantage. Any protection for these valuable assets will be lost if a company fails to make reasonable efforts to maintain the information as confidential.

At a minimum, contracts must be developed that commit employees not to disclose the trade secrets of the company, or any information legally mandated to be protected (e.g., individual health care or financial information). These agreements are often most effective if entered into at the time of, and as a condition to, employment. This is because most contracts require value to support enforceability and because a delay in requiring a non-disclosure agreement may allow sensitive information to be disclosed before the contract is in place.

Employment policies should reinforce the employee's obligation to maintain confidentiality. These policies should also provide clear guidance on procedures to use and maintain passwords and to responsibly use the information secured on the network. Regular interviews and employee training should be implemented to reinforce the notion that these requirements are mandatory and taken seriously by management. Vendors and service providers that may need to review confidential information should only be permitted access to such information under an agreement limiting the use of that information and agreeing to maintain its confidentiality. Hiring a consultant to perform a network security evaluation without a proper confidentiality agreement could later be found to be sufficient evidence that a company failed to take reasonable efforts to maintain information as confidential, with the result that the information is not longer a trade secret entitled to protection.

Use Qualified Third-party Professionals

Working with qualified information security professionals to implement proper hardware and software solutions to minimize a security breach is critical, but never enough. These functions need to be performed in conjunction with a system of evaluation testing and retesting that integrates legal considerations, and under the supervision and guidance of qualified and experienced legal counsel.

In addition, working with qualified and experienced outside counsel can substantially improve success in the event that claims of negligence are asserted (using attorneys and technical professionals trained to conduct comprehensive and ongoing systems assessments and evaluations is evidence of the reasonableness of the efforts to prevent the loss). Companies' internal staff may be equally competent to develop and implement the strategies of information security, but regulators, courts, and juries will look to whether or not a company retained qualified and experienced outside counsel and technical consultants before a problem arose. Working with these experts increases the probability that best practices are being followed and independent review is the best way to mitigate against foreseeable loss of sensitive information.

As discussed in more detail below, retaining outside professionals in a way that creates an attorney-client privilege may offer protection (in the event of civil litigation, regulatory, or even criminal, action) from disclosure of system vulnerabilities discovered in the information security assessment and evaluation processes. The privilege is not absolute, however, and may have different practical applications in the civil and criminal contexts and, in particular, when a customer elects to assert an "advice-of-counsel" defense.

A key requirement emerging as a critical part of the evolving information security standards of care is the requirement to get an external review by qualified, neutral parties.[60] These requirements are based on the sound theory that, no matter how qualified, expert, and well intentioned an entity's information technology and information security staff is, it is impossible for them to be truly objective. Moreover, the "fox in the hen house" problem arises, leaving senior management to wonder whether those charged with creating and maintaining information security can and will fairly and impartially assess the effectiveness of such security. Finally, qualified and experienced outside legal counsel and technical consultants bring perspective, breadth of experience, and currency with the latest technical and legal developments that in-house staff normally cannot provide cost-effectively.

Making Sure Your Standards-of-Care Assessments Keep Up with Evolving Law

As suggested above, the legal definition of a "reasonable" standard of care is constantly evolving. Policymakers take seriously the threats and the substantial economic loss caused by cyber-attacks. New laws are continually being enacted to punish attackers and to shift liability to companies that have failed to take reasonable information security measures. Contractual obligations can now be formed instantly and automatically simply by new customers accessing your customer's Web sites and using their services, all over the Internet and, thus, all over the world. As new vulnerabilities, attacks, and countermeasures come to public attention, new duties emerge. In short, what was "reasonable" last month may not be reasonable this month.

Information security assessments and evaluations provide a tool to evaluate, and enhance compliance with, best practices in protecting critical information; however, they are, at best, only snapshots unless they are made regular, ongoing events. Best practices begin with understanding and complying with applicable laws, but can only be maintained through tracking and implementing evolving statutory requirements. Working with qualified and experienced counsel to follow new legal developments in this fast-moving area of the law and advise on the proper interpretation and implementation of legislative requirements is becoming essential to navigate through this ever-changing landscape.

Plan for the Worst

Despite all best efforts, nothing can completely immunize a company from liability. Failing to plan a crisis management and communications strategy in the event of lost or compromised information can invite lawsuits and create liability despite a track record showing your company exercised a reasonable standard of care in trying to protect information. Avoiding liability involves planning for problems. For example, one class action filed against ChoicePoint alleges that shareholders were misled when the company failed to disclose (for several months) the existence of its security breach and the true extent of the information that was compromised. Having had policies in place to provide guidance to executives in communicating with customers and prospective shareholders may well have avoided these allegations. California currently has a Notice of Security Breach law that was enacted in 2002.[61] As of May 2005, Arkansas, Georgia, Indiana, Montana, North Dakota, and Washington have followed suit by enacting some form of legislation requiring disclosure relating to breaches of security, and bills have been introduced in not less than 34 other states to regulate in this area.[62] As of mid-2005, there was no similar federal regulation, although, several disclosure bills have been introduced in Congress.

A strategic policy to deal with crisis management must take into account disclosure laws in all states in which a company operates. Making disclosures that comply with multiple laws and that minimize the adverse impact of information security breaches and disclosures of them must be planned far in advance of a crisis. Again, this is a constantly changing landscape, and these policies need to be reviewed and updated on a regular basis. It is critical that these policies and plans are developed and carried out with the assistance of qualified and experienced counsel.

Insurance

As more information security breaches occur and are disclosed, the cost to businesses and individuals will continue to rise. In 2002, the Federal Trade Commission (FTC) estimated that 10 million people were victims of identity theft. According to Gartner, Inc., 9.4 million online users in the U.S. were victimized between April 2003 and April 2004 with losses amounting to $11.7 billion.[63] Costs to business from these losses will likely grow to staggering levels in the coming years, and this trend is capturing the attention of some of the more sophisticated insurance companies. Some companies are developing products to provide coverage for losses resulting from breaches of information security. Companies should contact their carriers and do their own independent research to determine what coverage, if any, is or will become, available.

Customers of information security consultants, with the advice of qualified and experienced counsel, must take into account all of these issues in determining how best to mitigate their legal risk. A key component of mitigating that risk is the relationships established with information security consultants, including qualified and experienced counsel and skilled and respected technical consultants. Those relationships, of course, must be established and governed by written contracts (discussed in the next section).

What to Cover in Security Evalutaion Contracts[64]

The contract is the single most important tool used to define and regulate the legal relationship between the information security consultant and the customer. It protects both parties from misunderstandings and should clearly allocate liability in case of unforeseen or unintended consequences, such as a system crash, access to protected, proprietary, or otherwise sensitive information thought secure, and damage to the network or information residing on the network. The contract also serves as a roadmap through the security evaluation cycle for both parties. A LOA (described in the next section) serves a different purpose from a contract and often augments the subject matter covered in a contract or deals with relationships with third parties not part of the original service contract. In most evaluations, both will be required.

The contract should spell out each and every action the customer wants the provider to perform. Information security consultants should have a standard contract for a packages of services, but should be flexible enough for negotiation in order to meet the specific needs of the customer. What is, or is not, covered in the contract, and how the provisions should be worded, are decisions both parties must make only with the advice of qualified and experienced counsel familiar with this field. As with any other legal agreement between parties, both signatories should fully understand all the terms in the contract, or ask for clarification or re-drafting of ambiguous, vague, or overly technical language. Contract disputes often arise in situations where two parties can read the same language in different ways. Understand what you are signing.

What, Who, When, Where, How, and How Much

The following paragraphs provide an overview of what should be included in security evaluation and information security service contracts. They include checklists of questions that the contract should answer for both parties; however, remember that each assessment is different because customer's needs and the facts of each evaluation process will differ. Make sure the contract you sign clearly covers each of the topics suggested here, but keep in mind that this is not an exhaustive list and cannot replace the specific advice of your own legal counsel for your specific circumstances.

What

The first general requirement for a contract for information security evaluation services is to address the basic services the consultant will perform. What are the expectations of both parties in performing the non-technical aspects of the business relationship, such as payment, reporting, and documentation? What services does the contract cover? What does the customer want? What can the information security consultant provide? A number of categories of information should appear in this first section.

Description of the Security Evaluation and Business Model

In the initial part of the contract, the information security consultant should describe the services to be provided and, generally, how its business is conducted. This information provides background on the type of contract that is to be used by the parties (e.g., a contract for services or a contract for services followed by the purchase and installation of software to remediate any identified vulnerabilities). This initial section should also identify the customer and describe its business model. For example, is the customer a financial organization, a healthcare organization, an organization with multiple geographic locations under evaluation, or subject to specific legal requirements and/or industry regulations?

Definitions Used in the Contract

Each contract uses terms that will need further explanation so that the meaning is clear to both parties. Technical terms such as "vulnerability" and "penetration" should be spelled out. Executives sign contracts. Attorneys advise executives whether or not to sign the contracts. Both must understand what the contract means.

Description of the Project

The contract should provide a general statement of the scope of the project. If the project is a long-term endeavor or a continuing relationship between the two parties, this section should also include a description of how each part of the project or phase in the relationship should progress and what additional documents will cover each phase or part of the project. This section also clearly defines what the information security consultant will and will not do throughout the evaluation. Also, in the description of the project, the customer should clearly define the objectives it wants the information security consultant to accomplish. Are all the entity's networks included? What types of testing are required? This section should also include the types of vulnerabilities that the information security consultant is not likely to discover based on the types of testing, the networks tested, and the scope of the overall evaluation, as permitted by the customer.

Assumptions, Representations, and Warranties

In every assessment, the parties must provide or assume some basic information. These assumptions should appear in the contract. Assumptions are factual statements, not a description of conversations the parties have had (e.g., "The schedule in this contract is based on the assumption that all members of the evaluation team will work from 8:30 A.M. to 5:30 P.M. for five days per week for the full contract period."). With regard to the network assumptions, the customer should provide basic information on network topology upon which the assessment team can base assumptions for the types of vulnerabilities they will look for and testing methodologies that will successfully achieve the customer's objectives (e.g., "The evaluation methodology applied to the customer network under this contract relies on the assumption that the customer maintains servers in a single geographic location, physically secured, and logically segregated from other networks and from the Internet.")[65] The language in this section should also address responsive actions should the assumptions prove false: Under what circumstances is the contract voided? What can make the price go up or down? In the event of unexpected security or integrity problems being created during an evaluation, when should the testing be stopped? Who decides? When should the customers' management be informed? At what levels?

IEM contracts should include "representations and warranties" by the customer spelling out certain critical information that the customer "warrants" to be true such as: descriptions of the customer's business operations and information they hold within their systems; what agreements the customer has with third-party vendors and/or holders of their information; what information systems external to those controlled by the customer, if any, could be impacted by the evaluation and testing to be done, and what measures the customer has taken to eliminate the possibilities of such impact; and the degree to which the customer exclusively owns and controls information and systems to be evaluated and/or tested or has secured written agreements explicitly authorizing evaluation and testing by others that do own or control such information and systems.[66]

Boundaries and Limitations

In addition to stating what the evaluation will cover, this initial section should also address what the assessment will not cover in terms of timing, location, data, and other variables. The general goal of the evaluation cycle is to provide a level of safety and security to the customer in the confidence, integrity, and availability of its networks. However, some areas of the network are more sensitive than others. Additionally, each customer will have varying levels of trust in the evaluation methodology and personnel. Not all evaluation and testing methodologies are appropriate for all areas of a network. The customer should give careful consideration to what is tested, when and how, as well as what the evaluators should do in the event of data contamination or disclosure.

If a customer runs a particular type of report on a specific date to meet payroll, accounting, regulatory, or other obligations, that date is not a very good time to engage in network testing. Even if the testing methodology is sound and the personnel perform at peak efficiency and responsibility levels, human nature will attribute any network glitch on that date to the testing team. Sensitive data requires an increased level of scrutiny for any measure taken that could damage or disclose the information, or make the use of the information impossible for some period of time. Such actions could result in administrative or regulatory penalties and expensive remediation efforts.

Data privacy standards vary by industry, state, country, and category of information. A single network infrastructure may encompass personnel records, internal audits or investigations, proprietary or trade secret information, financial information, and individual and corporate information records and databases. The network could also store data subject to attorney-client or other legal privilege. Additionally, customers should consider where and how their employees store data. Does the customer representative negotiating the scope of the project know where all the sensitive data in his/her enterprise are stored, and with what degree of certainty? Does the customer have a contingency plan for data contamination or unauthorized access? How does the security evaluation account for the possibility that testing personnel will come into contact with sensitive data (see Non-Disclosure and Secrecy Agreements section below)? In this portion of the contract, the customer should specify any areas of the network where testing personnel may not conduct evaluations, either for a period of time or during specific phases.

Both parties should be sensitive to the fact that the customer may not own and control all areas of the network. A customer can only consent to testing those portions of the network it owns and controls.

> **NOTE**
>
> Evaluation of other portions of a larger corporate network or where the evaluation proceeds through the Internet, requires additional levels of authorization from third parties outside the contractual relationship, and should never be carried out without explicit agreements negotiated and reviewed by qualified and experienced counsel.

In some cases, the evaluation can continue through these larger networks, but will require additional documentation, such as a LOA (see " Where the Rubber Meets the Road: the Letter of Authorization as Liability Protection" below).

Identification of Deliverables

Without feedback to the customer presented in a usable format, evaluating and testing the network is a waste of resources. The contract should state with a high degree of specificity what deliverables the customer requires and for what level of audience. For example, a 300-page technical report presented to a board of directors is of little use. A ten-slide presentation for the officers of a customer company that focuses on prioritizing the vulnerabilities in terms of levels of risk is far more valuable. Conversely, showing those same ten slides to the network engineering team will not help them. The key in this section of the contract is to manage expectations for the various levels of review within the customer's structure.

Who

The second general requirement for a contract for security evaluation services is to spell out the parties to the agreement and specify the roles and responsibilities of each (including specific names and titles of responsible individuals) for successfully completing the evaluation. This identity and role information is critical for reducing the likelihood of contract disputes due to unmet expectations.

Statement of Parties to the Contractual Agreement

Each party should be clearly identified in the contract by name, location, and principal point of contact for subsequent communications. Often, the official of record for signature is not the same person who will be managing the contract or engaged in day-to-day liaison activities with the evaluation personnel. Additionally, this section should spell out the procedures for changing the personnel of record for each type of contact.

Authority of Signatories to the Contractual Agreement

Ideally, the level of signatory to the contract should be equal, and, in any event, the signing official must be high enough to bind the entities to all obligations arising out of the contractual relationship. It is often also helpful for the customer signatory to be a person empowered to make changes based on recommendations resulting from the evaluation.

Roles and Responsibilities of Each Party to the Contractual Agreement

Spelling out the levels of staffing, location of resources, who will provide those resources, and the precise nature of other logistical, personnel, and financial obligations is critical. It allows both sides to proceed through the evaluation cycle with a focus on the objectives, rather than a daily complication of negotiating who is responsible for additional, unforeseen administrative issues. Some common areas of inclusion in this section are:

- Who provides facilities and administrative support?
- Who is responsible for backing up critical data before the evaluation begins?
- Who is responsible for initiating communication for project status reports. Does the customer call for an update, or does the evaluation team provide regular reporting? Must status reports be written or can they be oral and memorialized only in the information security consultants' records?
- Who is responsible for approving deviations from the contract or evaluation plan and how will decisions about these be recorded?

- Who will perform each aspect of each phase of the evaluation (will the customer provide any technical personnel)?

- Who is responsible for mapping the network before evaluation begins (and will those maps be provided to the evaluation team, or kept in reserve for comparison after the evaluation ends)?

- Who is responsible for briefing senior officers in the customer organization?

- Who is responsible for reporting discrepancies from the agreed project plan to evaluation POCs and executives?

- Who is responsible for reporting violations of policies, regulations, or laws discovered during the evaluation?

- Who has the authority to terminate the evaluation should network irregularities arise?

- Who bears the risk for unforeseen consequences or circumstances that arise during the evaluation period?

Non-disclosure and Secrecy Agreements

Many documents and other information pertaining to information security evaluations contain critical information that could damage one or both parties if improperly disclosed. Both parties bear responsibility to protect tools, techniques, vulnerabilities, and information from disclosure beyond the terms specified by a written agreement. Non-disclosure agreements should be narrowly drawn to protect sensitive information, yet allow both parties to function effectively. Specific areas to consider including are: ownership and use of the evaluation reports and results; use of the testing methodology in customer documentation; disclosures required under law; and the time period of disclosure restrictions. It is often preferable to have non-disclosure/secrecy agreements be separate, stand-alone documents so that, if they must be litigated later in public, as few details as possible of the larger agreement must be publicly exposed.

Assessment Personnel

A security evaluation team is composed of a variety of expert personnel, whether from the customer organization or supplied by the contractor. The contract should spell out the personnel requirements to complete each phase of the assessment successfully and efficiently. Both parties should have a solid understanding of each team member's skills and background. Where possible, the contract should include information on the personnel conducting the assessment. Both parties should also consider who would fund and who would perform any background investigations necessary for personnel assigned to evaluate sensitive networks.

Crisis Management and Public Communications

Network security evaluations can be messy. No network is 100 percent secure. The assessment team will inevitably find flaws. The assessment team will usually stumble across unexpected dangers, or take actions that result in unanticipated results that could impact the network or the data residing on the network. Do not make the mistake of compounding a bad situation with a poor response to the crisis. Implementing notification procedures at the contract phase often saves the integrity of an evaluation should something go wrong. The parties also should clearly articulate who has the lead role in determining the timing, content, and delivery mechanism for providing information to the customer's employees, customers, shareholders, and so forth. This section should also spell out what role, if any, the customer wants the assessment team or leader to play in the public relations efforts. A procedure for managing crisis situations is also prudent. Qualified and experienced legal counsel must be involved in these processes.

Indemnification, Hold Harmless, and Duty to Defend

Even more so than in many other types of contracts for services, the security evaluation contract should include detailed provisions explicitly protecting the information security consultants from various types of contract dispute claims. In addition to standard contract language, these sections should specifically spell out the responsibilities (and their limits) of both the customer and the information security consultants to defend claims of damage to external systems or information and intellectual property or licensing infringement for software, if any, developed by the information security consultant for purposes of the evaluation.

Ownership and Control of Information

The information contained in the final report and executive level briefings can be extremely sensitive. Both parties must understand who owns and controls the disclosure and dissemination of the information, as well as what both parties may do with the information following the review process. Any proprietary information or processes, including trade secrets, should be marked as such, and covered by a separate section of the contract. Key topics to cover include: use of evaluation results in either party's marketing or sales brochures; release of results to management or regulatory bodies; and disclosure of statistics in industry surveys, among other uses. The customer should spell out any internal corporate controls for the information in this section. If the customer requires encryption of the evaluation data, this section should clearly spell out those requirements and who is responsible for creating or providing keys.

One important ownership area that must be specifically covered in information security evaluation contracts is how reports and other resulting documentation from the evaluation are to be handled. May the information security consultants keep copies of the documents, at least for a reasonable period of time following the conclusion of the evaluation (e.g., in case the customer takes legal action against the consultant)? Who is responsible for destroying any excess copies of such information? May the information security consultant use properly sanitized versions of the reports as samples of work product?

Intellectual Property Concerns

Ownership and use of intellectual property is a complicated area of the law. However, clear guidance in the prior section on the ownership and use of evaluation information will help the parties avoid intellectual property disputes. The key to a smooth legal relationship between the parties is to clearly define expectations.

Licenses

The evaluation team must ensure that they have valid licenses for each piece of software used in the evaluation. The customer should verify valid licensing.

When

The third general requirement for a security evaluation services contract is to create a schedule for conducting the evaluation that includes all of the phases and contingency clauses to cover changes to that schedule. At a minimum, the contract should state a timeline for the overall evaluation and for each phase, including:

- A timeline for completing deliverables in draft and final formats
- Estimated dates of executive briefings, if requested
- A timeline for any follow-up work anticipated

Actions or Events that Affect Schedule

Inevitably, something will happen to affect the schedule. Personnel move, network topography changes a variety of unforeseen factors can arise. While the contract team cannot control those factors, it can draft language in the contract to allow rapid adaptation of the schedule, depending on various factors. Brief interruptions in assessments can mean long-term impacts if the team is at a sensitive point in the assessment. At the contracting phase, both sides should consult with other elements in their companies to determine what events could affect the schedule. Failure to plan adequately for scheduling conflicts or disruptions could result in one party breaching the contract. Both parties should agree on a contingency plan if the evaluation must terminate prematurely. Contingency plans could include resuming the evaluation at a later time or adjusting the total amount of the contract cost based on the phases completed.

Where

The fourth general requirement for a contract for security evaluation services is to define the location(s), both geographic and logical, subject to the evaluation. Where, precisely, are you testing? To create boundaries for the evaluation and prevent significant misunderstandings on the scope of the assessment or evaluation, list each facility, the physical address and/or logical location, including the Internet Protocol (IP) address range. Make sure that each machine attached to that IP space is within the legal and physical control of the customer. If any of the locations are outside the U.S., seek the immediate advice of counsel on this specific point. While covering the rapid developments in overseas law of this field is beyond the scope of this section, understand that many countries are implementing computer crime laws and standing up both civil and criminal response mechanisms to combat computer crime. Various elements of a network security evaluation can look like unauthorized access to a protected computer. Both the evaluation provider and the customer need to take additional cautionary measures and implement greater notification procedures when considering an evaluation of a system located even partially abroad. Additionally, this section should cover the location the evaluation team will use as their base of operations. If the two locations are separate geographically, the parties must address the electronic access needed for the evaluation.

Exercise an extra level of caution if the evaluation traverses the Internet. Use of the Internet to conduct evaluations carries an additional level of risk and legal liability because neither party owns or controls all of the intermediate network structures.

WARNING

Do not act where your evaluation and testing must traverse the Internet without the advice of qualified and experienced counsel.

How

The fifth general requirement for a contract for security evaluation services is to map out a methodology for completing the evaluation. This section should identify and describe each phase of the evaluation and/or the overall testing cycle if the contract will cover a business relationship that will span multiple assessments. The key is to prevent surprises for either party. Breaking complex assessments and/or evaluations up into phases in the contract allows the reviewing officials to understand what they are paying for and when they can expect results. State with precise language what the evaluator will be doing at each phase, the goals and objectives of each phase, each activity the evaluation team will complete during that phase, and the deliverables expected. Do not use technical slang. A separate background document on evaluation and testing methodology (i.e., NSA/IAM, IEM, ISO 17799, and so on) is often more useful than cluttering the contract with unnecessary technical detail. This section should also state and describe the standards the evaluation team will use for measuring the evaluation results. Testing should bear results on a measurement scale that allows for comparisons over time and between locations.

How Much

The sixth, and final, general requirement for a contract for security evaluation services is to spell out the costs of the evaluation and other associated payment terms. This section is similar to any other business service contract. At a minimum, it should include the following five elements.

Fees and Cost

The parties should discuss and agree to a fee structure that meets the needs of both parties, which in most cases will call for multiple payments based on phase completion. A helpful analogy is the construction of a house. At what phases will the homeowner pay the general contractor: excavation and clearing the lot; completion of the foundation; framing; walls and fixtures; or final walkthrough? Also, consider the level of customer management that must approve phase completion and payment. In most cases, the final payment on the contract will be tied in some way to the delivery of a final report. Both parties should also carefully discuss the costs for which the customer is responsible. If evaluation teams must travel to the customer's location, who pays for the travel, food, lodging, and other non-salary costs for those personnel, and what level of documentation will be needed to process payment? Do the costs include airfare, lodging, mileage, subsistence (meals and incidentals), and other expenses? Does the customer require that the expenses be "reasonable" or must a customer representative authorize the expenses in advance? To avoid disputes that detract the team's attention from the assessment, spell out the parties' expectations in the contract. The parties should also cover who pays for extraordinary unanticipated expenses such as equipment failure. In some circumstances, the best method for dealing with truly unexpected expenses is to state affirmatively in the contract that the parties will negotiate such costs as they arise.

Billing Methodology

In order for the customer's accounting mechanisms to adequately prepare for the obligations in the contract, the billing or invoicing requirements should be spelled out. If the customer requires a specific type of information to appear on the invoice, that information should be provided to the contractor in writing, preferably in the contract. The types of fees and costs that will appear on the invoice should also be discussed, and the customer should provide guidance on the level of detail they need, while the contractor should explain the nature of their billing capabilities.

Payment Expectations and Schedule

The contract should clearly represent both parties' expectations for prompt payment. Will the contractor provide invoices at each phase or on a monthly cycle? Are invoices due upon receipt or on a specific day of the month? Where does the contractor send the invoice and to whom within the customer's structure? Does the contractor require electronic payment of invoices, and if so, to what account? What penalties will the contractor assess for late payments or returned checks? Again, the key factor is to address both parties' expectations to prevent surprises.

Rights and Procedures to Collect Payment

In the event of problems in the contractual relationship or changes in management that affect the contract, what are the parties' rights? As with other commercial contracts, articulating the rights and remedies is essential to minimize or avoid altogether the expense of disputes.

Insurance for Potential Damage During Evaluation

Which party, if either, will carry insurance against damage to the customer's systems and information as well as to those of third parties?

Murphy's Law (When Something Goes Wrong)

The final standard set of clauses for the contract deals with the potential for conflict between the parties or modifications to the contract.

Governing Law

Where both parties are in the same state, and the evaluation is limited to those facilities, this clause may not be necessary. However, in most cases, the activities will cross state borders. The parties should agree on which state's law applies to the contract and under which court's jurisdiction parties can file lawsuits. Determining venue for disputes before they arise can reduce legal costs.

Acts of God, Terror Attacks, and other Unforeseeable Even

Attorneys and network engineers share at least one common trait; neither can predict with any certainty when things will go wrong, but all agree that something will eventually happen that you did not expect. Natural disasters, system glitches, power interruptions, military coups, and a thousand other events can affect a project. Where the disruption is the fault of neither party, both sides should decide in advance on the appropriate course of action.

When Agreement is Breached and Remedies

When one party decides not to fulfill or becomes incapable in some way of performing, the terms of the contract, or believes the other party has not met its contractual obligations, a party can claim a breach (breaking) of the agreement and demand a remedy from the opposing party. Many types of remedies exist for breach of a contract. Either party can also take the matter to court, which can be very messy and extremely expensive. Anticipating situations such as these and inserting language in the contract to deal with potential breaches could save thousands of dollars in attorney fees and court costs. Both parties should discuss the following options with counsel before negotiating a contract for security evaluation services. First, are arbitration or mediation options appropriate or desirable? Second, should the matter proceed to court, one party will inevitably claim attorney's fees as part of the damages. Anticipate this claim and include language that specifies what fees are part of the remedy and whether the party who loses the dispute will reimburse attorney's fees, or whether each side will be responsible for its own attorney's fees.

Liquidated Damages

Liquidated damages are an agreed, or "liquidated," amount that one party is required to pay the other in the event of a breach or early termination of a contract. Liquidated damages are valuable to bring certainty to a failed relationship but are not appropriate if used to create a windfall or punish a party for not completing their contractual obligations. Instead, to be legally enforceable, a liquidated damages clause must estimate the parties' reasonably anticipated damages in the event of a breach or early termination of the contract. Liquidated damages cannot be a penalty and are not appropriate if actual damages can be readily determined.[67] Courts in Colorado, for example, generally will enforce a liquidated damages clause in a contract if: (1) at the time contract was entered into, anticipated damages in case of breach were difficult to ascertain; (2) parties mutually intended to liquidate them in advance; and (3) the amount of liquidated damages, when viewed as of the time the contract was made, was a reasonable estimate of potential actual damages a breach would cause.[68] If these factors apply to your transaction, liquidated damages should be considered to avoid protracted debates regarding the parties' harm when a breach occurs.

Limitations on Liability

Limitations on liability should always be considered and, if possible, incorporated in any contract for evaluation services. Typical clauses might state that liability is limited to an amount equal to the total amount paid by the customer under the contract. Other limitations on damages may require the customer to waive incidental or consequential damages or preclude recovery arising from certain conduct by the information security consultant. Like liquidated damages, however, the ability to limit or waive damages may be restricted by both statute and court decisions. For example, in some states, contractual provisions that purport to limit liability for gross negligence or for willful or wanton conduct are not enforceable.[69] In most states, limitations of liability are acceptable and will be enforced if the agreement was properly executed and the parties dealt at arms length.[70] Accordingly, you should try to limit the customer's right to recover consequential damages, punitive damages, and lost profits. Working with qualified counsel will assist in determining what limitations are enforceable in each specific transaction.

Survival of Obligations

This section makes clear what happens to specific contractual obligations, such as duties of non-disclosure and payment of funds owed, following the expiration of the contract.

Waiver and Severability

This section of the contract describes what happens if either party wants to waive the application of a portion of the contract, and allows for each section of the contract to be severable from the contract as a whole should a court rule that one clause or section is not enforceable. This section is also standard contract language and should be supplied by the attorney for the party drafting the contract.

Amendments to the Contract

For contracts that span significant periods of time, it is likely that one or both parties may require modifications to the contract. To avoid disputes, the original contract should spell out the format for any amendments. Amendments should be in writing and signed by authorized representatives of both parties. The parties should also discuss the financial arrangements surrounding a change to the contract. Proposed amendments to the contract must be accepted by the receiving party.

Where the Rubber Meets the Road: The LOA as Liability Protection

The contract functions as the overall agreement between the organization performing the security assessment and the company or network that will be tested or assessed. A LOA should be used between any two parties, whether party to the same original evaluation contract or not, to document consent to specific activities and protect against different types of adverse liability. For example, Widgets-R-Us contracts with Secure-Test to test the security of a new online shipping management network linked to Widgets' warehouses. ISP-anywhere provides the bandwidth for Widgets' east coast warehouses. Widgets should provide a LOA to Secure-Test consenting to specific network traffic that could trigger ISP-anywhere guards or intrusion detection systems. A copy of the letter should be provided to ISP-anywhere, in advance of the testing, as notice of the activity and a record of Widgets' consent. Additionally, depending on the language of the service agreement between Widgets and ISP-anywhere, Widgets may need to ask ISP-anywhere to provide a LOA for any of Secure-Test's activities that could impact their network infrastructure or otherwise void the bandwidth service agreement. ISP-anywhere was not a party to the original information security evaluation contract and, therefore, Secure-Test needs this additional form of agreement for the activities.

It is an unusual case in which a customer is the sole user of a third-party network system. Accordingly, the network hosts information for businesses and individuals that may maintain confidential information or information not owned by the customer. Merely accessing this information without proper authorization can result in both criminal and civil penalties. In addition, agreements between the customer and the network host may prohibit such access to the system altogether. You, along with your counsel, must always review these relationships with your customer, comply with contractual limitations, and obtain appropriate authorizations.

In many cases, the LOA will turn out to be the single most important document you sign. In addition to the potential civil liability for any damage to your customer's or third parties' systems that occur during periods when you arguably exceed your authorized access, failing to obtain adequate authorization may result in the commission of a crime. As discussed in "Legal Standards Relevant to Information Security" above, the federal Computer Fraud and Abuse Act imposes criminal liability for unauthorized access to computer systems and for exceeding the scope of authorization for accessing certain computers. Every state has passed some form of law that prohibits access to computer systems without proper authority.[71] Working with qualified and experienced legal counsel is vital to assure that your work avoids violation of law and the potential for criminal liability.

Another typical use of a LOA is augmentation of a part of the evaluation or correction of unforeseen technical challenges during the course of the contract (e.g., Widgets-R-Us acquires a warehouse on the west coast after the security evaluation begins, and wants to add this warehouse to the list of facilities Secure-Test will review). Widgets-R-Us does not need a new contract, and most likely does not need to amend the current contract, so long as both parties will accept a LOA to expand the scope of the security assessment. Whether or not to allow LOA amendments to a standing contract should be a term written into the original contract itself.

An important section of a LOA (similar to the overall contract itself) is a comprehensive and detailed statement of what a customer is not authorizing (i.e., certain systems or databases that are off limits, specific times that testing is not to be done, the tools the information security consultant will, and will not use, security measures that the customer will not permit the consultant to take, and so forth). This is equally important for the customer and the information security consultant.

LOAs should be signed by officials for each party with sufficient authority to agree to all specified terms. Importantly, LOAs between a customer and information security consultant should identify any and all types of information or specific systems for which the customer does not have the authority to authorize access. While LOA provisions can be part of the basic contract itself, as with non-disclosure agreements, it is often preferable to have the LOA be a separate, stand-alone agreement so that, if the LOA must be litigated later in public, as few details as possible of the larger agreement must be publicly exposed.

Beyond You and Your Customer

Simply obtaining your customer's consent to access their computer systems is necessary, but it is not always enough. Your customer has obligations to its customers, licensors, and other third parties. Honoring these commitments will avoid potential liability for both you and your customer.

Software License Agreements

Typically, software used by the customer will be subject to a license agreement that governs the relationship between the customer and the software provider. It is not uncommon for software license agreements to prohibit decompilation, disassembly, or reverse engineering of the software code, and to limit access to the software.

The use of tools to penetrate computer systems can constitute the use, access, and running of executable software using the computer's operating system and other programs in a manner that may violate the license agreement. To avoid civil liability, the consultant should have qualified and experienced legal counsel review applicable license agreements and, where appropriate, obtain authorization from the licensor prior to conducting tests of the customer's system.

Your Customer's Customer

To avoid creating liability for your customer, you need to understand your customer's customers and their expectations. Your customer should be able to identify their customer's confidential information and any specific contractual requirements. Understanding the source of third-party information (how it is stored and where appropriate or required), and obtaining consent to access their information is essential. To maintain the integrity of your work, you must respect the confidentiality of your customer and third party-information available to your customer. This is true even if no formal demand is made or no written agreement is entered into. You will be perceived as an agent of your customer; professionalism requires discretion and maintaining privacy.

Similarly, you need to recognize and honor intellectual property rights of your customer and its customers. In general, to protect your customer, you must also protect its customers with the high standards of respect for information privacy and security you provide to your customer.

The First Thing We Do…? Why You Want Your Lawyers Involved From Start to Finish

Few of Shakespeare's words have been more often quoted (and misquoted) than the immortal words of "Dick the Butcher": "The first thing we do, let's kill all the lawyers."[72] What generally is left out by modern lawyer bashers cheering Dick on in his quest is that Dick, and the band of rogues to which he belonged, were planning to overthrow the English government when this battle plan was suggested. The group followed up the lawyer killing idea shortly thereafter by hanging the town clerk of court.

The most reasonable reading of this passage is that Shakespeare intended to demonstrate that those who helped people interpret and litigate the law were, in fact, necessary to the orderly functioning of society. This interpretation is not without fierce challenge, however. In fact, a cottage industry emerges from time-to-time on the Internet debating whether Shakespeare was pro- or anti-lawyer. One prolific Internet lawyer-basher even suggests that the fact that lawyers use Shakespeare to justify our existence is conclusive evidence both of our ignorance and, to put it more charitably than the author, willingness to twist the facts to our own ends.[73]

Two things are certain. First, lots of people hate lawyers, some with very good reason. Second, the only thing worse than your own lawyer is the other guy's lawyer.

Having litigated numerous cases, and advised information security professionals inside and outside the federal government, we can assure information security professionals and their customers that, if and when you are sued by victims of attack or identify theft, or find yourselves in the sights of regulators or prosecutors, you will look to your lawyer as, if not a friend, at least a most necessary evil. And you will wish you had consulted that lawyer much, much sooner. Here's why.

It would seem obvious that, when the task is to determine how an entity may most effectively come into compliance with the numerous and complex legal requirements for information security, a qualified and experienced attorney should be involved. Surprisingly, this often does not appear to be the case today with information security evaluations. Most assessments and evaluations are conducted by computer engineers, accounting, and consulting firms. To be sure, that each of these professional competencies plays a necessary role in information security evaluations. However, since a key question is how to best comply with the current standards of care and, thus, mitigate potential legal liability, experienced and qualified counsel should be quarterbacking this team, much as a surgeon runs an operating room, even though nurses, anesthesiologists, and other competent professionals are crucial parts of the operating team.

WARNING: DO NOT PRACTICE LAW WITHOUT A LICENSE

In virtually every U.S. state, individuals are legally prohibited from practicing law without a license. For example, in Colorado, "practicing law" is defined, by law, to include, "counseling, advising and assisting [another] in connection with" legal rights and duties.[74] Penalties for the unauthorized practice of law in Colorado can include fines or imprisonment.[75] Information security consultants should not, under any circumstances, purport to advise customers as to the legal implications of statutes such as the HIPAA, Gramm-Leach-Bliley financial information privacy provisions, or other federal, state, or local laws or regulations. First, the consultants risk legal action against them by doing so. Second, they do their customers a grave disservice by leading them to believe that the customers can take any legal comfort from advice given them by non-lawyers.

Beyond this seemingly obvious reason for including the services and expertise of experienced and qualified legal counsel in conducting information security evaluations, a number of other factors also support doing so.

Attorney-Client Privilege

The so-called attorney-client privilege is one of the oldest protections for confidential information known to the law, and it is quite powerful. In every state, though with varying degrees of ease in establishing the privilege and differing degrees of exception to it, communications of legal advice from legal counsel to a client are "privileged," that is, protected, from compelled disclosure, including in civil lawsuits.[76] Information given by the client to the lawyer for the purpose of seeking legal advice is similarly protected.[77] In many, but not all jurisdictions, at least in civil litigation, once a court finds that the privilege applies, no amount of need for the privileged information claimed by a legal adversary cannot outweigh the protection created by the privilege.[78] This near-absolute protection is less certain, however, in at least some jurisdictions, in the criminal context.[79]

Further, courts in many states appear to apply a heightened level of scrutiny to corporate counsel and other "in-house" attorneys than they do to outside law firms retained by a corporation to perform particular legal services.[80] That is, courts force corporations to jump through more evidentiary "hoops" before allowing the attorney-client privilege for communications with in-house counsel than they do to communications with outside law firms.[81]

Importantly for information security consultants, courts have held (albeit in contexts analogous, but not identical, to information security, such as work with environmental consultants and accountants) that technical work performed by expert consultants can also enjoy attorney-client privilege protection.[82] Critically, though, this protection can attach to the consultant's work if, and only if, the client hires the attorney to perform a legal service (i.e., advising the client on how best to comply with HIPAA and/or other laws, and then the attorney hires the consultant to provide the attorney with technical information needed to provide accurate legal advice).[83] And this chain of employment cannot be a sham or mere pass-through used by the client to get the technical information but improperly cloak that data improperly with the privilege protection.[84]

The potential for the technical aspects of information security evaluations to enjoy enhanced protection from disclosure has obvious implications for information security evaluation results. If done honestly and correctly, the "chain of employment" (the hiring of a lawyer to provide legal advice which, in turn, requires assessment/evaluation work by technical experts) can protect all of the work. The legal advice, as well as, for example, technical reports showing identified potential vulnerabilities in the client's information security, may be protected under the attorney-client privilege.

It is important to recognize that, like information security measures, the attorney-client privilege is never "bullet proof." It is not absolute and there are, in every jurisdiction, well-recognized exceptions and ways to waive the protection (e.g., information provided to an attorney for the purpose of perpetrating a crime or fraud is not protected).[85] The protected nature of appropriately privileged information may disappear if the client or the attorney reveals that information to third parties outside the communication between the attorney (and consultants hired by the attorney) and certain company personnel (or in the presence of such third parties, even if the attorney is also present).[86] There are also times when it is appropriate to waive the privilege (e.g., a business or educational institution may choose to waive the privilege in order to assert an "advice-of-counsel" defense.) Also, the so-called Thompson Memorandum, issued by U.S Deputy Attorney General Larry Thompson in January 2003,[87] encourages companies to cooperate with the government in investigations by setting forth factors that are used to determine whether the government will pursue criminal prosecution. One important factor is whether the company is willing to waive the attorney-client and other privileges. Still, it is better to have these privileges to waive in an effort to encourage the government not to prosecute than not to have the privileges at all.

Courts have concluded that the societal benefit of not discouraging entities from conducting their own assessments of their compliance with applicable law outweighs any potential downside of the privilege, such as preventing all relevant information from coming out at trial.[88] This also makes good common sense. Entities will be far more likely to initiate their own compliance assessments/evaluations in information security, as in numerous other areas, if they are confident the results will be protected.[89]

Advice of Counsel Defense

Unfortunately, many information security consultants, auditors, and others attempt to advise customers about how to comply with laws and regulations they believe are applicable. This is problematic for several important reasons. First, generally speaking, experienced and qualified attorneys will be better able than others to accurately interpret and advise concerning the law.

Second, as noted several times already, non-attorneys may run afoul of state law by purporting to provide legal advice.

In addition to these reasons, following the advice of non-lawyers as to how to comply with the law does not provide the same level of legal defense in future lawsuits, regulatory proceedings, or prosecutions as following an attorney's advice. In general, a client who provides full and accurate information to an attorney in the course of seeking advice on how to comply with information security law, and makes a good faith effort to follow that advice, can enjoy what is known as the "advice of counsel" defense.[90] This defense is a significant protection against legal liability. Following an attorney's advice on information security legal compliance can protect the client, even if that advice turns out to have been in error.[91]

Establishment and Enforcement of Rigorous Assessment, Interview, and Report-Writing Standards

Important components of information security evaluations and assessments are the interviews of key customer personnel and reviews of their documents. While this work can be, and often is, performed exclusively by engineers or other consultants, interviewing and document review are skills in which lawyers tend to be particularly proficient. These two tasks form major portions of the daily work of many lawyers. As important as actually conducting interviews and reviewing documents is making certain that the right people are interviewed and that all relevant documents are located and carefully reviewed. These tasks, in turn, require the evaluation team to be flexible and alert to new avenues of inquiry that arise during the course of an evaluation (as well as during preparation for, and follow up to, the evaluation). Again, these skills are ones that lawyers exercise virtually every day in their ordinary practices.

Regardless of how much information is collected, it is useless to the customer until it is put into a form that is clear, understandable, and placed in its appropriate context. Extraneous information must be removed. Simple, declarative language must be used. The implications of each piece of information included in the report must be clearly identified. Here again, clear, understandable writing is the stock-in-trade of good lawyers. Attorney involvement in the drafting, or at least reviewing and editing, of information security evaluation reports can add significantly to the benefit of the process, and the final product, to the customer.

Creating a Good Record for Future Litigation

Many qualified and experienced lawyers also know how to write for judges and juries. There is a flip side of the coin of attorney-client privilege to help protect confidential results of information security evaluations from compelled disclosure in court. That is, the benefit of managing the process so that the resulting reports will work well in court in the event that the privilege fails for some reason (inadvertent waiver of it by the client, for example) and a report must be disclosed, *or* a report ends up being helpful in litigation and you *want* to disclose it. In such circumstances, two things will be important. First, the evaluation process and resulting report(s) must stand up under the evidentiary standards imposed by the civil litigation rules. For example, good records of interviews and document reviews should be kept in such a way as to prove a defensible "paper trail" that will convince the court that the information is reliable enough to be allowed into evidence in a trial. Second, reports should be written in a way to clearly describe threats and vulnerabilities, but not overstate them or speak of them in catastrophic terms when such verbiage is not warranted.

Lawyers, and especially experienced trial lawyers, tend to be skilled at both tasks.

Maximizing Ability to Defend Litigation

In a real sense, all of the benefits of involving qualified and experienced counsel previously discussed will help information security professionals and their customers defend against future litigation and, as important, deter would-be litigants from suing in the first place. There is an additional benefit for defense of potential litigation, often phrased as "in on the takeoff, in on the landing." Particularly in business areas with a significant inherent risk of litigation or enforcement action, having qualified and experienced trial lawyers involved early in the business process and throughout that process, will help maximize the ability of the work of information security consultants and their customers stand up to future litigation.

Dealing with Regulators, Law Enforcement, Intelligence, and Homeland Security Officials

Your meeting with Uncle Sam could happen in at least two ways: you may call him, or he may call you. The first is preferable.

The first scenario may unfold in several ways. Your customer may believe it is a victim of an attack on its information systems, terrorism-related or otherwise, and either not be able to stop the attack as it unfolds, not be able to ascertain its origin after it is over, or not be able to determine whether the attackers left behind surprises for further attack at a later time. Or your customer may simply believe contacting the authorities is the right thing to do. In any event, those authorities may want to talk with you—and potentially subpoena you to testify in court—as part of their investigation. Alternatively, an attack may take place while you are working on the customer's systems, making you, in effect, the "first responder."

The second scenario, Uncle Sam reaching out affirmatively to you and/or your customers, also may unfold in multiple ways, but two things are fairly constant. One, the government will be looking at your customer's systems well before they contact your customer. Two, when they come, they generally will get the information they need, even if a subpoena or warrant is necessary. As demonstrated by the National Strategy to Secure Cyberspace, and, particularly since 9/11, the existence of some type of "cyber unit" at many national law enforcement, intelligence, and homeland security organizations, Uncle Sam is keenly interested in any breaches of cyber security that could threaten our national security. This interest, and the government's aggressiveness in pursuing it, is likely only to increase.

In either scenario (voluntary or involuntary contact with the government, including state law enforcement agencies), what you and/or your customers do in the first few hours may be critical to how intact their information systems and sensitive information are when the process is complete. Who has the authority to speak to government authorities? What can and cannot be said to them? How much legal authority (request vs. search warrant vs. subpoena) will be required before allowing them in? Is there any information that they should not be allowed to review? What is the potential legal liability for sharing too much information? Too little? Obviously, your customers (and you, if you are involved) will want to cooperate with legitimate requests and, in fact, may have requested the government's help, but all businesses, educational institutions, and information security consultants must take care not to create civil or criminal liability for themselves by how they conduct their contacts with governmental authorities.

Here again, the keys are: (1) immediately gain the assistance of qualified legal counsel experienced both in information security law and in dealing with law enforcement, intelligence, and homeland security officers; and (2) have a plan in place beforehand for how such authorities will be dealt with, including having legal counsel retained and ready to go.

Notes from the Underground…

What to Look For in Your Attorneys

There are a number of obvious characteristics one should seek in any attorney retained for any purpose. These include integrity, a good reputation in the legal community, and general competence. You also want to consider an attorney with a strong background in corporate and business transactions who is familiar with the contracting process. One useful tool for evaluating these qualities as you attempt to narrow your list of potential attorneys to interview is a company called Martindale Hubbell (*www.martindale.com*). Look for lawyers with an "AV" rating (Martindale's highest).

(Note: Never hire any attorney without at least one face-to-face meeting to learn what your gut tells you about whether you could work with him or her.)

In the area of information security evaluation, you will want to look for attorneys with deep and broad expertise in the field. The best way to do so is to look for external, independently verifiable criteria demonstrating an attorney or law firm's tested credentials (e.g., is the lawyer you seek to retain listed on the National Security Agency Web site as including individuals certified as having been trained in NSA's Information Security

Continued

Assurance Methodology (IAM)? If so, on the appropriate NSA Web page (e.g., www.iatrp.com/indivu2.cfm#C), you will find a listing similar to this: Cunningham, Bryan, 03/15/05, (303) 743-0003, bc@morgancunningham.net)

Has an attorney you are considering authored any published works in the area of information security law? Has he or she held positions, in the government or elsewhere, related to information security? Finally, there's the gut check. How does your potential lawyer make you feel? Are you comfortable working with him or her? Does he or she communicate clearly and concisely? Does he or she seem more interested in covering their own backside than in providing you with legal counsel to protect your interests?

The Ethics of Information Security Evaluation[92]

The eighteenth century philosopher, Immanuel Kant, observed, "[i]*n law a man is guilty when he violates the rights of others. In ethics he is guilty if he only thinks of doing so.*"[93] To think and act ethically requires more than just strict compliance with the law. It requires an understanding of your customer, their business environment, and the duties your customer owes to others, under statutory requirements as well as private contracts. The reward is an increased likelihood of compliance with laws and establishing credibility in the community that will reduce the likelihood of disputes with customers and increase your marketability. Ethics relate to your conduct and not to the conduct of those with whom you are transacting business. However, it is not unethical to be alert to the possibility that others with whom you are dealing are themselves unethical. Do not be naive. Pursuit of an ethical practice does not replace the need to protect yourself through reliable processes, consistent methodologies, and properly drafted contracts that include defined work, limitations on liability, and indemnifications.

Do not think of violating the rights of others. Do not take short cuts. Do not assume that you can conduct your work without understanding the needs and rights of others and acting to protect them. Failing to understand the rights of customers you have been retained to help, or of those involved with your customers is tantamount to thinking of violating their rights. Ethical business, therefore, requires you understand the players and whose rights are at stake.

Finally, though it sounds obvious, do your job well. Martin Van Buren counseled that "[i]t is easier to do a job right than to explain why you didn't." Customers often insist on short cuts and reject proposals that require time delays to document the relationship and obtain the appropriate consents before the work begins. Customers soon forget their front-end demands for cost savings and expedience in completing the project. Hold firm. Do the job right and avoid having to explain to an angry customer, a prosecutor, a judge, or a jury why you did not.

Solutions Fast Track

Uncle Sam Wants You: How Your Company's Information Security Can Affect U.S. National Security (and Vice Versa)

☑ The U.S. Government has announced both the possibility of a significant information security attack on our U.S. critical infrastructure, and its intent to respond forcefully to such an attack if necessary, and the duty of the private sector to better secure its portion of cyberspace.

☑ Although no one can predict when and how severe such an attack may be, prudent commercial and educational entities, after the attacks of September 11, 2001, also should assume it will happen and act accordingly.

☑ This is an additional reason, beyond business operational needs, legal and regulatory requirements, and customer confidence, why commercial and educational entities should engage qualified and experienced legal counsel and technical information security providers sooner rather than later.

Legal Standards Relevant to Information Security

☑ A complex web of federal, state, and international statutes, regulations, and common law is evolving to create legal duties for commercial and educational entities in the area of information security.

☑ Non-lawyer consultants, even knowledgeable ones, cannot lawfully give advice on compliance with these laws, and commercial and educational entities should not rely on them to do so.

☑ This chapter cannot provide commercial and educational entities (or anyone else) with legal advice. Only qualified, licensed, and experienced legal counsel in a direct relationship with individual corporate and educational clients can do so.

Selected Laws

☑ At the U.S. federal level, HIPAA, GLBA, SOX, the Computer Fraud and Abuse Act, and other statutes and the regulations under them, as well as new ones yet to emerge, are constantly creating new information security legal obligations.

☑ State laws and "common law" theories such as negligence also may result in liability for failing to follow emerging "standards of care."

☑ Civil damages, regulatory action and, in some cases, even criminal liability, may result from failure, on the part of commercial and educational entities and the information security consultants who provide services to them, to seek (and follow) the advice of qualified and experienced legal counsel concerning these many emerging legal obligations.

Do It Right of Bet the Company: Tools to Mitigate Legal Liability

☑ Hire qualified, outside, legal and technical professionals.

☑ Effectively manage your contractual relationships to minimize liability.

What to Cover in IEM Contracts[94]

☑ Information security consultants must ensure that their legal obligations and rights, and those of their customers, are clearly spelled out in detailed written agreements.

☑ At a minimum, these should cover the topics discussed in the body of the chapter.

☑ In most cases LOAs, which are separate documents appended to an overall contract, should be used to clearly establish the authority, and any limitations on it, of information security consultants, to access and conduct testing on all types of information, systems, and portions of the Internet necessary to carry out the requested work.

The First Thing We Do...? Why You Want Your Lawyers Involved From Start to Finish

☑ Lawyers are a necessary evil to all information security consultants and their customers.

☑ Lawyers add value by, among other things: (1) helping to establish protection from disclosure, both for discovered customer information security vulnerabilities and the trade secrets and working methodology of information security consultants; (2) creating additional legal defenses against future liability.

☑ Lawyers (and only lawyers) may lawfully advise clients as to how best to comply with HIPAA, GLBA, SOX, and other federal and state statutory, regulatory, and common law legal requirements.

Frequently Asked Questions

The following Frequently Asked Questions, answered by the authors of this book, are designed to both measure your understanding of the concepts presented in this chapter and to assist you with real-life implementation of these concepts. To have your questions about this chapter answered by the author, browse to **www.syngress.com/solutions** and click on the **"Ask the Author"** form.

Q: Why can't I advise customers about compliance with HIPAA or SOX information security requirements if I'm a knowledgeable information security consultant?

A: Doing so would not only put you at risk for violating state law prohibitions against the unauthorized practice of law, but also fail to provide your customers either with attorney-client privilege protection against disclosure of vulnerabilities information or an "advice of counsel" defense.

Q: Why doesn't my in-house lawyer's involvement give me sufficient attorney-client privilege protection?

A: Contracting information security evaluations through in-house counsel is better than not having that involvement. However, as discussed, courts in multiple jurisdictions impose a higher standard for allowing attorney-client privilege for in-house counsel than for outside, retained lawyers.

Q: How often do I need to have information security evaluations?

A: Courts and regulators will apply a "reasonability" determination on this question, and it will be fact-specific, depending on the industry you are in, the types and amount of sensitive information you hold, and the then-current status of legal and regulatory requirements applicable to your business. In general, however, they should probably be no less frequently than once a year and, in many cases, more often.

Q: How much does having a lawyer involved add to the cost of information security evaluations?

A: Assuming you locate qualified and experienced counsel working with equally qualified technical consultants, and those two groups, in partnership, provide an integrated product that is priced in a reasonable and packaged way, your costs may well be less than using large, expensive, hourly rate-based consulting companies alone.

Q: How likely is a catastrophic information attack on our country?

A: There is a great deal of disagreement on this question, including among the authors of this chapter. However, the U.S. government has based a publicly stated policy on the possibility of such an attack and, post-9/11, it is prudent to assume such an attack could take place. Perhaps most importantly, assuming such an attack could occur only supports the myriad other business reasons to take reasonable information security measures, including one that lawyers rarely talk about: it is the right thing to do.

Q: Why are scientists now using lawyers more than rats for experiments?

A: (1) There are now more lawyers available than there are rats;(2) it is possible for scientists to get emotionally attached to the rats; and (3) there are some things you just can't get a rat to do.

References

[1] This chapter was written jointly by: Bryan Cunningham, Principal at Morgan & Cunningham LLC, a Denver-based homeland security consulting and law firm, and formerly Deputy Legal Adviser to the U.S. National Security Council and Assistant General Counsel, Central Intelligence Agency; C. Forrest Morgan, Principal at Morgan & Cunningham LLC, and Amanda Hubbard, Trial Attorney, U.S. Department of Justice with extensive experience in the U.S. Intelligence Community. The authors also gratefully acknowledge the research and analysis assistance of Nir D. Yarden. The views expressed herein are solely those of the authors and do not necessarily represent the views of the publisher or the U.S. government.

[2] This section drew, in part, from portions of pages 7–11 of *Security Assessment: Case Studies for Implementing the NSA IAM*, used by permission of Syngress Publishing, Inc.

[3] *Kennedy v. Mendoza-Martinez, 372 U.S. 144, 160 (1963).*

[4] *See, e.g.*, the 1993 opinion of the U.S. Department of Justice Office of Legal Counsel: "The concept of 'enforcement' is a broad one, and a given statute may be 'enforced' by means other than criminal prosecutions brought directly under it. " *Admissibility of Alien Amnesty Application Information in Prosecutions of Third Parties*, 17 Op. O.L.C. (1993); *see also* the 1898 opinion of Acting Attorney General John K. Richards:

> The preservation of our territorial integrity and the protection of our foreign interests is intrusted, in the first instance, to the President. . . . In the protection of these fundamental rights, which are based upon the Constitution and grow out of the jurisdiction of this nation over its own territory and its international rights and obligations as a distinct sovereignty, the President is not limited to the enforcement of specific acts of Congress. [The President] must preserve, protect, and defend those fundamental rights which flow from the Constitution itself and belong to the sovereignty it created.

Foreign Cables, 22 Op. Att'y Gen. 13, 25-26 (1898); *see also Cunningham v. Neagle*, 135 U.S. 1, 64 (1890).

[5] As Discussed in FN 13.

[6] United States National Strategy to Secure Cyberspace, February 14, 2003 (hereinafter "National Strategy") at 10. The National Strategy is available at: *http://www.whitehouse.gov/pcipb/*.

[7] See Testimony of Keith Lourdeau, Deputy Assistant Director, Cyber Division, FBI Before the Senate Judiciary Subcommittee on Terrorism, Technology, and Homeland Security, February 24, 2004 ("The FBI assesses the cyberterrorism threat to the U.S. to be rapidly expanding, as the number of actors with the ability to utilize computers for illegal, harmful, and possibly devastating purposes is on the rise. Terrorist groups have shown a clear interest in developing basic hacking tools and the FBI predicts that terrorist groups will either develop or hire hackers, particularly for the purpose of complimenting large physical attacks with cyber attacks."); Robert Lenzner and Nathan Vardi, Cyber-nightmare, http://protectia.co.uk/html/cybernightmare.html.

[8] *Id.*

[9] *Frontline* interview conducted March 18, 2003, at *http://www.pbs.org/wgbh/pages/frontline/shows/cyberwar/interviews/clarke.html.*

[10] *http://www.pbs.org/wgbh/pages/frontline/shows/cyberwar/interviews/clarke.html.*

[11] *http://www.pbs.org/wgbh/pages/frontline/shows/cyberwar/interviews/clarke.html;* Hildreth, CRS Report for Congress, *Cyberwarfare,* Updated June 19, 2001, at 18, at http://www.fas.org/irp/crs/RL30735.pdf

[12] *Cyberwarfare.* at 2.

[13] The idea of a catastrophic cyber attack against the U.S. by terrorist groups is far from universally accepted. *See, e.g.,* James A. Lewis, *Assessing the Risks of Cyber Terrorism, Cyber War and Other Cyber Threats,* Center for Strategic and International Studies, December 2002, at *http://www.csis.org/tech/0211_lewis.pdf.* Indeed, as noted above, one of the three authors of this chapter believes that, while technically possible, this threat is often overstated, at least as a near-term possibility. For information security professionals and their customers, however, the prudent course—given our adversaries' capability, intent, and opportunity and the stated U.S. Government policy of being prepared to respond to cyber attack—is to assume the possibility of such an attack. In addition, the plethora of known active threats to information security, including extortionists, identity thieves, gangs attempting to amass and sell financial and other valuable personal information, malicious hackers, and others, provide precisely the same incentive to secure information systems' as do would-be cyber-terrorists.

[14] *See, e.g., Law of Armed Conflict and Information Warfare—How Does the Rule Regarding Reprisals Apply to an Information Warfare, Attack?,* Major Daniel M. Vadnais, March 1997, at 25 ("To the extent that information warfare is manifested by traditionally understood damage to sovereign integrity, the law of armed conflict should apply, and proportional reprisals may be justified. On the other hand, to the extent that damage to a sovereign's integrity is not physical, there is a gap in the law."). *http://www.fas.org/irp/threat/cyber/97-0116.pdf.*

[15] *Id.*

[16] National Strategy at p. 59 (A/R 5-4).

[17] National Strategy at p. 49 (Priority V: National Security and International Cyberspace Security Cooperation).

[18] Nearly as dangerous for our Nation as attacks from within the U.S. directed *at us,* would be if zombied servers here were being used to launch an attack *against another nation.* Imagine the reaction of China or Iran if servers inside the U.S. were being used to damage their infrastructure or harm their people. First, they likely would not believe denials by our government that these acts of war were being carried out deliberately by our government. Second, even if they did believe such denials, they still might feel compelled to respond with force to disable or destroy the systems of, and/or punish, those they perceived to be their attackers.

[19] Particularly in the wake of the 2005 publicity surrounding security breaches at ChoicePoint, LexisNexis, MasterCard, major banks, other commercial entities, and universities, a number of pieces of legislation requiring disclosure of information security breaches and/or enhanced information security measures were working their way through the U.S. Congress, or were threatened in the near future. *See* Roy Mark, *Data Brokers Step Into Senate Panel's Fire,* e-Security Planet.com, http://66.102.7.104/search?q=cache:REXdffBCvEYJ:www.esecurityplanet.com/trends/article.php/3497591+specter+and+information+security+and+disclosure&hl=en.

[20] 15 U.S.C. §§ 6801, et. seq.

[21] 15 U.S.C. § 6801(b).

[22] 15 U.S.C. §§ 6804 - 6805.

[23] Available at *http://www.ffiec.gov/ffiecinfobase/resources/elect_bank/ frb-12_cfr_225_appx_f_bank_holding_non-bank_affiliates.pdf.*

[24] *Guidelines.*

[25] *Id.*

[26] *Id.*

[27] *Id.*

[28] *Id.*

[29] EPHI is defined in the law as individually identifiable health information that is transmitted by, or maintained in, electronic media, except several narrow categories of educational, employment, and other records. 45 C.F.R. part 106.103. Note, however, that the separate HIPAA Privacy Rule also requires "appropriate security" for all PHI, even if it is not in electronic form.

[30] 45 C.F.R. part 164.

[31] Compliance with the Security Rule became mandatory for all but small health care plans in April 2005. "Small" health care plans have until April 2006 to comply.

[32] 45 C.F.R. part 164.

[33] *Id.* One reason it is crucial for information security professionals to retain, on an ongoing basis, qualified, experienced counsel is that "reasonably anticipated" is essentially a legal standard best understood and explained by legal counsel and because what is "reasonably anticipated" is constantly evolving as new threats are discovered and publicized, and information security programs

must evolve with it in order to mitigate legal liability,

[34] *Id.*

[35] *Id.*

[36] It is worth remembering that a significant majority of the process and procedural requirements are *not* technical. This, among other considerations, counsels the use of multidisciplinary teams, of which technical experts are only one part, to conduct and document information security evaluations.

[37] 45 C.F.R. Part 164.308.

[38] 45 C.F.R. Part 164.310.

[39] 45 C.F.R. Part 164.312.

[40] 18 U.S.C. § 1350.

[41] SOX § 404.

[42] SOX § 302.

[43] FISMA, Title III of the E-Government Act of 2002, Public Law No. 107-347.

[44] FN: 20 U.S.C § 1232g

[45] As enacted, the TEACH Act amended Section 110 of the Copyright Act. 17 U.S.C. §110.

[46] 18 U.S.C. § 2510, *et. seq.*

[47] 18 U.S.C. § 1030, *et. seq.*

[48] Other federal laws and regulations potentially relevant to the work of information security professionals and their customers include, but are not limited to, the Children's Online Privacy Protection Act of 1998, information security standards promulgated by the National Institute of Standards, Presidential Decision Directive 63 (May 22, 1998), and Homeland Security Presidential Directive 7 (December 17, 2003). In addition, numerous state laws, including provisions of the Uniform Commercial Code and Uniform Financial Transactions Act, as enacted in the various states, implicate information security requirements for specific economic sectors and/or types of transactions.

[49] Colorado Revised Statutes § 18-5.5-102.

[50] Colorado Revised Statutes § 6-1-105.

[51] Colorado Revised Statutes § 6-1-105(e).

[52] Colorado Revised Statutes § 6-1-105(u).

[53] Between 2001 and 2005 such actions included those against: Microsoft Corporation, Victoria's Secret, Eli Lilly, and Ziff Davis Media, Inc., among others. *See, e.g.,* http://www.ftc.gov/os/2002/08/microsoftagree.pdf; http://www.oag.state.ny.us/press/2002/aug/aug28a_02_attach.pdf.

[54] *Directive 95/46/EC of the European Parliament and of the Council of 24 October 1995 on the protection of individuals with regard to the processing of personal data and on the free movement of such data, Official Journal of the European Communities of 23 November 1995 No L. 281, 31, available at* http://www.cdt.org/privacy/eudirective/EU_Directive_.html.

[55] *See, e.g.,* Transcript of Hearing Before U.S. District Judge Royce Lamberth, in which an information security consultant is examined and cross-examined under oath, in public, for multiple days, concerning penetration test work done for the U.S. Bureau of Indian Affairs. http://66.102.7.104/search?q=cache:d30x73ieDSwJ:www.indiantrust.com/_pdfs/3am.pdf+lamberth+and+cobell+and+transcript+and+miles&hl=en

[56] For example, B. Grimes *The Right Ways to Protect Your Net* PC World Magazine, September 2001, offers tips for tightening your security and protecting your enterprise from backdoor hackers and thieves.

[57] *http://wsbradio.com/news/0223choicepointsuit.html.*

[58] *Harrington v. ChoicePoint Inc.,* C.D. Cal., No. CV 05-1294 (SJO) (JWJx), 2/22/05).

[59] Generally, a post-hoc calculation of "reasonability" will be based on balancing such factors as: (1) the probability of reasonably anticipated damage occurring; (2) the expected severity of the damage if it does occur; (3) reasonably available risk mitigation measures; and (4) the cost of implementing such measures.

[60] *See, e.g., Assurance of Discontinuance, In the Matter of Ziff Davis Media Inc.,* at 7, available at *http://www.oag.state.ny.us/press/2002/aug/aug28a_02_attach.pdf.; Agreement Containing Consent Order, In the Matter of Microsoft Corporation,* at 5, available at *http://www.ftc.gov/os/2002/08/microsoftagree.pdf.*

[61] California Civil Code Sections 1798.29 and 1798.82 accessible at *http://www.leginfo.ca.gov/calaw.html.*

[62] 2005 Breach of Information Legislation. http://www.ncsl.org/programs/lis/CIP/priv/breach.htm.

[63] P. Britt, *Protecting Private Information* Information Today (Vo. 22 No. 5 May, 2005) *http://www.infotoday.com/it/may05/britt.shtml.*

[64] This section drew, in part, from portions of pages 7-11 of *Security Assessment: Case Studies for Implementing the NSA IAM,* used by permission of Syngress Publishing, Inc.

[65] Assuming the NSA IAM is used, of course, much of this critical work will already have been documented prior to initiation of the IEM.

[66] The issue of securing complete authorization for all types of information and systems (internal and external) that may be impacted by evaluation and testing, is intentionally covered in multiple parts of this section. It is absolutely critical to the legal well being of both the consultant and the customer to ensure clarity of responsibility for these, which is why this section provides multiple different avenues for addressing this problem. Equally critical is a clear understanding of the "divi-

sion of liability" for any damage that, notwithstanding best efforts of both sides, may result to external systems. This should be taken care of through a combination of indemnification (described below), clear statements of responsibility in the contract, written agreements with third parties, and insurance.

[67] *See, e.g., Management Recruiters, Inc. v. Miller, 762 P.2d 763, 766 (Colo.App.1988).*

[68] *Board of County Commissioners of Adams County v. City and County of Denver, 40 P.3d 25 (Colo.App.,2001).*

[69] *See, e.g., Butler Manufacturing Co. v. Americold Corp., 835 F.Supp. 1274 (D.Kan. 1993).*

[70] *See, e.g., Elsken v. Network Multi-Family Sec. Corp., 838 P.2d 1007 (Okla.1992)*

[71] National Conference of State Legislatures information page accessible at *http://www.ncsl.org/programs/lis/cip/hacklaw.htm.*

[72] *Henry VI*, Part 2, act iv, scene ii.

[73] *See, e.g.,* Seth Finkelstein, "The first thing we do, let's kill all the lawyers" – It's a Lawyer Joke, *The Ethical Spectator,* July 1997., available at: *http://*www.sethf.com/essays/major/killlawyers.php.

[74] *Koscove v. Bolte, 30 P.3d 784* (Colo.App. 2001*).*

[75] *See, e.g.* Rule 238(c), Colorado Court Rules (2004).

[76] *See, e.g., Pacamor Bearings, Inc. v. Minebea Co., Ltd.,* 918 F.Supp. 491, 509-510 (D. N.H. 1996).

[77] *Id.*

[78] *See, e.g., Diversified Indus., Inc. v. Meredith,* 572 F.2d 596, 602 (8th Cir. 1978*).*

[79] *See, e.g., People v. Benney, 757 P.2d 1078* (Colo.App. 1987*).*

[80] *See, e.g., Southern Bell Telephone & Telegraph Co. v. Deason,* 632 So. 2d 1377 (Fla. 1994); *McCaugherty v. Sifferman,* 132 F.R.D. 234 (N.D. Cal. 1990). *United States v. Davis* 132 F.R.D. 12 (S.D.N.Y. 1990).

[81] *See, e.g., United States v. Chevron,* No. C-94-1885 SBA, 1996 WL 264769 (N.D. Cal. Mar. 13, 1996).

[82] *See, e.g., Gerrits v. Brannen Banks of Florida* 138 F.R.D. 574, 577 (D. Colo. 1991).

[83] *See, e.g., id.*

[84] *See, e.g., Sneider v. Kimberly-Clark Corp.,* 91 F.R.D. 1, 5 (N.D. Ill. 1980)

[85] *See, e.g., In re Grand Jury Proceedings,* 857 F.2d 710, 712 (10th Cir. 1988).

[86] *See, e.g., Winchester Capital Management Co. vs. Manufacturers Hanover Trust Co.,* 144 F.R.D.170, 174 (D. Mass. 1992).

[87] U.S. Department of Justice, *Federal Prosecution of Business Organizations* in *Criminal Resource Manual* No. 162 (2003) available at *http://www.usdoj.gov/usao/eousa/foia_reading_room/usam/title9/crm00162.html* and amended and available at *http://www.usdoj.gov/dag/cftf/corporate_guidelines.html.*

[88] *See, e.g., Union Carbide Corp. v. Dow Chem. Co.,* 619 F. Supp. 1036, 1046 (D. Del. 1985)

[89] A related protection to that of the attorney-client privilege is the so-called "work product" doctrine. This protection for materials that might tend to show the strategies or other "mental impressions" of attorneys when such materials are prepared "in anticipation of litigation" would cover the work of information security consultants assisting attorneys in preparing materials for use at a trial or to deal with regulators or law enforcement officials. Work-product protection is significantly more susceptible to being held inapplicable by the court, upon a sufficiently high showing of need by your adversary, than is the attorney-client privilege.

[90] *See, e.g., United States v. Gonzales*, 58 F.3d 506, 512 (10th Cir. 1995).

[91] *Id.*

[92] Entire books could be written on this topic, and some have, at least on the broader topic of IT ethics. *See, e.g., IT Ethics Handbook: Right and Wrong for IT Professionals*, Syngress Publishing, Inc. A comprehensive discussion of Information Security Evaluation ethics is beyond the scope of this book. This discussion is simply to remind us all of some things we learned from our parents that translate into our business relationships.

[93] Available at
http://en.thinkexist.com/quotation/in_law_a_man_is_guilty_when_he_violates_the/7854.html.

[94] This section drew, in part,, from portions of pages 7-11 of Security Assessment: Case Studies for Implementing the NSA IAM, used by permission of Syngress Publishing, Inc.

Examples of INFOSEC Tools by Baseline Activity

Solutions in this chapter:

- Port Scanning
- SNMP Scanning
- Enumeration and Banner Grabbing
- Wireless Enumeration
- Vulnerability Scanning
- Host Evaluation
- Network Device Analysis
- Password-Compliance Testing
- Application-Specific Scanning
- Network Protocol Analysis

NOTE

No specific tools are implied or endorsed.
No specific brands are implied or endorsed.
CVE/CAN relation is strongly recommended.
Tool versions are current as of the writing of this book.

Port Scanning

Tool Name: Nmap (v.3.81)

Developer: Fyodor (Insecure.org)

Platform/OS: UNIX, Linux, FreeBSD, NetBSD, OpenBSD, Solaris, OS X, Microsoft Windows, HP-UX, AIX, DigUX, Cray UNICOS

Commercial or Freeware? Freeware (GPL)

URL: www.insecure.org/nmap/

Notes: Microsoft Windows XP SP2 disabled the ability to use RAW sockets, it throttled the number of permitted outbound TCP connections, and disabled the ability to send spoofed UDP packets. This is "fixed" in Nmap version 3.55 and newer. Nmap is a tool that fits into more than one baseline activity. It can provide a wealth of information.

Tool Name: ScanLine (v.1.01)

Developer: McAfee (formerly FoundStone)

Platform/OS: Microsoft Windows

Commercial or Freeware? Freeware

URL: www.foundstone.com/resources/proddesc/scanline.htm

Notes: ScanLine is the replacement for Fscan. This is a command-line scanner for the MS Windows platform; it can handle scanning in a highly parallel fashion and provides more scanning capabilities than Fscan did.

Tool Name: Scanrand (part of paketto v.2.0p3)

Developer: Dan Kaminsky

Platform/OS: Compiles on Linux (RedHat, Mandrake, and Debian), FreeBSD, MinGW (on MS Windows)

Commercial or Freeware? Freeware

URL: www.doxpara.com

Notes: Libnet (v1.0.2) and libpcap are *required*.

Tool Name: SuperScan (v.4.0)

Developer: McAfee (formerly FoundStone)

Platform/OS: Microsoft Windows

Commercial or Freeware? Freeware

URL: www.foundstone.com/resources/proddesc/superscan4.htm

Notes: SuperScan v3.0 and v4.0 are available from this site. Version 4.0 provides more functionality but doesn't seem as fast as version 3.0.

Tool Name: MingSweeper (v.1.0alpha5, build 130)

Developer: HooBie

Platform/OS: Microsoft Windows NT/2000/XP

Commercial or Freeware? Freeware

URL: www.hoobie.net/mingsweeper/index.html

Notes: MingSweeper is a network reconnaissance tool. It is designed for scanning large address spaces and for high-speed node discovery and identification. It is capable of doing ping sweeps, reverse DNS sweeps, TCP scans, and UDP scans as well as OS and application identification.

SNMP Scanning

Tool Name: SolarWinds Network Management Toolset

Developer: SolarWinds.net Network Management

Platform/OS: Microsoft Windows

Commercial or Freeware? Commercial

URL: www.solarwinds.net/Toolsets.htm

Notes: SolarWinds toolset is much more than a simple SNMP scanner. Considering how much functionality this application suite provides, it could be considered a one-stop shop when it comes to network management and troubleshooting.

Tool Name: Snscan (v.1.05)

Developer: McAfee (formerly FoundStone)

Platform/OS: Microsoft Windows

Commercial or Freeware? Freeware

URL: www.foundstone.com/resources/proddesc/snscan.htm

Notes: Snscan is a decent SNMP scanning tool but limited in its capabilities and information it provides.

Tool Name: GetIF (v.2.3.1)

Developer: Philippe Simonet

Platform/OS: Microsoft Windows

Commercial or Freeware? Freeware

URL: www.wtcs.org/snmp4tpc/getif.htm

Notes: This is an excellent freeware SNMP tool for MS Windows. Very handy and easy to use.

Tool Name: Braa (v.0.8)

Developer: Mateusz "mteg" Golicz

Platform/OS: Linux, FreeBSD, OpenBSD

Commercial or Freeware? Freeware

URL: http://s-tech.elsat.net.pl/braa/

Notes: Braa is a mass SNMP scanner. What separates this tool from the rest is the way it handles multiple queries simultaneously. According to the author of this tool, it is able to scan dozens or even hundreds of hosts simultaneously, in a single process. Braa implements its own SNMP stack and requires a system that implements BSD sockets and supports POSIX syscalls.

Enumeration and Banner Grabbing

Tool Name: Winfingerprint (v.0.6.2)

Developer: Vacuum

Platform/OS: Microsoft Windows

Commercial or Freeware? Freeware

URL: http://winfingerprint.sourceforge.net

Notes: Winfingerprint is a host/network enumeration and scanning tool. It is capable of the following scan types: TCP, UDP, ICMP, RPC, SMB, and SNMP. If you ant to do TCP SYN scans, you must have WinPcap installed as well. Otherwise the scans will be non-blocking connect() based.

Tool Name: NBTScan (v.1.5.1)

Developer: Alla Bezroutchko (Inetcat.org)

Platform/OS: Microsoft Windows NT/2000/XP, OS X, Linux, Solaris, FreeBSD, OpenBSD, HP-UX, AIX

Commercial or Freeware? Freeware

URL: www.inetcat.org/software/nbtscan.html

Notes: This is an easy-to-use NetBIOS scanner. It is used for enumerating resources available via NetBIOS on the network.

Tool Name: Xprobe2 (v.0.2.2)

Developer: Fyodor Yarochkin and Ofir Arkin

Platform/OS: Linux, Solaris, FreeBSD, OpenBSD, NetBSD

Commercial or Freeware? Freeware

URL: http://sys-security.com/index.php?page=xprobe

Notes: Xprobe2 is a remote active OS fingerprinting tool. It does its OS fingerprinting a bit differently than other tools. Xprobe2 relies on fuzzy fingerprint matching, guesswork (based on probabilities), simultaneous multiple matches, and a signature database.

Tool Name: hping2 (v.2.0.0-rc3)

Developer: Lead Maintainer: Salvatore Sanfilippo (see www.hping.org/authors.html for additional contributors)

Platform/OS: Linux, OS X, Solaris, FreeBSD, OpenBSD, NetBSD

Commercial or Freeware? Freeware

URL: www.hping.org

Notes: hping2 is a command-line-oriented TCP/IP packet assembler and analyzer. Hping2 supports the following protocols: ICMP, TCP, UDP, and RAW-IP. Additionally, it has a *traceroute* mode. Hping2 has so many features, it would take up too much space to list them all. Note: at press time hping3 was still in development.

Tool Name: Netcat (*NIX: v1.10, Windows: v1.11)

Developer: Hobbit

Platform/OS: Linux, Solaris, SunOS, OS X, AIX, HP-UX, Irix, Ultrix, BSDi, FreeBSD, NetBSD, OpenBSD, UnixWare, NeXT, Microsoft Windows

Commercial or Freeware? Freeware

URL: www.vulnwatch.org/netcat/

Notes: Netcat is *essential* for every INFOSEC toolbox. There's a reason people call it the "Swiss army knife of TCP/IP"—it can do so much. Read up on this tool and you will see how useful it is. Simply put, Netcat is a UNIX utility for reading and writing data across network connections, using TCP or UDP for its protocol. Netcat can act as a client *or* a server and can be used directly or accessed via programs or scripts. Flexibility is the best word to describe Netcat.

Wireless Enumeration

NOTE

Wireless Ennumeration has privacy concerns/issues, as well as potential "theft of service." Be aware!

Tool Name: Kismet

Developer: Kismetwireless.net

Platform/OS: Linux (preferred), OS X, FreeBSD, OpenBSD, NetBSD, and limited support on Microsoft Windows

Commercial or Freeware? Freeware

URL: www.kismetwireless.net/

Notes: Kismet is a passive wireless network detector, protocol analyzer, and intrusion detection system. Kismet works with any wireless card that supports raw monitoring mode (rfmon). Kismet can capture and analyze 802.11a, 802.11b, and 802.11g traffic. Kismet on Windows works only with remote captures, since there are no public rfmon drivers for Windows (win32). Furthermore, Kismet on Windows requires Cygwin to provide the necessary POSIX layer.

Tool Name: Netstumbler

Developer: Marius Milner

Platform/OS: Microsoft Windows 2000/XP/2003, PocketPC 2002, 2003

Commercial or Freeware? Freeware (not open source)

URL: www.stumbler.net (Netstumbler forums: http://www.netstumbler.net)

Notes: Netstumbler is a Microsoft Windows-only wireless network detector. It is free but not open source. It's a very popular freeware wireless network detector and does its job pretty well. But unlike Kismet, Netstumbler isn't passive. It uses active probing to detect wireless networks.

Tool Name: Airsnort

Developer: Snax

Platform/OS: Linux, Microsoft Windows

Commercial or Freeware? Freeware

URL: http://airsnort.shmoo.com/

Notes: Airsnort is a wireless network tool designed to recover wireless encryption keys. Airsnort passively monitors for wireless transmissions, and when it has enough packets gathered, it computes the encryption key (in less than a second!). Airsnort requires approximately 5–10 million encrypted packets to guess the encryption key.

Tool Name: AiroPeek NX

Developer: WildPackets

Platform/OS: Microsoft Windows XP (SP1), 2000 (SP3)

Commercial or Freeware? Commercial

URL:
www.wildpackets.com/products/airopeek/airopeek_nx/overview

Notes: AiroPeek NX is an expert wireless network analyzer that provides expert diagnostic tools for troubleshooting and managing your wireless infrastructure. AiroPeak can do site surveys, wireless LAN analysis, wireless LAN monitoring, and application layer protocol analysis.

Vulnerability Scanning

Tool Name: Nessus (v.2.2.4)

Developer: Renaud Deraison

Platform/OS: n/a

Commercial or Freeware? Freeware

URL: www.nessus.org

Notes: Nessus is probably the most popular open source vulnerability scanner in use today. It is used for remote vulnerability scanning and can be used for local host scanning too. It has an up-to-date CVS/CAN-compliant vulnerability database and built-in scripting capabilities (via NASL), and each security test is written as a plug-in in NASL, so you are able to view the code being executed and modify it to fit your needs or the needs of the organization you are evaluating. There are over 6000 plug-ins (vulnerability checks) available with the default install of Nessus.

Tool Name: NeWT (v.2.1)

Developer: Tenable

Platform/OS: Microsoft Windows

Commercial or Freeware? Commercial

URL: www.tenablesecurity.com

Notes: NeWT stands for *Nessus Windows Technology*. As the name states, this is a version of Nessus built to run on Microsoft Windows platforms. It has the same capabilities and checks as Nessus.

Tool Name: Retina (v5.2.12)

Developer: eEye

Platform/OS: Microsoft Windows

Commercial or Freeware? Commercial

URL: www.eeye.com/html/products/retina/

Notes: Retina is a really good vulnerability scanner, but it is commercial and somewhat pricey. It has an excellent vulnerability database, and the reporting capabilities are much more flexible than in previous versions.

Tool Name: SAINT (v.5.8.4)

Developer: Saint Corporation

Platform/OS: UNIX, Linux, OS X, FreeBSD, Solaris, HP-UX 11

Commercial or Freeware? Commercial

URL: www.saintcorporation.com/saint/

Notes: SAINT stands for *Security Administrators Integrated Network Tool*. SAINT is a vulnerability assessment tool that is also CVE/CAN compliant (as well as IAVA). This tool is excellent for measuring compliance (for example, for GLBA, SOX, and HIPAA), and the reporting capabilities are quite good.

Tool Name: VLAD the Scanner (v.0.9.2)

Developer: BindView

Platform/OS: Linux, OpenBSD, FreeBSD, OS X

Commercial or Freeware? Freeware

URL:
www.bindview.com/Services/RAZOR/Utilities/Unix_Linux/
vlad.cfm

Notes: VLAD is an open source vulnerability scanner that tests for the SANS Top 10 vulnerabilities
(http://www.sans.org/top20/top10.php). VLAD requires several Perl modules: LWP::UserAgent, HTTP::Request, HTTP::Response, Net::DNS::Resolver, IO::Socket, IO::Pty, IO::Stty, Socket, Net::SNMP, Net::Telnet, Expect, File::Spec, and Time::HiRes.

Tool Name: LANGuard Network Security Scanner (v6.0).

Developer: GFi

Platform/OS: Microsoft Windows

Commercial or Freeware? Commercial

URL: www.gfi.com/lannetscan/

Notes: LANGuard NSS is primarily a Microsoft Windows vulnerability scanner, but GFi recently added some Linux checks/scans to the product. LANGuard NSS is an excellent vulnerability scanner and enumeration tool for Microsoft Windows platforms. Not only does it do vulnerability scanning and enumeration activities, but it can handle patch management as well.

Tool Name: Typhoon III

Developer: NGS Software

Platform/OS: Microsoft Windows NT/2000/XP

Commercial or Freeware? Commercial

URL: www.nextgenss.com/typhon.htm

Notes: Typhoon is another vulnerability scanner that provides much of the same information as other scanners, but it goes about it differently; using NGS's spidering technique. Typhoon is a high-speed scanner and can do application-level checks as well (such as cross-site scripting attack checks and SQL injection checks).

Host Evaluation

Tool Name: CIS Benchmark Tools/Scripts

Developer: Center for Internet Security (CIS)

Platform/OS: Microsoft Windows NT, 2000, 2000 Pro, 2000 Server, 2003 Server, and XP Pro; OS X, FreeBSD, Solaris 2.5.1-10, Linux, HP-UX, AIX, wireless networks, Cisco IOS Router, Cisco PIX, Oracle Database 8a, 9a, and 10g, and Apache Web Server

Commercial or Freeware? Free for noncommercial use

URL: www.cisecurity.org/benchmarks/

Notes: The CIS Benchmark Tools measure the assessed system or application against widely accepted security benchmarks and best-practice security configuration for computers connected to the Internet.

Tool Name: Microsoft Security Baseline Analyzer (v.1.2.1)

Developer: Microsoft

Platform/OS: Microsoft Windows 2000, XP and 2003

Commercial or Freeware? Freeware

URL: www.microsoft.com/technet/security/tools/mbsahome.mspx

Notes: The Microsoft Baseline Security Analyzer (MSBA) is an easy-to-use tool that helps determine the security state of the evaluated machine, in accordance with Microsoft security recommendations, and offers remediation guidance.

Tool Name: HFNetChk / HFNetChkPro (v.5.0)

Developer: Shavlik

Platform/OS: Microsoft Windows 2000, XP and 2003

Commercial or Freeware? Commercial (demo available)

URL: www.shavlik.com/hf.aspx

Notes: Though HFNetChkPro is listed as a patch management solution, it is also very good at checking for vulnerabilities and missing patches and security updates and provides a method for mitigating many issues remotely. That's why we listed this tool in the Host Analysis section—it covers more baseline activities in this section.

Network Device Analysis

Tool Name: Firewalk (v5.0)

Developer: Mike Schiffman

Platform/OS: n/a

Commercial or Freeware? Freeware

URL: www.packetfactory.net/firewalk/

Notes: Firewalk is an active reconnaissance network security tool that attempts to determine what layer 4 protocols an IP forwarding device will allow to pass through. Firewalk is designed for testing firewalls and other IP forwarding devices. Building Firewalk requires libnet 1.1.x, libpcap, and libdnet.

Tool Name: RAT (Router Audit Tool)

Developer: CIS (Center for Internet Security)

Platform/OS: Microsoft Windows, UNIX, Linux

Commercial or Freeware? Free for noncommercial use

URL: www.cisecurity.org/rat/

Notes: The Router Audit Tool from CIS can download the configuration from the device to be evaluated (router, PIX firewall) and check the configuration against the settings defined in the provided benchmarks. RAT provides a list of all the rules to be checked, along with a pass/fail score for each, the raw overall score, the weighted score (scale of 1–10), and a list of IOS/PIX commands that will correct the issues identified.

Password-Compliance Testing

Tool Name: Brutus (v.AET2)

Developer: HooBie

Platform/OS: Microsoft Windows

Commercial or Freeware? Freeware

URL: www.hoobie.net/brutus/

Notes: Application still is in development. It's a remote password cracker.

Tool Name: L0phtCrack (v.5.0)

Developer: Symantec (formerly @Stake)

Platform/OS: Microsoft Windows

Commercial or Freeware? Commercial

URL: www.atstake.com/lc/

Notes: L0phtCrack (LC5) has been around for quite some time and is very well known. LC5 can test the password strength of Windows and UNIX passwords. Now LC5 comes with tables of precomputed password hashes, which makes the password-testing phase go quicker.

Tool Name: OPHCrack (v.2.0)

Developer: Philippe Oechslin

Platform/OS: Microsoft Windows, Linux

Commercial or Freeware? Freeware

URL: http://ophcrack.sourceforge.net/

Notes: OPHCrack is also referred to as the "time-memory tradeoff cracker." It uses precomputed hash tables loaded into memory to dramatically speed the password-cracking process. OPHCrack can obtain the password hash in any one of three ways: through the encrypted SAM file, through the local SAM file, and through the remote SAM file.

Tool Name: John the Ripper (v.1.6)

Developer: Openwall Project

Platform/OS: UNIX (11 flavors), Microsoft Windows, OS X, Linux, BeOS, FreeBSD, OpenBSD, NetBSD

Commercial or Freeware? Freeware

URL: www.openwall.com/john/

Notes: John the Ripper is a fast password cracker that was developed for the task of detecting weak UNIX passwords. Since then, John the Ripper has expanded to test not only UNIX passwords (several of the most common crypt() password hash types) but Kerberos AFS and Microsoft Windows NT/2000/XP/2003 LM hashes as well. Contributors to the project have submitted patches to test the password strength of several applications and services.

Application-Specific Scanning

Tool Name: WebInspect

Developer: SPI Dynamics

Platform/OS: Microsoft Windows 2000/XP/2003

Commercial or Freeware? Commercial

URL: www.spidynamics.com/products/webinspect/

Notes: WebInspect is an application security assessment tool. It identifies vulnerabilities at the Web application layer. WebInspect is great for measuring compliance, making Web application vulnerability assessments, or checking the configuration of a Web application. SPI Dynamics provides the industry's largest Web application vulnerability database with WebInspect.

Tool Name: AppDetective

Developer: Application Security Inc.

Platform/OS: Microsoft Windows 2000/XP/2003

Commercial or Freeware? Commercial

URL: www.appsecinc.com/products/appdetective/

Notes: AppDetective is a network-based vulnerability scanner for database applications. It supports the scanning of MySQL, Oracle, Sybase, IBM DB2, MSSQL, Oracle Application Server, and Lotus

Notes/Domino. AppDetective allows you to assess the three primary application tiers: Web front-end, application/middleware, and back-end database. AppDetective locates, examines, reports, and fixes security holes and configuration issues.

Tool Name: Wikto (v.1.6)

Developer: SensePost

Platform/OS: Microsoft Windows

Commercial or Freeware? Freeware

URL: www.sensepost.com/research/wikto/

Notes: Wikto is a port to Microsoft Windows of the tool Nikto (www.cirt.net/code/nikto.shtml). Wikto has three main sections of functionality: back-end miner, Nikto-like functionality, and Googler. It is a Web server scanner that performs comprehensive tests against Web servers for multiple issues. Including over 3,200 potentially dangerous files/CGI/scripts, it obtains the versions on over 625 servers and version-specific problems on over 230 servers.

Something to keep in mind: Neither Nikto or Wikto are stealthy at all.

Tool Name: Achilles

Developer: Robert Cardona of Systegra

Platform/OS: Microsoft Windows

Commercial or Freeware? Freeware

URL: www.mavensecurity.com/achilles

Notes: Achilles is a general-purpose Web application security assessment tool. Achilles acts as a HTTP/HTTPS proxy that permits the user to intercept, log, and modify Web traffic on the fly.

Tool Name: IKE–Scan (v.1.7)

Developer: NTA Monitor Limited

Platform/OS: Linux, FreeBSD, OpenBSD, NetBSD, Solaris, OS X, HP-UX, Microsoft Windows (via Cygwin)

Commercial or Freeware? Freeware

URL: www.nta-monitor.com/ike-scan/

Notes: The IKE-scan tool scans IP addresses for VPN servers by sending a specially crafted IKE packet to each host within a network. Most hosts running IKE will respond, identifying their presence. The tool then remains silent and monitors retransmission packets. These retransmission responses are recorded, displayed, and matched against a known set of VPN product fingerprints.

Tool Name: k0ld (v.1.9)

Developer: FX

Platform/OS: Requires the OpenLDAP libraries

Commercial or Freeware? Freeware

URL: www.phenoelit.de/kold/

Notes: k0ld, or Knocking 0n LDAP's Door, is a dictionary attack against an LDAP server. It queries the LDAP server, dumps all users from a given DN, and tries to find the password for each user account. The newest version includes Windows 2000 AD attacks and a list of default DNs to attack.

Tool Name: SPIKE Proxy (v.1.4.8)

Developer: Immunity

Platform/OS: Linux, Microsoft Windows

Commercial or Freeware? Freeware

URL: www.immunitysec.com/resources-freesoftware.shtml

Notes: SPIKE Proxy is a tool for looking at application-level vulnerabilities in Web applications. It covers such things as SQL injection and cross-site-scripting attacks, but it's written in a completely open Python infrastructure, so it's customizable for Web applications that other tools break on.

Network Protocol Analysis

Tool Name: Ethereal (v.0.10.11)

Developer: Gerald Combs and the Ethereal dev community

Platform/OS: Microsoft Windows 98/ME/2000/XP/2003, Linux, Solaris, OS X, BeOS, FreeBSD, OpenBSD, NetBSD, AIX, HP-UX

Commercial or Freeware? Freeware

URL: http://ethereal.com/

Notes: Ethereal is probably the most popular open source network protocol analyzer. It can dissect over 680 protocols and has a very comprehensive feature-set. Ethereal is the network protocol analyzer of choice for many folks.

Tool Name: Ettercap (v.NG-0.7.3)

Developer: Alberto Ornaghi and Marco Valleri

Platform/OS: Linux, OS X, Solaris, FreeBSD, OpenBSD, NetBSD, Microsoft Windows 2000/XP/2003

Commercial or Freeware? Freeware

URL: http://ettercap.sourceforge.net/

Notes: Ettercap is a suite for conducting man-in-the-middle attacks on local area networks (LANs). Ettercap provides for the capture of live connections, content filtering on the fly, and several other interesting features. It supports active and passive protocol dissection and has many features that contribute to the network and host analysis portions of evaluation efforts.

Tool Name: Sniffer (v.4.7.5)

Developer: Network General

Platform/OS: Microsoft Windows NT, 2000, XP

Commercial or Freeware? Commercial

URL: www.networkgeneral.com

[1] Network sniffing has privacy issues in that all cleartext protocols are visible. The organization might not want you to see their data "up close and personal."

Notes: Network General's Sniffer is one of the more well-known commercial network protocol analyzers. This product has been around for a long time and provides excellent expert decodes and analysis. The Network General Sniffer product line consists of Sniffer Distributed, Sniffer Portable, Sniffer Mobile, Sniffer Voice, and Sniffer Wireless.

Tool Name: EtherPeek NX (v.3.0.1)

Developer: WildPackets

Platform/OS: Microsoft Windows 2000, XP

Commercial or Freeware? Commercial

URL:
www.wildpackets.com/products/etherpeek/etherpeek_nx/overview

Notes: EtherPeek NX claims to be the first network protocol analyzer to offer both expert diagnostics and frame decoding in real time during packet capture. It is fast and accurate, and the interface is easy to navigate. WildPackets offers four different protocol analyzers: EtherPeek NX, EtherPeek SE, EtherPeek VX, and EtherPeek for Mac.

Tool Name: Snoop

Developer: Sun Microsystems

Platform/OS: SunOS, Solaris

Commercial or Freeware? Freeware (comes with the OS)

URL: N/A

Notes: Snoop is a network analysis tool that comes with the Solaris operating system. Snoop captures packets from the network and displays their contents. If you are working on a Solaris machine, Snoop is essential.

Tool Name: Tcpdump (v.3.8.3)

Developer: Originally Lawrence Berkeley National Lab (LBNL); now maintained at Tcpdump.org

Platform/OS: UNIX, Linux, *BSD, OS X, Microsoft Windows

Commercial or Freeware? Freeware

URL: www.tcpdump.org

Notes: Tcpdump, simply put, dumps traffic from the network. It prints out the packet headers on the monitored network interface. You can also match on Boolean expressions or pipe the output to "grep." It is a very flexible and easy-to-use network troubleshooting tool.

Index

C

Syngress: *The Definition of a Serious Security Library*

Syn·gress (sin-gres): *noun, sing.* Freedom from risk or danger; safety. See *security*.

Phishing Exposed

Lance James, Secure Science Corporation,
Joe Stewart (Foreword)

If you have ever received a phish, become a victim of a phish, or manage the security of a major e-commerce or financial site, then you need to read this book. The author of this book delivers the unconcealed techniques of phishers including their evolving patterns, and how to gain the upper hand against the ever-accelerating attacks they deploy. Filled with elaborate and unprecedented forensics, Phishing Exposed details techniques that system administrators, law enforcement, and fraud investigators can exercise and learn more about their attacker and their specific attack methods, enabling risk mitigation in many cases before the attack occurs.

ISBN: 1-59749-030-X

Price: $49.95 US $69.95 CAN

Penetration Tester's Open Source Toolkit

Johnny Long, Chris Hurley, SensePost,
Mark Wolfgang, Mike Petruzzi

This is the first fully integrated Penetration Testing book and bootable Linux CD containing the "Auditor Security Collection," which includes over 300 of the most effective and commonly used open source attack and penetration testing tools. This powerful tool kit and authoritative reference is written by the security industry's foremost penetration testers including HD Moore, Jay Beale, and SensePost. This unique package provides you with a completely portable and bootable Linux attack distribution and authoritative reference to the toolset included and the required methodology.

ISBN: 1-59749-021-0

Price: $59.95 US $83.95 CAN

Google Hacking for Penetration Testers

Johnny Long, Foreword by Ed Skoudis

Google has been a strong force in Internet culture since its 1998 upstart. Since then, the engine has evolved from a simple search instrument to an innovative authority of information. As the sophistication of Google grows, so do the hacking hazards that the engine entertains. Approaches to hacking are forever changing, and this book covers the risks and precautions that administrators need to be aware of during this explosive phase of Google Hacking.

ISBN: 1-93183-636-1

Price: $44.95 U.S. $65.95 CAN

Syngress: *The Definition of a Serious Security Library*

Syn·gress (sin-gres): *noun, sing.* Freedom from risk or danger; safety. See *security*.

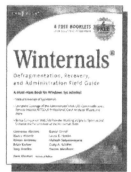

Syngress: *The Definition of a Serious Security Library*

Syn·gress (sin-gres): *noun, sing.* Freedom from risk or danger; safety. See *security*.

How to Cheat at Designing Security for a Windows Server 2003 Network

Neil Ruston, Chris Peiris

While considering the security needs of your organiztion, you need to balance the human and the technical in order to create the best security design for your organization. Securing a Windows Server 2003 enterprise network is hardly a small undertaking, but it becomes quite manageable if you approach it in an organized and systematic way. This includes configuring software, services, and protocols to meet an organization's security needs.

ISBN: 1-59749-243-4

Price: $39.95 US $55.95 CAN

How to Cheat at Designing a Windows Server 2003 Active Directory Infrastructure

Melissa Craft, Michael Cross, Hal Kurz, Brian Barber

The book will start off by teaching readers to create the conceptual design of their Active Directory infrastructure by gathering and analyzing business and technical requirements. Next, readers will create the logical design for an Active Directory infrastructure. Here the book starts to drill deeper and focus on aspects such as group policy design. Finally, readers will learn to create the physical design for an active directory and network Infrastructure including DNS server placement; DC and GC placements and Flexible Single Master Operations (FSMO) role placement.

ISBN: 1-59749-058-X

Price: $39.95 US $55.95 CAN

How to Cheat at Configuring ISA Server 2004

Dr. Thomas W. Shinder, Debra Littlejohn Shinder

If deploying and managing ISA Server 2004 is just one of a hundred responsibilities you have as a System Administrator, "How to Cheat at Configuring ISA Server 2004" is the perfect book for you. Written by Microsoft MVP Dr. Tom Shinder, this is a concise, accurate, enterprise tested method for the successful deployment of ISA Server.

ISBN: 1-59749-057-1

Price: $34.95 U.S. $55.95 CAN

Syngress: *The Definition of a Serious Security Library*

Syn·gress (sin–gres): *noun, sing.* Freedom from risk or danger; safety. See *security*.

Syngress: *The Definition of a Serious Security Library*

Syn·gress (sin–gres): *noun, sing.* Freedom from risk or danger; safety. See *security*.

Syngress IT Security Project Management Handbook
Susan Snedaker

The definitive work for IT professionals responsible for the management of the design, configuration, deployment and maintenance of enterprise-wide security projects. Provides specialized coverage of key project areas including Penetration Testing, Intrusion Detection and Prevention Systems, and Access Control Systems.

ISBN: 1-59749-076-8

Price: $59.95 US $77.95 CAN

Combating Spyware in the Enterprise
Paul Piccard

Combating Spyware in the Enterprise is the first book published on defending enterprise networks from increasingly sophisticated and malicious spyware. System administrators and security professionals responsible for administering and securing networks ranging in size from SOHO networks up to the largest enterprise networks will learn to use a combination of free and commercial anti-spyware software, firewalls, intrusion detection systems, intrusion prevention systems, and host integrity monitoring applications to prevent the installation of spyware, and to limit the damage caused by spyware that does in fact infiltrate their networks.

ISBN: 1-59749-064-4

Price: $49.95 US $64.95 CAN

Practical VoIP Security
Thomas Porter

After struggling for years, you finally think you've got your network secured from malicious hackers and obnoxious spammers. Just when you think it's safe to go back into the water, VoIP finally catches on. Now your newly converged network is vulnerable to DoS attacks, hacked gateways leading to unauthorized free calls, call eavesdropping, malicious call redirection, and spam over Internet Telephony (SPIT). This book details both VoIP attacks and defense techniques and tools.

ISBN: 1-59749-060-1

Price: $49.95 U.S. $69.95 CAN

Syngress: *The Definition of a Serious Security Library*

Syn·gress (sin-gres): *noun, sing.* Freedom from risk or danger; safety. See *security.*

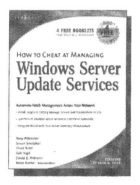

Syngress: *The Definition of a Serious Security Library*

Syn·gress (sin–gres): *noun, sing.* Freedom from risk or danger; safety. See *security*.

Managing Cisco Network Security, Second Edition

Offers updated and revised information covering many of Cisco's security products that provide protection from threats, detection of network security incidents, measurement of vulnerability and policy compliance, and management of security policy across an extended organization. These are the tools that you have to mount defenses against threats. Chapters also cover the improved functionality and ease of the Cisco Secure Policy Manager software used by thousands of small-to-midsized businesses, and a special section on Cisco wireless solutions.

ISBN: 1-931836-56-6

Price: $69.95 USA $108.95 CAN

How to Cheat at Managing Microsoft Operations Manager 2005

Tony Piltzecker, Rogier Dittner, Rory McCaw, Gordon McKenna, Paul M. Summitt, David E. Williams

My e-mail takes forever. My application is stuck. Why can't I log on? System administrators have to address these types of complaints far too often. With MOM, system administrators will know when overloaded processors, depleted memory, or failed network connections are affecting their Windows servers long before these problems bother users. Readers of this book will learn why when it comes to monitoring Windows Server System infrastructure, MOM's the word.

ISBN: 1-59749-251-5

Price: $39.95 U.S. $55.95 CAN

Syngress: *The Definition of a Serious Security Library*

Syn·gress (sin-gres): *noun, sing.* Freedom from risk or danger; safety. See *security*.

How to Cheat at Designing a Windows Server 2003 Active Directory Infrastructure

This book will start off by teaching readers to create the conceptual design of their Active Directory infrastructure by gathering and analyzing business and technical requirements. Next, readers will create the logical design for an Active Directory infrastructure. Here the book starts to drill deeper and focus on aspects such as group policy design. Finally, readers will learn to create the physical design for an active directory and network Infrastructure including DNS server placement; DC and GC placements and Flexible Single Master Operations (FSMO) role placement.

ISBN: 1-59749-058-X

Price: $39.95 US $55.95 CAN

Exam 70-291: Implementing, Managing, and Maintaining a Microsoft Windows Server 2003

ISBN: 1-931836-92-2

Price: $59.95 US

Exam 70-293: Planning and Maintaining a Microsoft Windows Server 2003 Network Infrastructure

ISBN: 1-931836-93-0

Price: $59.95 US

Exam 70-294: Planning, Implementing, and Maintaining a Microsoft Windows Server 2003 Active Directory Infrastructure

ISBN: 1-931836-94-9

Price: $59.95 US

SYNGRESS®

Syngress: *The Definition of a Serious Security Library*

Syn·gress (sin-gres): *noun, sing.* Freedom from risk or danger; safety. See *security*.

Syngress: *The Definition of a Serious Security Library*

Syn·gress (sin-gres): *noun, sing.* Freedom from risk or danger; safety. See *security*.

"Thieme's ability to be open minded, conspiratorial, ethical, and subversive all at the same time is very inspiring." –*Jeff Moss, CEO, Black Hat, Inc.*

Richard Thieme's Islands in the Clickstream: Reflections on Life in a Virtual World

Richard Thieme is one of the most visible commentators on technology and society, appearing regularly on CNN radio, TechTV, and various other national media outlets. He is also in great demand as a public speaker, delivering his "Human Dimension of Technology" talk to over 50,000 live audience members each year. *Islands in the Clickstream* is a single volume "best of Richard Thieme."

ISBN: 1-931836-22-1

Price: $29.95 US $43.95 CAN

"Thieme's Islands in the Clickstream is deeply reflective, enlightening, and refreshing." —*Peter Neumann, Stanford Research Institute*

"Richard Thieme takes us to the edge of cliffs we know are there but rarely visit ... he wonderfully weaves life, mystery, and passion through digital and natural worlds with creativity and imagination. This is delightful and deeply thought provoking reading full of "aha!" insights." —*Clinton C. Brooks, Senior Advisor for Homeland Security and Asst. Deputy Director, NSA*

"WOW! You eloquently express thoughts and ideas that I feel. You have helped me, not so much tear down barriers to communication, as to leverage these barriers into another structure with elevators and escalators."
—*Chip Meadows, CISSP, CCSE, USAA e-Security Team*

"Richard Thieme navigates the complex world of people and computers with amazing ease and grace. His clarity of thinking is refreshing, and his insights are profound." —*Bruce Schneier, CEO, Counterpane*

"I believe that you are a practioner of wu wei, the effort to choose the elegant appropriate contribution to each and every issue that you address." —*Hal McConnell (fomer intelligence analyst, NSA)*

"Richard Thieme presents us with a rare gift. His words touch our heart while challenging our most cherished constructs. He is both a poet and pragmatist navigating a new world with clarity, curiosity and boundless amazement." —*Kelly Hansen, CEO, Neohapsis*

"Richard Thieme combines hi-tech, business savvy and social consciousness to create some of the most penetrating commentaries of our times. A column I am always eager to read." —*Peter Russell, author "From Science to God"*

"These reflections provide a veritable feast for the imagination, allowing us more fully to participate in Wonder. This book is an experience of loving Creation with our minds." —*Louie Crew, Member of Executive Council of The Episcopal Church*

"The particular connections Richard Thieme makes between mind, heart, technology, and truth, lend us timely and useful insight on what it means to live in a technological era. Richard fills a unique and important niche in hacker society!" —*Mick Bauer, Security Editor, Linux Journal*

SYNGRESS®

Syngress: *The Definition of a Serious Security Library*

Syn·gress (sin–gres): *noun, sing.* Freedom from risk or danger; safety. See *security*.

Syngress: *The Definition of a Serious Security Library*

Syn·gress (sin-gres): *noun, sing.* Freedom from risk or danger; safety. See *security*.

Skype Me! From Single User to Small Enterprise and Beyond

Michael Gough

This first-ever book on Skype takes you from the basics of getting Skype up and running on all platforms, through advanced features included in SkypeIn, SkypeOut, and Skype for Business. The book teaches you everything from installing a headset to configuring a firewall to setting up Skype as telephone Base to developing your own customized applications using the Skype Application Programming Interface.

ISBN: 1-59749-032-6

Price: $34.95 US $48.95 CAN

Securing IM and P2P Applications for the Enterprise

Brian Baskin, Marcus H. Sachs, Paul Piccard

As an IT Professional, you know that the majority of the workstations on your network now contain IM and P2P applications that you did not select, test, install, or configure. As a result, malicious hackers, as well as virus and worm writers, are targeting these inadequately secured applications for attack. This book will teach you how to take back control of your workstations and reap the benefits provided by these applications while protecting your network from the inherent dangers.

ISBN: 1-59749-017-2

Price: $49.95 US $69.95 CAN

SYNGRESS®

Syngress: *The Definition of a Serious Security Library*

Syn·gress (sin–gres): *noun, sing.* Freedom from risk or danger; safety. See *security*.

Made in the USA
San Bernardino, CA
08 January 2016